BRITISH GOVERNMENT PUBLICATIONS

An index to
chairmen and authors

VOLUME IV: 1979–1982

Compiled by
Stephen Richard

THE LIBRARY ASSOCIATION · LONDON

First published 1984

British Library Cataloguing in Publication Data
Richard, Stephen
  British government publications.
  Vol. 4 : 1979–1982
  1. Governmental investigations—Great
  Britain—Bibliography 2. Great Britain—
  Government publications—Bibliography

  I. Title
  015.41′053   Z2009
  ISBN 0 85365 756 4

Designed by Ron Jones

Contents

Introduction

This index of chairmen and authors for the period 1979 to 1982, continues the series of indexes of chairmen of British government publications published by the Library Association in 1982. In this index coverage has been extended to include authors as well as chairmen. There is no easily available and relatively inexpensive source to enable identification of government reports known by the authors name alone. The British National Bibliography does not include a large number of reports for a variety of reasons; the HMSO catalogues of course only include reports published by HMSO; while the *Catalogue of British Official Publications Not Published by HMSO* includes only those reports identified as being published by departments and other official organizations. HMSO also issues a quarterly index of reports listed by chairmen's names covering HMSO published reports for £5.00 a year. This is very useful, but covers only a minority of official reports. Coverage has also been extended to include Northern Ireland reports. In previous indexes the publications of Northern Ireland government organizations have been excluded.

A new definition of official organizations has been used in the compilation of this index, which extends its coverage to the whole range of British official publications. The criteria to be satisfied in determining which organizations are to be considered official are as follows:
a) Central Government departments and those organizations funded directly by Parliament through the Annual Vote.
b) Organizations which form an integral part of, or are directly maintained by a government department or other organization directly and wholly financed by Parliament or a government department.
c) Organizations which were originally formed by government action (whether by statute, delegated legislation or other exercise of ministerial authority) or government bodies and which maintain a direct link by reporting, representational or financial arrangements with the parent organization. This definition includes the group of organizations popularly known as quangos.

Users of the series of indexes should note that this index includes pre-1979 committee reports which have been discovered since the publication of the previous indexes. The number is not great (about half a dozen), but may be of importance in particular instances.

Having discussed the inclusions in terms of authorship, areas, time and organizations, it is also necessary to outline the material excluded from the index. Certain types of material are excluded: catalogues, bibliographies, abstracts, calendars and similar listings, and speeches. The majority of publications of certain organizations are also excluded. In these cases, the committee reports emanating from the organizations are included, but none of the other reports and publications are included. The organizations concerned are libraries, museums, art galleries, broadcasting authorities, and government research stations. This means that reliance must be placed on the British Library Lending Division's *British Reports, Translations and Theses* for coverage of research reports from British government research stations. BRTT now contains indexes which makes it useful as a reference source.

The reports are listed alphabetically by the chairman's or author's name. If more than one report is concerned it is filed alphabetically by title. The exception to this is where such an arrangement would break up a numbered series, e.g. Law Commission reports. These are listed in numerical order.

Certain abbreviations are used in the index as follows:

ADAS	Agricultural Development and Advisory Service
Archbp.	Archbishop
Bp.	Bishop
Dept.	Department
DHSS	Department of Health and Social Security
DHSS for N.I.	Department of Health and Social Services for Northern Ireland
DoE	Department of the Environment
DoT	Department of Trade
DTp	Department of Transport
HIDB	Highlands and Islands Development Board
LGBCS	Local Government Boundary Commission for Scotland
MAFF	Ministry of Agriculture Fisheries and Food
Min.	Ministry
MSC	Manpower Services Commission
NEDO	National Economic Development Office
N.I.	Northern Ireland
OPCS	Office of Population Censuses and Surveys
Rep.	Report
SEPD	Scottish Economic Planning Department
Ser.	Series
SHHD	Scottish Home and Health Department
SSRC	Social Science Research Council

Stephen Richard
Oxford
January 1984

AARON, J. R.
Conifer bark: its properties and uses. (Forest Record 110)
Forestry Commission, 1982

The production of wood charcoal in Great Britain. (Forest Record 121)
Forestry Commission, 1980

ABBOTT, J.
On-line computing, a management guide
National Computing Centre, 1981

ABLETT, R. M.
Assessment of the capacity of the Daventry sectors at the London Air Traffic Control centre, October 1981. (CAA Paper 82018)
CAA, 1982

ABRAMS, M.
The elderly consumer. (Special Paper, no. 7)
National Consumer Council, 1982

ABRAMS, Michael
Recruitment to community medicine. Report of a joint working group
DHSS, 1980

ABSALOM, W. L. G.
A directors' guide to financing marketing co-operatives
Central Council for Agricultural and Horticultural Co-operation, 1981

ACHESON, E. D.
Cancer registration. Report of the advisory committee. Cancer registration in the 1980's. (Series MB1, no. 6)
OPCS, 1981

ACHESON, H. W. K.
Doctor patient relationship: a study in general practice, by F. Fitton and H. W. K. Acheson
DHSS, 1979

ACRES, B. D.
Yemen Arab Republic montane plains and Wadi Rima project; a land and water resources survey. (Project Record 52)
Land Resources Development Centre, 1980

ADAIR, John
Training for decisions. A tutor's manual. A course in decision making, problem solving, creative thinking
Chemical and Allied Products Industry Training Board, 1976

ADAMS, D. W.
Migration from Scotland to the rest of the United Kingdom. (Economics & Statistics Unit: Discussion Paper no. 10)
SEPD, 1980

Migration from Scotland to the rest of the UK revisited. (Economics & Statistics Unit: Discussion Paper no. 11)
SEPD, 1980

The relationship between employment and unemployment in Scotland in the post-war period. (Economics & Statistics Unit: Discussion Paper no. 5)
SEPD, 1980

ADAMS, E.
Art and the built environment; a teacher's approach, by E. Adams and C. Ward
Longman, for Schools Council, 1982

ADAMS, J. G. L.
Distribution and transport in the Highlands and Islands. Report by J. G. L. Adams and J. D. McCallum
HIDB, 1982

ADAMS, M. R.
Fermentation ethanol: an industrial profile, by M. R. Adams and G. Flynn. (Report G169)
Tropical Products Institute, 1982

The small-scale production of vinegar from bananas (G132)
Tropical Products Institute, 1980

ADAMS, S. C. M.
Automatic slurry handling and treatment processes, and hygiene in livestock buildings. Report of a study tour in Holland, Jan 1982, by S. C. M. Adams and R. Friman
ADAS, 1982

ADAMSON, A. H.
European grazing workshop group, 3rd. Report of a visit to Holland
ADAS, 1979

International grassland congress (14th), USA, June 1981, by A. H. Adamson and C. Dibb
ADAS, 1982

ADEANE, Michael Edward, Lord
Ancient monuments of York, V. 37th report of the Royal Commission on the Ancient and Historical Monuments and Constructions of England, Jan. 1979
Session 1978–79 Cmnd. 7435

Archaeological sites in north-west Northamptonshire. 38th interim report. Royal Commission on Ancient and Historical Monuments and Constructions of England, 1979
Session 1979–80 Cmnd. 7614

ADELSTEIN, A. M.
Perinatal and infant mortality: social and biological factors 1975–77, by A. M. Adelstein and others. (Studies on Medical and Population Subjects no. 41)
OPCS, 1980

ADELSTEIN, Richard P.
Institutional function and evolution in the criminal process. (Research Study no. 2)
SSRC, Institute of Socio-Legal Studies, 1980

ADLER, M.
Origins and consequences of default; an examination of the impact of diligence, by M. Adler and E. Wozniak (Res. Rep. for the Scottish Law Com., no. 5)
Scottish Office, 1981

AINGER, P. L.
Gilgate Holdings Limited. Raybourne Group Limited. Calomefern Limited. Desadean Properties Limited. Investigation under The Companies Act 1948
DoT, 1981

AINSWORTH, G.
Wastewater treatment. First biennial report of the committee (Standing Technical Committee Reports, no. 13)
National Water Council, 1979

AITKEN, G.
Pig production: report of a visit to Federal Republic of Germany, June 1981, by G. Aitken and P. Smith
ADAS, 1981

AITKEN, P. P.
Adults' attitudes towards drinking and smoking among young people in Scotland. Vol. IV, by P. P. Aitken and D. S. Leather
SHHD, 1981

Ten to fourteen year olds and alcohol. A developmental study in the central region of Scotland. Vol. III
SHHD, 1978

AITKEN, Robert
West highland way; official guide and official route map
Countryside Commission for Scotland, 1980

1

AITKEN-SWAN, J.
Male midwives; a report of two studies, by M. Speak and J. Aitken-Swan
DHSS, 1982

AITKENHEAD, P.
EPPO conference on pest and disease risks from imported exotic material, by P. Aitkenhead, C. R. B. Baker, R. A. Lelliott and A. W. Pemberton. (Report of a visit to Denmark, 25–27 November 1980)
ADAS, 1982

ALDERMAN, G.
CEC workshop of methodology of analysis of feeding stuffs for ruminants. Report of a visit to Holland, May 1980, by P. J. Ballinger and G. Alderman
ADAS, 1980

European Association for Animal Production, Munich, West Germany – 1–4 September 1980. Report by G. Alderman
ADAS, 1981

International workshop on the standardisation of techniques on feeding stuffs analysis. Report of a visit to Canada, March 1979
ADAS, 1979

Protein metabolism and nutrition. Report on 3rd symposium, May 1980 (European Association for Animal Production)
ADAS, 1980

ALDERSLADE, R
Standing committee on the disposal of sewage sludge. (Standing Technical Committee Report no. 21)
National Water Council, 1981

ALDERSON, J. C.
Issues in language testing, ed. by J. C. Alderson and A. Hughes. (ELT Documents 111)
British Council, 1981

ALFORD, D. V.
Pest and disease control in fruit and hops, by D. V. Alford and others
British Crop Protection Council, 1980

ALLAN, E. N. W.
Damage by insects to poultry house structures. Report of a visit to New Zealand, March 1980
ADAS, 1980

ALLEN OF ABBEYDALE, Lord
Greater security for the rights and expectations of members of occupational pension schemes. Occupational Pensions Board, 1982
Session 1981–2 Cmnd. 8649

ALLEN OF FALLOWFIELD, Lord
Chemicals: contraction or growth?
NEDO, 1981

ALLEN, David
Research and doctoral training
SSRC, 1981

ALLEN, F. H.
Selection procedure for the recruitment of administration trainees. Report of the committee
Civil Service Commission, 1979

ALLEN, K.
Regional development agencies in Europe; an overview, by D. Yuill and K. Allen (ESU Research Paper 4)
SEPD, 1981

ALLEN, P. G.
Mushroom production, by P. G. Allen and R. L. Tite. Report of a study tour in Holland, March 1980
ADAS, 1980

ALLEN, Patrick
Shared ownership: a stepping stone to home ownership. Report on a survey of local authority shared ownership schemes
DoE, 1982

ALLEN, Richard
Economic effects of a shorter working week (Government economic service working paper, no. 33; Treasury working paper, no. 14)
Treasury, 1980

ALVEY, J.
A programme for advanced information technology, the report of the Alvey Committee
Industry Dept., 1982

AMIES, S. J.
An analysis of FMS costed farms, 1978–79. (Report no. 22)
Milk Marketing Board, 1979

An analysis of FMS costed farms, 1979–80, by S. J. Amies and J. A. Craven. (Farm Management Service Information Unit Report no. 24)
Milk Marketing Board, 1980

Block calving the dairyherd. (Farm Management Services Information Unit Report no. 26)
Milk Marketing Board, 1981

Ireland and England and Wales: trends in dairy farming 1977–1981. (Information Unit Farm Management Services Report no. 27)
Milk Marketing Board, 1981
An analysis of FMS costed farms 1981–82, by S. J. Amies and J. A. Craven (Report no. 33)
Milk Marketing Board, 1982

AMOS, G. E.
Silage unloaders and feeders, by G. E. Amos and S. Fish. Report of a study tour undertaken in France
ADAS, 1979

ANAND, N.
Selected markets for ginger and its derivatives with special reference to dried ginger, by N. Anand. (Report G161)
London, Tropical Products Institute, 1982

ANDERSON, Alan
The supply and demand for computer related manpower to 1985. Final report of the manpower sub-committee of the electronic computers SWP and computer manpower in the '80's, by A. Anderson and A. Hersleb
NEDO, 1980

ANDERSON, Digby
Framework for a methodic approach to meetings with special reference to those attended by health education officers. (Occ. Paper, 1)
Health Education Council, 1980

ANDREWS, C. Leslie
Tenants and town hall
DoE, 1979

ANDREWS, Jane E.
Hostels for offenders. (Home Office Research Study, no. 52)
Home Office, 1979

ANDREWS, K.
Government policy towards assistance with heating costs. (Research note no. 57)
House of Commons, 1982

ANTHONY, Stewart
Birds: where to watch them in the Peak national park, by Philip Shooter and Stewart Anthony. Rev. ed.
Peak National Park, 1979

ANWAR, Muhammad
Between two cultures: a study of relationships between generations in the Asian community in Britain. 2nd ed.
Commission for Racial Equality, 1978

Television in a multi-racial society – a research report by M. Anwar and A. Shang
Commission for Racial Equality, 1982

APEA, E.
Development and production of school science equipment; some alternative approaches, by E. Apea and N. K. Lowe
Commonwealth Secretariat, 1979

APPLETON, W. J.
Benefits of data co-ordination. A survey and evaluation. (Standing Committee on Computing and Data Co-ordination)
DoE, 1979

Computers in the construction industry
1: Summary and recommendations
2: Pilot survey
3: Transfer of project data
4: Development and use of programs and systems
5: Building services
6: Architecture
7: Quantity surveying
8: Building contractors
(Standing Committee on Computing and Data Co-ordination)
DoE, 1979

Computing and communication in the construction industry. Final report of the Standing Committee on Computing and Data Co-ordination
DoE, 1979

Information systems for the construction industry; a review of progress. Standing Committee on Computing and Data Co-ordination
DoE, 1979

APTED, M.R.
Audley End House, Essex
DoE, 1982

Claypotts Castle. 2nd ed.
Scottish Development Dept., 1980

ARCHER, C. J.
Brucella ovis complement fixation test methods and standardisation procedures: report of a visit to France, 9–12 June 1981, by C. J. Archer and W. C. S. Read
ADAS, 1981

ARLINGTON, M.
A comparison of dairy farming in Bavaria and England and Wales. (Farm Management Services Information Unit Report no. 25)
Milk Marketing Board, 1981

ARMITAGE, Sir Arthur.
Child Benefit (Claims and Payments) Amendment Regulations, 1981. Report of the Social Security Advisory Committee
Session 1981–82 Cmnd. 8453

Child Benefit (General) Amendment Regulations, 1982. Report of the Social Security Advisory Committee. July 1982
Session 1981–2 Cmnd. 8586

Lorries, people and the environment. Report of the inquiry
D.Tp, 1980

Mobility Allowance (Motability Payment Arrangements) amendment regulations 1982. Report of the Social Security Advisory Committee. November 1982
Session 1982–3 Cmnd. 8754

Social Security (Claims and Payments) Amendment Regulations 1982; and the child benefit (claims and payments) amendment regulations, 1982. Report of The Social Security Advisory Committee. September 1982
Session 1981–2 Cmnd. 8656

Social Security (Claims and Payments) Amendment (no. 2) Regulations 1982 and the Social Security (Unemployment, Sickness and Invalidity Benefit) Amendment (No. 2) regulations, 1982. Report of the Social Security Advisory Committee, 1982
Session 1981–82 Cmnd. 8667

Social Security (Contributions) Amendment Regulations, 1983. Report of the Social Security Advisory Committee. January 1983
Session 1982–3 Cmnd. 8788

The Social Security (Maternity Grant) Regulations 1981. (S.I. 1981 no. 1157)
Session 1980–81 Cmnd. 8336.

The Social Security (Medical Evidence, Claims and Payments) Amendment Regulations 1982. (S.I. 1982 no. 699). Report of the Social Security Advisory Committee
Session 1981–82 Cmnd. 8560

Supplementary Benefit (Claims and Payments) Amendment Regulations, 1982. Report of the Social Security Advisory Committee. December 1982
Session 1982–83 Cmnd. 8772

Supplementary Benefit (Requirements and Resources) Amendment Regulations 1982, and the Supplementary Benefit (Miscellaneous Amendments) Regulations 1982. Report of the Social Security Advisory Committee. July 1982
Session 1981–82 Cmnd. 8598

ARMITAGE, Peter
Decisions in educational planning. (C.S.C. Working paper, no. 28)
Civil Service College, 1981

ARMSTRONG, A. C.
The hydrology and water quality of a drained clay catchment; a preliminary report on the Cockle Park drainage experiment. (Land Drainage Service Research and Development Report no. 3)
ADAS, 1980

Sedimentation of drain pipes; results of a national investigation (DW14). Preliminary report by A. J. Kellett and A. C. Armstrong. (Land Drainage Service R & D Report no. 2)
ADAS, 1980

ARMSTRONG, Adrian
The estimation of subsoil hydraulic conductivity; a preliminary report on the DW7 investigation, by A. Armstrong and I. Tring. (Land Drainage Service Research and Development Report no. 4)
ADAS, 1980

ARNDT, H. W.
The world economic crisis; a commonwealth perspective. Report by a group of experts
Commonwealth Secretariat, 1980

ARNOLD, E.
Designing the future; the implication of CAD interactive graphics for employment and skills in the British engineering industry, by E Arnold and P. Senker (Occasional Paper OP/9)
Engineering Industry Training Board, 1982

ARROWSMITH, G.
Sports usage and membership at a large urban leisure complex: Billingham Forum. (Research Working Papers 17)
Sports Council, 1979.

ASHBY, D. J.
Electroplating for engineering technicians
Industry Dept., 1982

ASHBY, D. J. (*continued*)
Hot dip coatings for engineering technicians
Industry Dept, 1982

ASHBY, S.
'I'll stay here if I can', ed. by S. Ashby (with) tutor's notes
MSC, 1981

ASHWORTH, L.
Better uses of resources in the manufacture of process plant. (Process Plant EDC)
NEDO, 1980

Technology prospects in the process industries, pt. 1: aluminium smelting; chemicals, including coal conversion; electricity generation, including nuclear fuel processing. Report of the competitiveness sub group
NEDO, 1979

ASKEW, M. F.
Oilseed rape and cereals. Report of a visit to France, 2–4 June 1981
ADAS, 1982

ASTIN, Alan E.
The management of schools in Northern Ireland. Report of the working party.
Dept. Education (N.I.), 1979

ATCHERLEY, Sir Harold
Review Body on Armed Forces Pay
8th report
Cabinet Office, 1979

Supplement to 8th report: Service medical and dental officers. June 1979
Session 1979–80 Cmnd. 7603

Second supplement to 8th report: I – pay of university cadets and of medical and dental cadets; II – London weighting. Nov. 1979
Session 1979–80 Cmnd. 7770

9th report. May 1980
Session 1979–80 Cmnd. 7899

Supplement to 9th report: Service medical and dental officers. July 1980
Session 1979–80 Cmnd. 7956

10th report. 1981
Session 1980–81 Cmnd. 8241

Supplement to 10th report: Service medical and dental officers. 1981
Session 1980–81 Cmnd. 8322

11th report. 1982
Session 1981–82 Cmnd. 8549

Supplement to 11th report: Service medical and dental officers. June 1982
Session 1981–82 Cmnd. 8573

ATHERTON, Graham
The book of the school; a study of Scottish school handbooks isued to pupils and their parents
Scottish Consumer Council, 1982

Paying for a warmer home; a review of the homes insulation scheme in Scotland
Scottish Consumer Council, 1980

Putting it to the test; testing facilities for consumer goods in Scotland. A directory and report
Scottish Consumer Council, 1979

ATKINSON, J.
The impact of neighbouring sports and leisure centres, by J. Atkinson and M. F. Collins. (Sports Council Research Working Papers 18)
Sports Council, 1980

ATKINSON, R. J. C.
Russian and Russian studies in British universities. Report
University Grants Committee, 1979

Stonehenge and its neigbouring monuments
DoE, 1981

What is Stonehenge? A guide for young people. 2nd ed
DoE, 1980

ATTERTON, D. V.
Strategy for steel. Summary of the 1979 progress report by the iron and steel SWP
NEDO, 1980

Iron and steel sector working party. Progress report
NEDO, 1980

ATWELL, John
Computer aided design and manufacture. Advisory Council for Applied Research and Development
Cabinet Office, 1980

Research and development for public purchasing. Advisory Council for Applied Research and Development
Cabinet Office, 1980

Technological change; threats and opportunities for the U.K. Advisory Council for Applied Research and Development
Cabinet Office, 1980

AULD, Robin
Ashbourne Investments Limited. Investigation under sections 164 and 172 of the Companies Act 1948. Report by Robin Auld and others
DoT, 1979

AUSTIN, R. B.
Decision making in the practice of crop protection. Proceedings of a symposium held at the University of Sussex, April 1982. (Monograph no.25)
British Crop Protection Council, 1982

AVENT, Richard
St. Cybi's Well, Gwynedd
Welsh Office, 1982

AVERY, D.
Nuclear power: is it the answer?
British Nuclear Fuels Ltd., 1982

AXON, P. E.
Improving company performance. A joint approach. Pumps and Valves SWP
NEDO, 1980

Pumps and valves sector working party. Progress report, 1980
NEDO, 1980

Pumps and valves sector working party. Progress report
NEDO, 1981

AYERS, R.
Skill shortages in the HVACR industry. Report of the Heating, Ventilating, Air Conditioning and Refrigeration Equipment SWP
NEDO, 1979

AYERST, Alice
Report of the investigations into the procedures for representations to the Electricity Council by area electricity consultative councils under the Electricity Act, 1947 (as amended). (Research Report no. 1)
Electricity Consumer Council, 1980

AYRES, R.
An approach to the development of staff with direct training roles. Discussion document. (Training of Trainers Committee)
MSC, 1979

BACHER, E.
Medieval stained glass restoration and conservation by Ernst Bacher. (Conservation Paper 5)
Crafts Advisory Committee, 1979

BACK, Philip
Talking about plastics; communications at company level. (Plastics Processing SWP)
NEDO, 1980

BADENOCH, J.
Whooping cough. Reports from the Committee on Safety of Medicines and the Joint Committee on Vaccination and Immunisation
DHSS, 1981

BAIGENT, Mark
Basic facts and figures. Sheffield development project for mentally handicapped people. (Mental Health Buildings Evaluation Report S1)
DHSS, 1979

BAILEY, A. D.
The American Society of Agricultural Engineers Winter Meeting. Report of a visit to USA, Dec. 1979
ADAS, 1979

BAILEY, S.
Collaborative international pesticides analytical council. Report on the 26th annual meeting, Italy, May 1982, by S. Bailey and F. J. Lovett
ADAS, 1982

Symposium on chemical signals in vertebrates and aquatic animals. Report of a visit to USA, May/June 1979
ADAS, 1979

BAIN, A. D.
Bank lending, monetary control and funding policy. (Panel of Academic Consultants, paper no. 19)
Bank of England, 1982

BAIN, George Sayers
Profiles of union growth; a comparative statistical portrait of eight countries, by G. S. Bain and R. Price. (Warwick Studies in Industrial Relations)
Social Science Research Council, Industrial Relations Research Unit, 1980

BAINBRIDGE, Sheila
National health surgical footwear, a study of patient satisfaction
OPCS, 1979

Restrictions at Stonehenge; the reactions of visitors to limitations in access. Report of a survey
OPCS, 1979

BAINES, Priscilla
Agricultural Marketing Bill (Bill 7 of 1982–83). (Reference Sheet no. 82/12)
House of Commons Library, 1982

Transport Bill (Bill 5 of 1982–83). (Reference Sheet no.82/11)
House of Commons Library, 1982

BAIRD, T. T.
You and your baby. Report of the advisory committee on infant mortality and handicap in Northern Ireland
DHSS for N.I., 1980

BAIRD, W.
Senior appointments in the police service in Scotland. Police advisory board for Scotland working party
SHHD, 1981

BAKER, A. T.
Report of the working party on rail access to Stansted
D.Tp, 1981

BAKER, C. R. B.
Entomology. Report on 16th international congress, Kyoto, Japan, August 1980, by C. R. B. Baker and D. G. H. Halstead
ADAS, 1980

BAKER, F. A.
A strategy for the automation and instrumentation industry. Automation and Instrumentation SWP. Progress report 1978.
NEDO, 1980

BAKER, John
The future for coal – a consumer's view (G1069)
CEGB, 1982

BAKER, R. D. H.
Investment appraisal and monitoring procedures for administrative computer projects. Report of the Computer Investment Appraisal Working Party
Civil Service Dept., 1980

BALDRY, A. F.
Farm animal welfare. Report of a study tour undertaken in Holland and Switzerland, March 1980
ADAS, 1980

BALDWIN, J. H.
Trials concerned with VCU (variety for cultivation and use) and DUS (distinctness and uniformity and stability) testing at Wageningen and Emmeloord. Report of a visit to Holland, June 1980
ADAS, 1980

BALDWIN, John
Confession in crown court trials, by J. Baldwin and M. McConville. (Research Study no. 5)
Royal Commission on Criminal Procedure, 1980

BALDWIN, John
Construction equipment and mobile cranes productivity. (Productivity Steering Group)
NEDO, 1979

BALDWIN, Peter
Transport without handicap – progress seminar, 16 June 1982
D.Tp, 1982

BALE, John
The development of soccer as a participant and spectator sport; geographical aspects. (State of the Art Review, no. 20)
Sports Council, 1979

BALL, Colin
Ethnic minorities and the special programmes for the unemployed; the problems, the needs and the responses. Report of a working group
MSC, 1979

BALLINGER, P. J.
CEC workshop on methodology of analysis of feedingstuffs for ruminants. Report of a visit to Holland, May 1980, by P. J. Ballinger and G. Alderman
ADAS, 1980

BALLS, R. C.
Potato harvesting, handling, storage and marketing in USA. Report of a study tour undertaken in USA, Sept./Oct. 1979, by J. S. Gunn and R. C. Balls
ADAS, 1979

Report on the national potato damage awareness campaign 1981, by R. C. Balls, J. S. Gunn and A. J. Starling. A joint project by the PMB and ADAS
Potato Marketing Board, 1982

BALSTON, H. R.
Recruitment and training in the paper and board industry. Report of the Manpower Sub-committee of the Paper and Board SWP
NEDO, 1979

BAMFORD, C.
An account of a rehabilitation programme with a group of long stay psychiatric patients. (Social Work Advisory

BAMFORD, C. *(continued)*
Group: Personal Social Services in Northern Ireland no. 12)
DHSS for N.I., 1981

BANCROFT, B.
Dust helmet in mining; a review of experience and possible future development, by G. K. Greenough and B. Bancroft. (Research Paper 12)
Health and Safety Executive, 1980

BANHAM, M.
A critical view on Wole Soyinka's 'The Lion and the Jewel'. (Nexus Books 02)
London: Rex Collings for British Council, 1981.

BARBER, Ann
Labour force information from the National Dwelling and Housing Survey. (Research Paper 17)
Employment Dept., 1981

BARBER, W. P.
Feed evaluation. Report of a study tour undertaken in Norway, Holland and France, 1979 series
ADAS, 1979

The international network of Feed Information Centres: report of a study tour undertaken in USA, June 1981
ADAS, 1982

BARCLAY, C.
Enterprise zones. (Research Note no. 75)
House of Commons, 1982

BARCLAY, Richard H.
Dental services for children at school. A report by the child health programme planning group of the Scottish Health Service Planning Council
SHHD, 1980

Towards better health care for school children in Scotland. A report by the child health programme planning group of the Scottish Health Service Planning Council
SHHD, 1980

Vulnerable families. A report by the child health programme planning group of the Scottish Health Service Planning Council
SHHD, 1980

BARIC, L.
Primary socialisation and smoking. (HEC Monograph Series, no. 1)
Health Education Council, 1979

BARKER, A. M.
Tetney outmarsh reclamation 1974–1980: final report, by A. M. Barker and D. W. Dawson. (Land Drainage Service: R & D Report no. 10)
ADAS, 1981

BARKER, Anthony
Central-local government relationships in Britain as a field of study: a commentary and research register
SSRC, 1979

BARKER, F. A.
Seed production in Holland, Schleswig-Holstein and Denmark. A report of the study tour undertaken during May/June 1978. (James E. Rennie Awards report no. 7)
Potato Marketing Board, 1979

BARKER, M.
Council of Europe seminar on alternatives in farming, Bad Nauheim, June 1981. Report by M. Barker and others
ADAS, 1981

Investigation of work on organic farming systems and furtherance of Anglo-Netherlands cooperation in R & D. Report by R. C. Little and M. Barker
ADAS, 1982

OECD 8th working conference of directors of agricultural

advisory services, Paris, France, 20–24 October 1980. Report
ADAS, 1981

BARNES, B.
Cotton and Allied Textiles EDC progress report 1980 and summary
NEDO, 1980

The Cotton and Allied Textiles EDC summary of progress report 1980
NEDO, 1980

BARNES, J. A.
Police interrogation; tape recording, by J. A. Barnes and N. Webster. (Research Study no. 8)
Royal Commission on Criminal Procedure, 1980

BARNES, Michael
Efficiency and costs of the Central Electricity Generating Board. Memorandum relating to the Monopolies and Mergers Commission investigation
Electricity Consumers' Council, 1980

Review of the structure of the bulk supply tariff (Interim report by the ECC)
Electricity Consumers' Council, 1981

BARNES, R.
The census as an aid in estimating the characteristics of non-response in the GHS, by R. Barnes and F. Birch. (New Methodology Series No. NM1)
OPCS, 1980

The family expenditure and food survey feasibility study 1979–1981, by R. Barnes, R. Redpath and E. Breeze. (New Methodology Series no. NM12)
OPCS, 1982

BARTHOLOMEW, Richard
Study of long-term unemployed, by M. Colledge and R. Bartholomew
MSC, 1980

BARTLETT, D.
NTV exhibition. Report of a visit to Holland, Jan. and Feb. 1979
ADAS, 1979

BARTRAM, M. M.
Improving and profitable use of continuous research
English Tourist Board, 1982

BARTRIP, Peter W. J.
Safety at work: the factory inspectorate in the fencing controversy, 1833–1857. (Centre for Socio-legal Studies: Working Paper no. 4)
SSRC, 1979

BARTY, Euan
Safety and security in the home
Design Council, 1980

BASINGER, D.
International (7th) Pig Veterinary Society Congress. Report of a visit to Mexico, July to August 1982 by D. Basinger. (FR7181)
ADAS, 1982

Pig conference. Report of a visit to Italy, May 1979
ADAS, 1979

BASSEY, E. J.
The case for exercise, by P. H. Fenton and E. J. Bassey. (Research working paper 8)
Sports Council, 1979

BATE, Margaret
Liaison groups in early education, by M. Bate, M. Hargreaves and V. Gibson. (Transition and Continuity in Early Education Project)
Schools Council, 1982

BATES, Don
Research on the training of instructors. (EITB Occasional Paper 7)
Engineering Industry Training Board, 1979

BATES, J. A.
Industrial relations in Northern Ireland. Report of the review body 1971–74 with supplement
Manpower Services Department for Northern Ireland, 1979

BAXTER, M. J.
Measuring the benefits of recreational site provision, a review of techniques related to the Clawson method
Sports Council and SSRC, 1979

BAXTER, P. J.
Mortality in the British rubber industries 1967–76, by P. J. Baxter and J. B. Werner
Health and Safety Executive, 1980

BAYLEY, Stephen
In good shape: style in industrial products 1900–1960
Design Council, 1979

BAYNE, Rowan
An experimental comparison of board and sequential interviewing; preliminary report. (Recruitment Research Unit Report no. 10)
Civil Service Commission, 1979

Selection interviewing; some perspectives and proposals for research. (Recruitment Research Unit Report no. 9)
Civil Service Commission, 1979

Short-term follow-up of direct entry principal recruitment (1973–74 competitions), by D. McLeod and Rowan Bayne. (Recruitment Research Unit Report no. 7)
Civil Service Commission, 1979

BAYNES, K.
The shoe show; British shoes since 1790
Crafts Council, 1979

Gordon Russell
Design Council, 1980

BEAN, Charles R.
An econometric model of manufacturing investment in the UK. (Government Economic Service Working Paper no. 29)
Treasury, 1979

BEASTHALL, G. H.
An evaluation of the Innotron Hydrogamma 16 gamma counter, by H. Hughes and G. H. Beasthall Welsh Office, 1982

BEAUMONT, J. H.
Hand-operated bar mill for decorticating sunflower seed. (Rural Technology Guide 9)
Tropical Products Institute, 1981

Hand-operated disc mill for decorticating sunflower seed. (Rural Technology Guide 10)
Tropical Products Institute, 1981

Hand-operated winnower. (Rural Technology Guide 11)
Tropical Products Institute, 1981

BEAUMONT, P. B.
The determinants of bargaining structure; some large scale survey evidence for Britain, by D. R. Deaton and P. B. Beaumont (Industrial Relations Research Unit Discussion Paper no. 15)
SSRC, 1979

BEAVIS, John
Consultative committee on registration of tourist accommodation
British Tourist Authority, 1980

BEDEMAN, Trevor
Young people on YOP, by T Bedeman and J. Harvey (Special Programmes Research and Development Series no. 3)
MSC, 1981

BEDFORD, T.
Vocational guidance interviews. Report
Employment Dept., 1982

BEESLEY, Michael E.
Liberalisation of the use of British telecommunications network, a study
Industry Dept., 1981

BELL, J. C.
Veterinarians and public health – the American experience. Report of a visit to America
ADAS, 1982

BELL, J. R.
Survey of acrylonitrile and methacrylonitrile levels in food contact materials and in foods. The sixth report of the Steering Group on Food Surveillance. The working party on acrylonitrile and methacrylonitrile. (Food Surveillance Paper no. 6)
MAFF, 1982

BELL, Peter
Teaching slow learners in mixed ability classes, by Peter Bell and Trevor Kerry. (DES Teacher Education Project Focus books)
Macmillan for DES, 1982

BELLOCH, J. D.
Safe manriding in mines. 2nd report of the National Committee for Safety of Manriding in Shafts and Unwalkable Outlets
Health and Safety Executive, 1980

BENETT, Y.
Sidetracked?: a look at the careers advice given to fifth-form girls, by Y. Benett and D. Carter
Equal Opportunities Commission, 1981

BENHAM, C. L.
Mechanisation and microbiological aspects of chemical treatment of forage: report of a study tour undertaken in West Germany, Denmark and Norway, October 1980, by M. Jamieson and C. L. Benham
ADAS, 1981

BENN, J. M.
Voluntary schools. Report of the working party
Education Department for Northern Ireland, 1979

BENNER, P.
Study group on medical manpower: interim report
DHSS, 1982

BENNET, Donald J.
Scotland for hillwalking; a guide to some popular routes
Scottish Tourist Board, 1979

BENNETT, H. G.
Police interrogation procedures in Northern Ireland. Report of a committee of inquiry, March 1979
Session 1978–79 Cmnd. 7497

BENNETT, P. G.
Northampton fire priority demonstration scheme, by R. M. Griffin and P. G. Bennett. (Technical Paper 19)
DTp, 1979

BENNETT, R. A.
Initial review of electoral arrangements for the city of Dundee District. (Serial no.53)
LGBCS, 1980

BENNETT, R. A. *(continued)*
Initial review of electoral arrangements for Roxburgh District. (Serial no.54)
LGBCS, 1979

Initial review of electoral arrangements for Moray District. (Serial no.55)
LGBCS, 1980

Initial review of electoral arrangements for Gordon District. (Serial no. 56)
LGBCS, 1980

Initial review of electoral arrangements for Ross and Cromarty District. (Serial no. 57)
LGBCS, 1980

Initial review of electoral arrangements for Angus District. (Serial no. 58)
LGBCS, 1980

Initial review of electoral arrangements for Renfrew District. (Serial no. 59)
LGBCS, 1980

Initial review of electoral arrangements for Dumbarton District. (Serial no. 60)
LGBCS, 1980

Initial review of electoral arrangements for Monklands District. (Serial no.61)
LGBCS, 1980

Initial review of electoral arrangements for Eastwood District. (Serial no.62)
LGBCS, 1980

Initial review of electoral arrangements for Cumbernauld and Kilsyth District. (Serial no. 63)
LGBCS, 1980

Initial review of electoral arrangements for Lochaber District. (Serial no. 64) LGBC, 1980

Initial review of electoral arrangements for Bearsden and Milngavie District. (Serial no. 65)
LGBCS, 1980

Initial review of electoral arrangements for East Kilbride District. (Serial no. 66)
LGBCS, 1980

Initial review of electoral arrangements for Lothian Region: Designations of electoral divisions in the City of Edinburgh District. (Serial no. 67)
LGBCS, 1980

Initial review of electoral arrangements for Hamilton District. (Serial no. 68)
LGBCS, 1980

Initial Review of electoral arrangements for the City of Glasgow District (Serial no. 69)
LGBCS, 1980

Initial review of electoral arrangements for Cumnock and Doon Valley District. (Serial no. 70)
LGBCS, 1981

Initial review of electoral arrangements for Kyle and Carrick District. (Serial no. 71)
LGBCS, 1981

Initial review of electoral arrangements for Motherwell District. (Serial no. 72)
LGBCS, 1980

Initial review of electoral arrangements for Clydesdale District. (Serial no. 73)
LGBCS, 1981

Initial review of electoral arrangements for Inverclyde District. (Serial no. 74) LGBCS, 1981

Initial review of electoral arrangements for Argyll and Bute District. (Serial no. 75)
LGBCS, 1981

Electoral arrangements for Fife Region. Interim review of boundary of electoral division 2 at Raith, Kirkclady District. (Serial no. 76)
LGBCS, 1981

Initial review of electoral arrangements for Kilmarnock and Loudoun District. (Serial no. 77)
LGBCS, 1981

Initial review of electoral arrangements for Strathkelvin District. (Serial no. 78)
LGBCS, 1981

Initial review of electoral arrangements for Clydebank District. (Serial no. 79)
LGBCS, 1981

Review of the Central/Strathclyde regional boundary at Croftamie. (Serial no. 80)
LGBCS, 1982

BENSON, Henry
Legal services and lawyers – a summary of the Royal Commission on Legal Services Report
Royal Commission on Legal Services, 1979

Royal Commission on Legal Services. Final report. 2 volumes in 4
Session 1979–80 Cmnd. 7648

BENSON, I. A.
Electronic computers SWP manpower sub-committee second interim report.
NEDO, 1979

Electronic Computers SWP Manpower Sub-committee final report
NEDO, 1980

BENTLEY, J.
Arsenic-bearing wastes. A technical memorandum on recovery, treatment and disposal including a code of practice. (Sub-group of Land Wastes Working Group). (Waste Management Paper no. 20)
DoE, 1980

BENTLEY, P. R.
Blast overpresssure and fallout radiation dose models for casualty assessment and other purposes. (Home Office Research Report 10/81)
Home Office, 1982

Revised ed. (Scientific Research and Development Branch, Report 16/82)
Home Office, 1982

BERESFORD, J. C.
Variation in the use of in-patient services by place of residence. (Working Paper no. 31)
Civil Service College, 1982

BERESFORD, Shirley A.
Planning for stroke patients. A four-year descriptive study of home and hospital care, by J. M. Weddell and S. A. A. Beresford
DHSS, 1979

BERRILL, Kenneth
Climatic change: its potential effects on the UK and the implications for research. Report by the interdepartmental group on climatology
Cabinet Office, 1980

BERRY, R. L. P.
Waste paper supply. Report of the committee
Industry Dept., 1980

BERTHOUD, Richard
The education, training and careers of professional engineers, by Richard Berthoud and David J. Smith
Industry Dept., 1980

BETTEMBOURG, Jean-Marie
Conservation problems of early stained glass windows by Jean-Marie Bettembourg. (Conservation Paper 6)
Crafts Advisory Committee, 1979

BEVAN, D.
Control of pine beauty moth by fenitrothion in Scotland 1978, edited by A. V. Holden and D. Bevan
Forestry Commission, 1979

BEVERIDGE, W. T.
Room utilisation in educational institutions by W. T. Beveridge and J. Hay
Scottish Education Dept., 1979

BICKNELL, C.
Review of the country code: a consultation paper. Report by the study group
Countryside Commission, 1979

BIEBUYCK, Tony
A participant observation study of the single homeless. (Single and Homeless Working Paper 3)
DoE, 1982

Six discussion groups of single homeless people, by T. Biebuyck and M. Drake. (Single and Homeless Working Paper 4)
DoE, 1982

BIGGAR, W. A.
Animals Board. Final report
Agricultural Research Council, 1980

BIRCH, Francis
Age of buildings – a further check on the reliability of answers given on the GHS. (New Methodology Series no. NM7)
OPCS, 1980

The census as an aid in estimating the characteristics of non-response in the GHS, by R. Barnes and F. Birch (New Methodology series no NM1)
OPCS, 1980

Survey of rent rebates and allowances – a methodological note on the use of a follow-up sample. (New Methodology Series no. NM8)
OPCS, 1980

BIRD, A. F.
United States sheep experimental station: report of a visit to the USA 21–24 September 1981
MAFF, 1982

BIRKS, Michael
Small claims in the county court; how to sue and defend actions without a solicitor (Form EX50)
LCD, 1981

BIRLEY, A. R.
Hadrian's Wall: an illustrated guide
DoE, 1981

BIRLEY, E.
Chesters Roman Fort, Northumberland, by E. Birley. (Official Handbook)
DoE, 1982

BIRSE, D. G.
Starch extraction; a check list of commercially available machinery, by D. G. Birse and J. E. Cecil. (G142)
Tropical Products Institute, 1980

BISHOP, C. F. H.
Straw burning boilers and automatic stoking equipment. Report of a visit to Denmark, Jan. 1980
ADAS, 1980

BISHOP, D.
Underground services in the inner city, by D. Bishop, G. Blundell and B. Curtis. (Inner Cities Research Programme 3)
DoE, 1980

BLACK, Douglas
Inequalities in health. Report of a research working group
DHSS, 1980

BLACK, Harold
Children and young persons review group report December 1979
DHSS for N.I., 1979

BLACKBURN, Guy
Field surgery pocket book edited by Major General N. G. Kirby and G. Blackburn
Defence Ministry, 1981

BLACKBURN, R. H. A.
Intoxicating liquor licensing in Northern Ireland. Report of the Inter-departmental Review Body
DHSS for N.I., 1979

BLACKIE, Jonathan A.
The leisure planning process, by J. A. Blackie and others. (Review for the Sports Council/SSRC Joint Panel on Leisure and Recreation Research)
Sports Council, 1979

Tourism and recreation in the Chichester area: a basis for planning. A research study. (Research Report no. 35)
English Tourist Board, 1977

BLAIR, C. H. H.
Dunstanburgh Castle, by C. H, H. Blair and H. L. Honeyman. 3rd ed.
DoE, 1982

Warkworth Castle, Northumberland, by C. H. H. Blair and H. L. Honeyman
DoE, 1982

BLAKE, D. V.
Equipment interfaces. (Guide to Computing Standards no. 16)
National Computing Centre, 1981

BLAKE, R. E.
Retraining, alternative employment and career advice. (Socio-economics Paper no. 11; Booklet 2011)
ADAS, 1979

BLANCH, Stuart, Archbp. of York
Clergy Pensions (Amendment) Measure. 185th report by the Ecclesiastical Committee
Session 1981–2 HL141, HC360

BLAXTER, K.
Nutrient requirements of ruminant livestock. Report of an A. R. C. working party.
CAB, 1980

BLAXTER, Mildred
The health of the children: a review of research on the place of health in cycles of disadvantage, by Mildred Blaxter. (DHSS Studies in Deprivation and Disadvantage no. 3)
SSRC, 1981

BLOFIELD, John
Fourth City and Commercial Investment Trust Ltd.; Excelads Ltd.; Systematic Tooling Ltd.; Cambrian Ltd. Investigations under the Companies Act, 1948 by J. Blofield and B. Currie
Trade Dept., 1981

BLOOMFIELD, Barbara A.
Ability and examinations at 16+, by Barbara A. Bloomfield and others. (Schools Council Research Studies)
Schools Council, 1979

BLUME, H.
Fund raising, a handbook for minority groups, ed. by M. Norton and H. Blume
Commission for Racial Equality, 1979.

BLUME, S.S.
The commissioning of social research by central government
SSRC , 1982

BLUME, Stuart
Positive discrimination in health. (C.S.C. Working Paper no. 14)
Civil Service College, 1979

BOCHEL, Dorothy
The establishment and development of local health councils, by D. Bochel and M. MacLaran. (Scottish Health Service Studies, no. 41)
SHHD, 1979

BOHAN, W. J.
Road traffic law. Report of the Interdepartmental Working Party
D.Tp, 1981

BOLTON, Frederick
Commercial sail. Ship and marine technology requirements board. Proceedings of a symposium held at the Royal Institution of Naval Architects, June 1979
Industry Dept., 1980

Small ships' survival. Ship and marine technology requirements board. Proceedings of a seminar held at the National Maritime Institute, Feltham, May 1978
Industry Dept., 1979

BOND, D. E.
Asbestos wastes. A technical memorandum on arisings and disposal including a code of practice. Sub-group on asbestos waste disposal (Waste Management Paper no. 18)
DoE, 1979

Pesticide wastes; a technical memorandum on arisings and disposal including a code of practice. (Waste Management Paper no. 21)
DoE, 1980

BOND, I. D.
Determination of UK manufactured inport prices. (Bank of England Discussion Paper no. 16)
Bank of England, 1981

BOND, J.
Services for the elderly, by J. Bond and V. Carstairs. (Scottish Health Service Studies 42)
SHHD,

BOND, M. F.
The development of public information services at Westminster (Fact Sheets no. 5)
House of Lords, 1979

A short guide to the records of Parliament. 3rd ed.
House of Lords, 1980

Works of art in the House of Lords
House of Lords, 1980

BONE, Margaret
Empty housing in England. A report on the 1977 property survey carried out on behalf of the Department of the Environment, by M. Bone and V. Mason
OPCS, 1980

Measuring how long things last – some applications to a simple life table technique to survey data. (New Methodology Series, NM11)
OPCS, 1980

BONIFACE, Priscilla
The garden room
Royal Commission on Historical Monuments, 1982

Hotels and restaurants: 1830 to the present day
Royal Commission on Historical Monuments, 1981

BONNERJEA, Lucy
Changes in the resident population of inner areas, by David Eversley and Lucy Bonnerjea. (The Inner City in Context 2)
SSRC, 1980

BONSALL, P.
Organising a car sharing scheme
DTp, 1980

BOOTH, A. J.
Pig slaughtering and meat inspection: report of a study tour undertaken in Holland, 21–25 September 1981
ADAS, 1982

BOOTH, D.H.
Cable TV systems and the insulated wires and cables industry
NEDO, 1982

BORG, Alan
Arms and armour in Britain
DoE, 1979

BORRIE, G.
Advice agencies; what they do and who uses them
National Consumer Council, 1982

BOSTOCK, Geoffrey
Direct trainers. Second report of the Training of Trainers Committee
MSC, 1980

BOSWELL, C.
Construction safety research. (Report of Working Party no. 2 of the Construction Industry Advisory Committee)
Health and Safety Commission, 1979

BOUCHIER, Ian A. D.
Research into coronary heart disease in Scotland. Report by the Working Group on Ischaemic Heart Disease
SHHD, 1979

BOWEN, Sian
A study of the London labour market: what jobs are there for unqualified, unskilled 16–18 year olds? (Training Services Division Report no. DTP 16)
MSC, 1979

BOWERMAN, J. M.
The CEGB and nuclear power. Questions and answers, ed. by G. C. Dale and written and researched by J. M. Bowerman
Central Electricity Generating Board, 1979

The safety of the AGR
Central Electricity Generating Board, 1982

BOWETT, Derek W.
Report on the election in El Salvador on 28 March 1982, By Sir John Galsworthy and Prof. Derek W. Bowett, May 1982 Session 1981–82 Cmnd. 8553

BOWIE, Ian MacDonald
Bandara Investments Ltd., Bandara Ceylon Co. Ltd. Report of investigation under the Companies Act, by P. J. Millett and I. M. Bowie
Trade Dept., 1980

The Central Provinces Manganese Ore Co. Ltd., Data Investments Ltd., Vivella Ltd. Report of investigation under the Companies Act by P. J. Millett and I. M. Bowie
Trade Dept., 1980

Darjeeling Holdings Ltd. Report of investigation under the Companies Act by P. J. Millett and I. M. Bowie
Trade Dept., 1980

BOWMAN, C. E.
Report on international symposium on diagnosis and therapy of Varroa disease, West Germany, 29 September – 1 October 1980
ADAS, 1981

BOYCE, Walter E.
Forward with Jay. A response from the PSSC to the Jay report on mental handicap nursing and care. (People with Handicaps Group)
Personal Social Services Council, 1979

BOYLE OF HANDSWORTH, Lord
Ministers of the Crown and members of Parliament and the Peers' expenses allowance

Part 1. (Review Body on Top Salaries, Report no. 12, June 1979)
Session 1979–80 Cmnd. 7598

Part II. (Review Body on Top Salaries, Report no. 13, 1979)
Session 1979–80 Cmnd. 7825

Review body on Top Salaries, Report no. 15
Session 1979–80 Cmnd. 7953

Top salaries, 3rd report. (Review body on Top Salaries, report no. 11, May 1979)
Session 1979–80 Cmnd. 7576

Top salaries, 4th report, July 1980. (Review body on Top Salaries report no. 14)
Session 1979–80 Cmnd. 7952

BOYNTON, John
Southern Rhodesia: independence elections 1980. Report of the Election Commissioner, Salisbury, March 1980
Session 1979–80 Cmnd. 7935

BRADLAW, Robert
Review of the classification of controlled drugs and of penalties under the Misuse of Drugs Act, 1971. Report by the Advisory Council on the Misuse of Drugs
Home Office, 1979

BRADLEY, J.
Stretching the system; FE and related responses to students with special needs, by J. Bradley and S. Hegarty
DES, 1982

Students with special needs in further education: a review of current and completed research relating to young people in the 14–19 age range with special educational needs. (Project report 12)
Further Education Curriculum Review and Development Unit, 1981

BRADLEY, M. R.
Bridleways for recreation. (A Regional Strategy for Sport and Recreation, Report 6)
Eastern Council for Sport and Recreation, 1982

BRADLEY, R.
Muscle hypertrophy of genetic origin and its utilization to improve beef production. Report of a visit to France, June 1980, by R. Bradley and B. M. Scott
ADAS, 1980

BRADSHAW, A. D.
Land reclamation in cities. A guide to methods of establishment of vegetation on urban waste land, by R. A. Dutton and A. D. Bradshaw
DoE, 1982

BRADSHAW, E. S. R.
Food preparation aids for rheumatoid arthritis patients – screwtop jar and bottle openers, can openers, vegetable peelers, stabilizers. (DHSS Aids Assessment Programme)
DHSS, 1982

BRAGG, N. C.
Opencast mining. A review with specific interest on research and development work on restoration techniques. (Land Drainage Service Research and Development, Report no. 6)
ADAS, 1981

BRASIER, F.
The multi-purpose claim form trial in Brighton, by S. Graham, and F. Brasier
DHSS, 1979

BRAUN, E.
New technology and employment, by E. Braun and P. Senker
MSC, 1982

BRAYSHAW, Peter
The cost to firms of training professional engineers in 1976/7. (Working paper WP 3/79)
Engineering Industry Training Board, 1979

Manpower and training in the electronics industry, by P. Brayshaw and G. Lawson. (Reference Paper RP/5/82)
Engineering Industry Training Board, 1982

Women in engineering, by P. Brayshaw and C. J. Laidlaw. (Reference Paper RP/4/79)
Engineering Industry Training Board, 1979

Young people in engineering, by P. Brayshaw and C. J. Laidlaw. (Reference Paper RP/4/82)
Engineering Industry Training Board, 1982

BREAG, G. R.
Producer gas; its potential and application in developing countries, by G.R. Breag and A. E. Chittenden. (G.130)
Tropical Products Institute, 1979

Utilisation of waste heat produced during the manufacture of coconut shell charcoal for the centralised production of copra, by G. R. Breag and A. P. Harker. (G. 127)
Tropical Products Institute, 1979

BREECH, Michael
Direct access to financial markets for financing nationalised industries' investment, by M. Breech and J. Whiteman. (Economic Working Paper no. 6)
NEDO, 1981

Interdependence of the public and private sectors (Economic Working Paper no. 4)
NEDO, 1981

BREEZE, David J.
Roman Scotland: some recent excavations
Scottish Development Dept., 1979

BREEZE, Elizabeth
Rating lists – practical information for use in sample surveys. (New Methodology Series No. NM9)
OPCS, 1982

BRENCHLEY, G. H.
Potato diseases, by G. H. Brenchley and H. J. Wilcox. (RPD 1)
ADAS, 1979

BRENNAN, W. K.
Curricular needs of slow learners. Report of the Schools Council project. (Working Paper no. 63)
Schools Council, 1979

BRIAULT, C. B.
Portfolio model of domestic and external financial markets, by C. B. Briault and S. K. Howson. (Discussion Paper no. 20)
Bank of England, 1982

BRIDGE OF HARWICH, Nigel Cyprion Bridge
Report of an inquiry into the appointment as the Queen's police officer and the activities of Commander Trestrail; to determine whether security was breached or put at risk, and advise whether in consequence any change in security arrangements is necessary or desirable, November 1982
Session 1982–83 HC 59

BRIDGEMAN, C. J.
Community use of education facilities: management considerations, by C. J. Bridgeman. (Seminar report, Tuesday December 16th, 1980: ref. SCSR (81) 12)
Southern Council for Sport and Recreation, 1981

BRIDGER, G. A.
Sector appraisal manual: rural development, by G. A. Bridger (et al)
Overseas Development Admin., 1980

BRIDLE, J. R.
Target cost contracts, a worthwhile alternative. Civil Engineering E. D. C.
NEDO, 1982

BRIGDEN, Raymond J.
Shared treatment facilities; an evaluation
DHSS, 1980

Shared treatment facilities: an evaluation, by R. J. Brigden. (Summary – extract from main report)
DHSS, 1980

BRIGGS, M. H.
Structural steelwork productivity: a guide to the use of modern fabrication equipment. (Constructional steelwork SWP)
National Economic Development Office, 1981

BRIGGS, P. S.
Gloving, clothing and special leathers. (Report G135)
Tropical Products Institute, 1981

BRIMELOW, Thomas, Lord
Improved protection for the occupational pension rights and expectations of early leavers. A report of the Occupational Pensions Board, 1981
Session 1980–81 Cmnd. 8271

Occupational Pension Schemes (Connected Employers) Regulations, 1982. Report of the Occupational Pensions Board, August 1982
Session 1981–82 Cmnd. 8617

The Occupational Pensions Schemes (Public Service Pensions Schemes) (Amendment Regulations, 1979). Report of the Occupational Pensions Board, 1979
Session 1979–80 HC 320

The Occupational Pension Schemes (Public Service Pension Schemes) (Amendment) Regulations 1980. (S.1. 1980 no. 288). Report of the Occupational Pensions Board preceded by a statement in accordance with section 68(2) of the Social Security Act 1973 and section 61(3) of the Social Security Pensions Act 1975. March 1980
Session 1979–80 HC 472

BRITTAN, Y.
The effect of ill-health and subsequent compensation and support on household income: a logistic regression approach, by Y. Brittan and I. G. Vlachonikolis. (Centre for Socio-Legal Studies: Working Paper no. 6)
SSRC, 1980

BROAD, K. F.
Tree planting on man-made sites in Wales
Forestry Commission, 1979

BRODY, Stephen
Taking offenders out of circulation, by Stephen Brody and Roger Tarling. (Research Study no. 64)
Home Office, 1980

BROLON, William
The changing contours of British industrial relations: a survey of manufacturing industry
SSRC, Industrial Relations Research Unit, 1981

BROMELEY, Leonard
Scotia Investments Ltd. Report of investigation under the Companies Act of 1948, by L. Bromeley and J. S. Hillyer
Trade Dept., 1980

BROOKE, A. C.
Social entertainment in the Belfast city centre. Report of the working party
DoE for N.I., 1979

BROOKES, Christopher
Boards of directors in British industry. (Research Paper no. 7)
Employment Dept., 1979

BROOKING, A. J.
Training resources working party. Report
National Training Council for the National Health Service, 1981

BROPHY, J.
Study of information services on training matters in the NHS. Report by J. Brophy and R. B. Lovell
National Training Council for the National Health Service, 1980

BROSTER, W. H.
Feeding strategies for dairy cows. Report of a seminar, Harrogate, October 1979
Agricultural Research Council, 1980

BROWN, A. A. D.
Mechanical springs. (Engineering Design Guides 42)
Design Council, 1981

BROWN, A. H.
Commuter travel trends in London and the southeast 1966–79 – and associated factors
D.Tp, 1981

BROWN, C. A.
Drainage problems. Report of a study tour undertaken in Yugoslavia, 1979 series
ADAS, 1979

BROWN, George
Explanations and explaining, by George Brown and Neville Hatton. (DES Teacher Education Project Focus books)
Macmillan for DES, 1982

BROWN, L. C.
The land resources and agro-forestal development of St. Helena, Volume I: Prospects for development, Vol. 2 resources + (Vol. 3) Maps (9 maps in folder). (Land Resource Study 32)
Land Resources Development Centre, 1981

BROWN, M.
Despite the welfare state: a report on the SSRC/DHSS programme of research into transmitted deprivation, by M. Brown and N. Madge. (Studies in Deprivation and Disadvantage)
Heinemann for SSRC, 1982

BROWN, Sir Max
Electricity supply meters, report on the supply and export.
Monopolies and Mergers Commission, August 1979
Session 1979–80 Cmnd. 7639

Surrey Advertiser Newspaper Holdings Ltd. and the Guardian and Manchester Evening News Ltd. A report on the proposed transfer of 29 newspapers to the Guardian and Manchester Evening News Ltd. Monopolies and Mergers Commission report, May 1979
Session 1979–80 HC 100

BROWN, Michael B.
Isabella plantation: woodland garden; Richmond Park
DoE, 1980

BROWN, Paul Steven
Report of inquiry see: MORLAND, M

BROWN, R. A.
Orford Catle, Suffolk. 9th impr
DoE, 1982

BROWN, R. N.
The interrelationships between costs and prices in the U.K. (Discussion Paper no. 8)
Bank of England, 1980

BROWN, Sally
What do they know? A review of criterion-referenced assessment
Scottish Education Dept., 1980

BROWN, William
The changing contours of British industrial relations: a survey of manufacturing industry. (Warwick Studies in Industrial Relations)
SSRC, 1981

BROWNE, M.
Careers opportunities and education
Equal Opportunities Commission, 1982

BRUMFIT, C. J.
Readers for foreign learners of English. (ETIC Information Guide no. 7)
British Council, 1979

BRUNT, Harry
Camping and caravanning in and around the Peak District. Policy and recommendations. Report of the joint study officer working party
Peak Park Joint Planning Board, 1980

BUCK, W. E.
International dairy congress, 20th. Report of a visit to Paris
ADAS, 1978

BUCKLE, A. E.
Airborne bacteria, dust and manure gases in the animal environment. Report of a study tour undertaken in Canada and USA, September 1979
ADAS, 1979

BUDD, A.
Factors underlying the recent recession, by G. D. N. Worswick and Dr. A. Budd. (Papers Presented to the Panel of Academic Consultants no. 15)
Bank of England, 1981

BUIST, M.
Assessment of children; a follow-up survey, interim report, by E. Mapstone and M. Buist
Scottish Education Dept., 1980

BULL, D. A.
Fertiliser handling and distribution: report of a visit to Eire, 13–14 October 1980
ADAS, 1981

BULLEN, R. B.
Assessment of anthropomorphic dummies for fire service rescue training. (Report 9181)
Home Office, 1981

BULLER, A. J.
The support of health and personal social services research: a report by the Chief Scientists Advisory Group
DHSS, 1982

BUNTING, Claire
Public attitudes to deafness, a survey. (Social Survey 1117)
OPCS, 1981

BUNYAN, P. J.
International (5th) congress of pesticide chemistry, Kyoto, August – September 1982. Report of the meeting by P. J. Bunyan
ADAS, 1982

Study of the influence of pesticides on the natural ecosystem and different species of fauna and flora. Report of a visit to USSR, September 1979, by P. J. Bunyan and C. A. Edwards
ADAS, 1980

Survey of dieldrin residues in food. The seventh report of the steering group on food surveillance. The working party on pesticide residues. (Food Surveillance Paper no. 7)
MAFF, 1982

Survey of lead in food. Report of the working party on the monitoring of foodstuffs for heavy metals. (Food Surveillance Paper no. 10)
MAFF, 1982

Working party on pesticide residues (1977–81). Report. The ninth report of the steering group on food surveillance. (Food Surveillance Paper no. 9)
MAFF, 1982

BURCHELL, A.
Appraisal of development options in the National Health Service, by A. Burchell and B. K. Gilbert. (Review of Capricode Working Paper)
DHSS, 1982

The costs of alcohol misuse, by S. Holterman and A. Burchell. (Government Economic Service Working Paper no. 37)
DHSS, 1981

Inequalities in health; analysis of the 1976 general household survey. (Government Economic Service Working Paper 48)
DHSS, 1981

BURGH, J. C.
The self-regulatory system of advertising control. Report of the working party
Trade Dept., 1980

BURGOYNE, J. H.
Offshore safety. Report of the committee, March 1980
Session 1979–80 Cmnd. 7866

BURKITT, Ann.
Life begins at forty
Health Education Council, 1980

BURNSIDE, A. M.
The revised index of industrial production for Scotland for the period 1958 to 1970, by A. M. Burnside and D. S. Henderson. (Economics and Statistics Unit: Discussion Paper no. 6)
Scottish Economic Planning Dept., 1980

BURR, E. C.
Urban poverty: report by the Ministry of Overseas Development study group. (Overseas Development Paper no. 19)
Overseas Development Admin., 1979

BURRELL, N. J.
International symposium on controlled atmosphere storage of grains. Report of a visit to Italy, May 1980, by N. J. Burrell and S. W. Pixton
ADAS, 1980

BURRELL, T.S.
'A future for the village'. Working party on rural settlement policies interim report
DoE, 1979

BURRETT, F. G.
Rayner scrutiny of the departmental museums; Science Museum and Victoria and Albert Museum. Report by F. G. Burrett
DES, 1982

BURROWS, John
Crime prevention and the police, by J. Burrows. (Research Study no. 55)
Home Office, 1979

BURSTALL, Clare
Assessment – the American experience, by C. Burstall and B. Kay
Dept. Education and Science, 1979

BURTON, Paul
Skills in a thematic approach to C. D. T. (Schools Council Programme Three: Skills for Adult Working Life)
Schools Council, 1983

BUSBY, R. J. N.
Investment appraisal in forestry with particular reference to conifers in Britain, by R. J. N. Busby and A. J. Grayson. (Booklet 47)
Forestry Commission, 1981

BUSH, Peter
Postgraduate income and expenditure. A survey carried out on behalf of the Department of Education and Science and the Scottish Education Department, by Susan Dight and Peter Bush
OPCS, 1979

Undergraduate income and expenditure. A survey carried out on behalf of the DES and the SED, by P. Bush and S. Dight.
OPCS, 1979

BUSH, R.
Scarborough Castle
DoE, 1981

BUSH, R. P.
A disaggregated model of energy consumption in U.K. industry, by R. P. Bush and A. T. Chadwick. (ETSU R8)
Energy Technology Support Unit, 1979

The pattern of energy use in the UK – 1976, by R. P. Bush and B. J. Matthews (ETSU R7)
Energy Technology Support Unit, 1981

BUSS, B. P.
Status of standards in computing. Report by the national computer users forum (Standards Working Group)
National Computing Centre, 1979

BUSHELL, R.
Model to forecast payments from the Redundancy Fund. (Government Economic Service Working Paper 47)
Employment Dept., 1981

BUSWELL, Helen
What's where in Clwyd
Welsh Consumer Council, 1980

What's where in Gwent
Welsh Consumer Council, 1980

What's where in Mid Glamorgan
Welsh Consumer Council, 1980

What's where in West Glamorgan
Welsh Consumer Council, 1980

BUTCHER, B.
Electoral registration in 1981
OPCS, 1982

Variable quotas – an analysis of the variability. (New Methodology Series no. NM10)
OPCS, 1982

BUTLER, A. J.
11 to 16+ project fire; analysis of pupil questionnaires (Scotland). (Scientific Advisory Branch Memo. 2/80)
Home Office, 1980

Fire prevention publicity – an analysis of the 1979 fat campaign. (Home Office Scientific Advisory Branch Report 11/80)
Home Office, 1980

BUTLER, C. G.
Teacher training and staff development implications of the expansion of MSC-related programmes. Advisory Committee on the Supply and Education of Teachers
DES, 1982

BUTLER, Linda
Adult external candidates for GCE examinations
Advisory Council for Adult and Continuing Education, 1981

BUTLIN, J. A.
Welfare costs of structural adjustment in the UK fishing industry. (FERU Occas. Papers Series 1, 1979)
White Fish Authority, 1979

BUTTER, Neil
Ozalid Holdings Ltd. Report of investigation under the Companies Act, 1948, by N. Butter and B. A. Kemp
DoT, 1980

BUTTERWORTH, Keith
International conference of agricultural economists, 7th. Report of a visit to Canada.
ADAS, 1979

Microcomputer developments: report of a visit to Tasmania and Australia, November/December 1981
ADAS, 1982

Microcomputers on the farm. Report from ADAS investigation team, December 1979
ADAS, 1979

BUTTERY, P. J.
Protein metabolism in the ruminant. A seminar, Sutton Bonington, December 1978
Agricultural Research Council, 1979

BUTTIMER, James Michael
North Devon Railway Co. Ltd.; Words in Action Co. Ltd. Investigations under the Companies Act, 1948, by B. M. Hooper and J. M. Buttimer
Trade Dept., 1979

BYRNE, Donn
Communication games, by D. Byrne and S. Rixon. (ELT Guide 1)
British Council, 1979

BYRON, Reginald
Burra fishermen: social and economic change in a Shetland community. (North Sea Oil Panel Occasional Paper no. 9)
SSRC, 1981

Social change in Dunrossness; a Shetland study, by R. Byron and G. McFarlane. (North Sea Oil Panel Occasional Paper no. 1)
SSRC, 1980

CABLE, V.
Evaluation of the multifibre arrangement and negotiating options. (Commonwealth Economic Paper no.15)
Commonwealth Secretariat, 1981

CAIRNCROSS, Alec
Protectionism; threat to international order. The impact on developing countries
Commonwealth Secretariat, 1982

CAIRNS, Catherine
Experiment continued: countryside management in the urban fringe of Barnet and South Herefordshire
Countryside Commission, 1982

CALCUTT, David
Cornhill Consolidated Group Ltd. (in liquidation). Report of investigation under the Companies Act, 1948, by D. Calcutt and J. Whinney
Trade Dept., 1980

CALDWELL, J. B.
Small ships' survival. Ship and Marine Technology Requirements Board. Proceedings of a seminar held at the National Maritime Institute, Feltham, May 1978
Industry Dept., 1979

CALDWELL, T. H.
International congress of soil science, 11th. Report of a visit to Canada, by R. C. Little and T. H. Caldwell
ADAS, 1978

CALVERT, J. A.
Mid summer symposium Oslo and Tonsberg, Norway. Report of a visit to Norway, June 1980, by J. A. Calvert and others
ADAS, 1980

CAMERON, G. N.
The archives' programs for processing the general household survey. (SSRC Survey Archive Paper no.1)
SSRC, 1980

CAMERON, S. J.
Local authority aid to industry; an evaluation in Tyne and Wear. (Inner Cities Research Programme, 7)
DoE, 1982

CAMPBELL, Brian
Micro-electronics – a non-technical briefing for under secretaries. Summary of the proceedings of a seminar, June 1979. (C. S. C. Working Paper no. 16)
Civil Service College, 1979

CAMPBELL, G. G.
Fuel consumption targets. Interim report of the working group. (Automotive Energy Consultative Group)
Dept. of Energy, 1979

CAMPBELL, H.
Productivity, by H. Campbell and T. Craven. (Research Paper no. 4)
Labour Relations Agency, 1981

CAMPBELL, Stuart
Conversion for single persons. A report to the Housing Corporation
National Building Agency, 1979

CAMPBELL, W.
Engineering in the future
Southern Gas, 1980

CANNING, A. J.
Black dyes for coir fibre, 2: evaluation of selected dyes. (L52)
Tropical Products Institute, 1979

Black dyes for coir fibre, 3: practical considerations, by A. J. Canning, C. G. Jarman and S. M. Mykoluk. (Report L62)
Tropical Products Institute, 1982

The evaluation of some Phocion MX dyes for the dyeing of sisal, by M. Edwards and A. J. Canning. (L56)
Tropical Products Institute, 1981

CANTLEY, Sir Joseph Donaldson
Personal injuries litigation procedure working party. Report, March 1979
Session 1978–79 Cmnd. 7476

CAPLAN, D.
Independent review of the work of the Royal Commission of Historical Manuscripts: report
Civil Service Dept., 1980

CARD, Fred
Post Office; special agent. The report of a working party on the social service brief of the Post Office
National Consumer Council, 1979

CARDEN, P. W.
Integrated control in agriculture and forestry. Symposium, October 1979. Report of a visit to Austria, by K. S. George and P. W. Carden
ADAS, 1979

Integrated crop protection. Report on a symposium, Valance, France, June 1980, by P. W. Carden and H. J. Gould
MAFF, 1980

CARMICHAEL, C. L.
Redundancy, re-employment and the tyre industry, by C. L. Carmichael and L. M. Cook. (Manpower Intelligence and Planning)
MSC, 1981

CARNALL, C. A.
Women in the oil industry; attitude to work survey, by C. A. Carnall and V. J. Hammond
Petroleum Industry Training Board, 1979

CARRINGTON, Lord Peter Alexander Rupert, 6th Baron
Southern Rhodesia. Constitutional conference held at Lancaster House, London, September – December 1979. Report
Session 1979–80 Cmnd. 7802

CARSTAIRS, V.
Services for the elderly, by J. Bond and V. Carstairs. (Scottish Health Service Studies 42)
SHHD, 1982

CARTER, A.
Making the most of tax forms; a practical guide to P45, P2 and P15, by A. Corsini and A. Carter
Adult Literacy and Basic Skills Unit, 1982

CARTER, C. I.
Conifer lachnids in Britain, by C. I. Carter and N. R. Master. (Bulletin 58)
Forestry Commission, 1982

CARTER, D.
Sidetracked?: a look at the careers advice given to fifth-form girls, by Y. Benett and D. Carter
Equal Opportunities Commission, 1981

CARTER, I. R.
Social monitoring of oil developments in Scotland: an evaluation. (North Sea Oil Panel Occasional Paper no. 16)
SSRC, 1982

CARTER, P. D.
Man-made Fibre Production SWP: progress report
NEDO, 1981

CARTER, S.
Half a chance: a report on job discrimination against young blacks in Nottingham, by J. Hubbuck and S. Carter
Commission for Racial Equality, 1980

CASEBOW, A.
Devon Grassland Society tour of dairy farms in Brittany. Report of a visit to France, April 1981
ADAS, 1982

CASSELS, J. M.
Heat loads in British cities. Report of the heat load density working party of the combined heat and power group. (Energy Paper no. 34)
Energy Dept., 1979

CATTO, Gay
Higher education and the employment of graduates. (Research Paper 19)
Employment Dept., 1981

CAWSON, P.
Young offenders in care
DHSS, 1982

CECIL, J. E.
A stirrup-operated coconut grater, by J. E. Cecil and W. H. Timmins. (Rural Technology Guide 6)
Tropical Products Institute, 1980

Starch extraction: a check list of commercially available machinery, by D. G. Birse and J. E. Cecil. (G142)
Topical Products Institute, 1980

CHADWICK, A. T.
Dies and moulds: research on the problems involved in industry, by R. P. Bush and A. T. Chadwick. (ETSU R8)
Energy Technology Support Unit, 1979

CHALLIS, Harry
Dies and moulds: research on the problems involved in manufacture, by H. Challis, C. Stanton and P. Gough
Science and Engineering Research Council, 1982

Grinding: research on the problems of grinding technology, by H. Challis, C. Stanton and R. Palmer
Science and Engineering Research Council, 1982

Research in noise and vibration. A selection of short articles illustrating how basic research can be used to solve specific industrial problems by applying the latest scientific techniques, prepared by Harry Challis and Chris Stanton
Science Research Council, 1979

Research in tribology and bearings, by C. Stanton and H. Challis
Science Research Council, 1980

CHAMBERS, G. A.
Social enquiry reports in Scotland, pt. 1: social enquiry reports in two Scottish regions, by J. H. Curran, pt 2: sheriffs' perspective, by G. A. Chambers
Scottish Office, 1982

CHAMBERS, J.
Bromham pig study group visit: report of a visit to Denmark, 1–5 November 1981
MAFF, 1982

CHANDLER, G.
Energy task force. Report. (NEDC(81)15)
NEDO, 1981

CHANEY, Judith
Social networks and job information: the situation of women who return to work
Equal Opportunities Commision, 1981

CHAPLIN, M. F.
Project information; its context and arrangement. A report and proposals on the way forward. (Project Information Group)
DoE, 1979

CHAPMAN, P. J.
Acquisition of information on biology and distribution of pests etc.: report of a visit to USA and Canada, 6 days, August/September 1981
ADAS, 1982

CHAPPELL E. P.
Food and Drink Manufacturing EDC Progress Report 1980
NEDO, 1980

CHAPTER, J. F.
Southern region unusual services 1979, by B. W. Rayner and J. F. Chapter
Southern Electric Group, 1979

CHARLES, D. R.
Massey University annual poultry convention. Report of a visit to New Zealand, May/June 1979
ADAS, 1979

CHARLESWORTH, F. R.
Windscale; the management of safety
Health and Safety Executive, 1981

CHARLESWORTH, R. R.
Visit by the West Sussex Tomato Working Party to nurseries of prominent growers, by R. R. Charlesworth and A. P. Wareing. (Report of a visit to Holland, 18–19 September 1981)
ADAS, 1982

CHARLTON, John
The Banqueting House, Whitehall
DoE, 1981

Brougham Castle, Westmorland
DoE, 1981

Brougham Castle, repr
London, HMSO, for DoE, 1982

Broughton Castle, repr
DoE, 1982

Hampton Court Palace, by G. H. Chettle and John Charlton. 5th ed
DoE, 1982

Lancaster House St. James's
DoE, 1981

Osborne House
DoE, 1981

The Tower of London: its buildings and institutions
DoE, 1979

CHATFIELD, A. C.
Water spray from heavy goods vehicles; an assessment of some vehicle modifications, by A. C. Chatfield and others. (Vehicle Standards and Engineering Division, Report no. VSE 513)
DTp, 1979

CHERRY, G.
Effective writing in advisory work, by G. Cherry and N. Harvey
ADAS, 1981

CHETTLE, G. H.
Hampton Court Palace, by G. H. Chettle and John Charlton. 5th ed
DoE, 1982

Kirby Hall, Northamptonshire, 3rd ed., by G. H. Chettle and revised and expanded by Peter Leach. (Official handbook)
DoE, 1980

CHILD, S. C.
Ultrasonic river gauging in the U.K. (Instruments and Methods of Observation Group)
Thames Water Authority, 1979

CHILVER, Sir Henry
The future of higher education in Northern Ireland. Report of the Higher Education Review Group for Northern Ireland
Dept. of Education Northern Ireland, 1982

Joining and assembly: the impact of robots and automation. Report of the Advisory Council for Applied Research and Development working group
Cabinet Office, 1979

CHITTENDEN, A. E.
Anaerobic digesters for small-scale vegetable processing plants. (G139)
Tropical Products Institute, 1980

Producer gas: its potential and application in developing countries, by G. R. Breag and A. E. Chittenden. (G130)
Tropical Products Institute, 1979

CHIVERS, A. R. L.
Zinc diecasting. (Engineering Design Guides 41)
Design Council, 1981

CHRISTIE, A. N.
Welfare of pigs prior to slaughter: report of a study tour undertaken in Holland and West Germany, September 1980
ADAS, 1981

CHRISTIE, J. M.
Thinning control in British woodlands. Metric revision by G. J. Hamilton and J. M. Christie. (Booklet no. 32, 2nd impr.)
Forestry Commission, 1982

Yield models for forest management, by P. N. Edwards and J. M. Christie. (Booklet 48)
Forestry Commission, 1981

CHRISTIE, P. M.
Cairn Euny
DoE, 1981

CHRISTIE, T.
Defining public examination standards. (Schools Council Research Studies)
Schools Council, 1981

CHUKWUJEKWU, S. E.
Technical education and industry, 2: report of a commonwealth regional seminar, Ibadan, Nigeria, April – May 1978
Commonwealth Secretariat, 1979

CITRON K. M.
Tuberculosis today, by K. M. Citron and others. (Topics of Our Time, 3)
DHSS, 1981

CLABER, C. R.
Flexible magnetic disc cartridges, by C. R. Claber and J. B. Paterson. (Guides to Computing Standards no. 4)
National Computing Centre, 1981

Magnetic disc packs and rigid discs. (Guides to Computing Standards no. 5)
National Computing Centre, 1981

CLAPHAM, Alfred
Thornton Abbey, Humberside, by A. Clapham and P. K. B. Reynolds. 2nd ed., 8th pr
DoE, 1982

Whitby Abbey, Yorkshire
DoE, 1981

CLARK, A. B. E.
Brinkburn Priory, by A. B. E. Clark
DoE, 1982

CLARK, B. A.
North-south dialogue; making it work. Report by a Commonwealth group of experts
Commonwealth Secretariat, 1982

CLARK, M. W.
The strategic situation of the electronic capital goods industry in the U.K. A report by the radio communications, radar and navigational aids sector working party
NEDO, 1980

CLARK, Michael
Radio communications, radar, and navigational aids sector working party. Progress report
NEDO, 1979

CLARK, Sir Robert
Review body on doctors' and dentists' remuneration tenth report 1980
Session 1979–80 Cmnd. 7903

12th report, May 1982
Session 1981–82 Cmnd. 8550

CLARK, S.
A comparative evaluation of SIR, SAS, P-STAT and OSIRIS IV. (SSRC Data Archive, University of Essex, no. 6)
SSRC, 1982

An evaluation of OSIRIS IV. (SSRC Data Archive, University of Essex, no. 3)
SSRC, 1982

An evaluation of SAS 79. (SSRC Data Archive, University of Essex, no. 5)
SSRC, 1982

An evaluation of P-STAT 78. (SSRC Data Archive, University of Essex, no. 4)
SSRC, 1981

CLARKE, A. J.
Electricity supply and the environment
Central Electricity Generating Board, 1979

CLARKE, Darryn James
The actions of the authorities and agencies relating to D. J. Clarke. Report of the inquiry
See: HUGHILL, J

CLARKE, F. J. P.
Tidal power, the next step. Recommendations of the Ad Hoc Working Party on Tidal Power
Energy Dept., 1980

CLARKE, G. J.
Elderly farmers in the U.K. Report of an ADAS Socio-economic Group Working Party. (Socio-economic Paper 4)
MAFF, 1976

CLARKE, Linda
Occupational choice: a critical review of research in the United Kingdom. (DE Careers Service Branch)
Employment Dept., 1980

The practice of vocational guidance: a critical review of research in the United Kingdom. (DE Careers Service Branch)
Employment Dept., 1980

The transition from school to work: a critical review of research in the United Kingdom. (DE Careers Service Branch)
Employment Dept., 1980

CLARKE, M. T.
Men, women and post primary principalship in Northern Ireland, 1978.
Equal Opportunities Commission for Northern Ireland, 1978

CLARKE, P. A.
Industrial profile of rice milling, by G. Flynn and P. A. Clarke. (G148)
Tropical Products Institute, 1980

CLAYTON, Robert
Information technology. Advisory Council for Applied Research and Development. Working group report.
Cabinet Office, 1980

CLEGG, F. G.
Diseases and farming of red deer. Report of a visit to New Zealand, November/December 1979
ADAS, 1979

CLEGG, Hugh A.
British Waterways Board salaried staffs. (Standing Commission on Pay Comparability Report no. 5), March 1980
Session 1979–80 Cmnd. 7851

General report. (Standing Commission on Pay Comparability Report no. 9)
Session 1979–80 Cmnd. 7995

CLEGG, Hugh A. *(continued)*
Local authority and university manual workers; NHS ancillary staffs; and ambulancemen (statistical appendix). (Standing Commission on Pay Comparability Report no. 1), August 1979
Session 1979–80 Cmnd. 7641 and 7641–I

Local authority building workers. (Standing Commission on Pay Comparability Report no. 10)
Session 1979–80 Cmnd. 8014

Municipal airport manual workers. (Standing Commission on Pay Comparability Report no. 6) March 1980
Session 1979–80 Cmnd. 7852

Nurses and midwives. (Standing Commission on Pay Comparability Report no. 3), January 1980
Session 1979–80 Cmnd. 7795

Professions supplementary to medicine. (Standing Commission on Pay Comparability Report no. 4), March 1980
Session 1979–80 Cmnd. 7850

Teachers. (Standing Commission on Pay Comparability Report no. 7), April 1980
Session 1979–80 Cmnd. 7880

University technicians. (Standing Commission on Pay Comparability Report no. 2)
Session 1979–80 Cmnd. 7640

University technicians. (Standing Commission on Pay Comparability Report no. 8), July 1980
Session 1979–80 Cmnd. 7974

CLEMENTS, R.
By-election results since the General Election of May 1979, by J. Tanfield and R. Clements. (Research Note no. 79)
House of Commons, 1982

Statistical digest of by-election results since the General Election of May 1979, by J. Tanfield and R. Clements. (Fact Sheet no. 16)
House of Commons, 1982

CLEMINSON, J.
Improving productivity in the food and drink manufacturing industry: the case for a joint approach. (Food and Drink Manufacturing EDC)
NEDO, 1982

CLIFFORD, Brian
Job design and new factories. A review of the literature. (Work Research Unit Information System Review no. 1)
Employment Dept., 1980

CLIFT, P.
Record keeping in primary schools, by P. Clift, G. Weiner and E. Wilson. (SC Research Studies)
Schools Council, 1981

CLIFTON, Richard
Impact of employment legislation on small firms, by R. Clifton and C. Tatton-Brown. (Research Paper, no. 6)
Employment Dept., 1979

CLUCAS, I. J.
Fish handling, preservation and processing in the tropics: part 1. (G144)
Tropical Products Institute, 1981

An introduction to fish handling and processing, by I. J. Clucas and P. J. Sutcliffe. (G143)
Tropical Products Institute, 1981

COAD, J. G.
Fort Brockhurst
DoE, 1981

COBB, H. S.
Parliamentary history, libraries and records. Essays presented to Maurice Bond. (House of Lords Record Office)
House of Lords, 1981

COCKCROFT, J. R.
Effect of the milk marketing scheme on consumers. Report. (Agricultural Marketing Act 1958: Consumers' Committee for England and Wales)
MAFF, 1981

COCKROFT, W. H.
Mathematics counts. Report of the Committee of Inquiry Into the Teaching of Mathematics in Schools
DES, 1982

COGGAN, Donald, Archbp. of Canterbury
Deaconesses and Lay Workers (Pensions) Measure. (182nd Report of the Ecclesiastical Committee), December 1979
Session 1979–80 HC 325; HL 120

COGHLAN, R. T.
A small monetary model of the U.K. economy. (Discussion Paper no. 3)
Bank of England, 1979

COHEN, Gaynor
The controversy over bilingual education in California and the implications for Britain. (Working Paper no. 24)
Civil Service College, 1980

The crisis in affirmative action in the USA. (CSC Working Paper no. 9)
Civil Service College, 1979

Educational vouchers; some thoughts from California (Civil Service College Working Paper no. 32)
Civil Service College, 1982

Proposition 13 in California: the background and the effects. (CSC Working Paper no. 13)
Civil Service College, 1979

Youth policies in the USA: employment and preparation for employment. (CSC Working Paper no. 21)
Civil Service College, 1980

COLE, Lyndis
Wildlife in the city; a study of practical conservation projects
Nature Conservancy Council, 1980

COLE, W. Owen
World religions; a handbook for teachers. (4th ed.)
Commission for Racial Equality, 1979

COLEMAN, D. E.
Recreation footpaths. (A regional strategy for sport and recreation. Subject report 1 with summary)
Eastern Council for Sport and Recreation, 1979

COLES, G. J. K.
United Industrial Company Ltd. Investigation under the Companies Act, 1948. Report by G. J. K. Coles and P. H. Dobson
Trade Dept., 1981

COLLARD, A. J.
Co-operative production and marketing: report of a visit to France, 25–28 April 1982
ADAS, 1982

COLLEDGE, Maureen
Study of the long-term unemployed, by M. Colledge and R. Bartholomew
MSC, 1980

COLLINGRIDGE, J.
Review of assistance for disabled people; a report to the commission (Employment Service ESP 109)
MSC, 1982

COLLINS, M. F.
The impact of neighbouring sports and leisure centres, by J. Atkinson and M. F. Collins. (Sports Council Research Working Paper 18)
Sports Council, 1980

COLLINS, M. F. *(continued)*
Integrated facilities (priority theme IV). Report of the seminar, 29 October to 1 November 1979 (Committee for the Development of Sport)
Sports Council, 1980

CONGDON, P. L.
Flight path deviations due to cumulo-nimbus activity in the U.K. controlled airspace, by J. B. Critchley and P. L. Congdon. (CAA Paper 79005)
Civil Aviation Authority, 1979

CONNELL, David
The U.K.'s performance in export markets; some evidence from international trade data. (Discussion Paper 6)
NEDO, 1979

CONNOR, Anne
Arrestments of wages and salaries; a review of employers' involvement. (Research report for the Scottish Law Commission no. 4)
Scottish Office, 1980

Characteristics of warrant sales. (Research report for the Scottish Law Commission no. 2)
Scottish Office, 1980

COOK, L. M.
Redundancy, re-employment and the tyre industry by C. L. Carmichael and L. M. Cook. (Manpower Intelligence and Planning)
MSC, 1981

COOK, V. A.
International symposium on the diagnosis and treatment of varroasis, West Germany, September – October 1980
ADAS, 1980

COOKE, Kenneth R.
The impact of the mobility allowance; an evaluation study, by K. R. Cooke and F. M. Stader. (Research Report no. 7)
DHSS, 1981

COOKE, Lord Samuel
Family law: illegitimacy, 1979
see: CRETNEY, S. M

COOMES, T. J.
Survey of mycotoxins in the U. K. Report of the working party. (Food Surveillance Paper no. 4)
MAFF, 1980

COOPER, C. L.
Practical approaches to women's career development. Report of the conference 16–17 November 1981, Oxford
MSC, 1982

COOPER, F. B.
Anglo French collaboration in agricultural research: discussion meeting on 'forage brassicas': report of a visit to France, 14–17 September 1981
ADAS, 1982

COOPER, N.
School-industry link schemes, a study and recommendations. (Standard Telephones and Cable Ltd.)
Dept. Education and Science, 1981

COPE, C. D.
Health capital programme in Wales. Report of the capital formula sub-group
Welsh Office, 1981

Speech therapy staffing in Wales. Report of a working party
Welsh Office, 1979

COPEMAN, Harold
The national accounts: a short guide. (Studies in Official Statistics no. 36)
Central Statistical Office, 1981

COPLAND, I. A. M.
Metallurgical training requirements in the iron and steel industry. A report of a research study carried out by Incubon/AIC
Iron and Steel Industry Training Board, 1980

CORBEL, M. J.
Diagnostic procedures for non-smooth Brucella strains, by M. J. Corbel and others. (Booklet 2074)
ADAS, 1979

CORBEN, A. E.
Terrestrial land mobile services: spectrum requirements and availability to the end of the century. Report of the Mobile Radio Committee
Home Office, 1982

CORBIN, Robert
Commonwealth youth affairs council, London, May 1980. (Commonwealth Youth programme)
Commonwealth Secretariat, 1980

CORFIELD, Gerry
Starting and stopping. (Open Science)
Schools Council, 1979

CORFIELD, K. G.
Design for success. A summary of 'product design', a report
NEDO, 1979

Product design. (Industrial Strategy Special Topics)
NEDO, 1979

CORINA, Lewis
Oldham CDP: the final report. (Papers in Community Studies no. 23)
Dept. Social Administration and Social Work, for Home Office, 1979

CORK, Sir Kenneth
Bankruptcy. Interim report of the Insolvency Law Review Committee. July 1980
Session 1979–80 Cmnd. 7968

Insolvency law and practice. Report of the review committee
Session 1981–82 Cmnd. 8558

CORMACK, Keith
Household consumption of frozen fish and frozen fish products in Great Britain. (Fishing Economics Research Unit: Occasional Paper Series no. 1, 1980)
White Fish Authority, 1980

CORMACK, R. J.
Into work? Young school leavers and the structure of opportunity in Belfast, by R. J. Cormack and others. (Research Paper 5)
Fair Employment Agency, 1980

CORNEILLE, J. P.
A manpower planning model for the science group. (ORUR 1/79)
Industry Dept., 1979

CORNEY, Graham
Teacher education and geography, 16–19. (Occasional Paper no. 1)
Schools Council, 1981

CORSINI, I.
Making the most of tax forms; a practical guide to P45, P2 and P15 by I. Corsini and A. Carter
Adult Literacy and Basic Skills Unit, 1982

COSGROVE, D. F.
Community councils in Strathclyde region 1976–79, by D. F. Cosgrove and H. N. Shelden. (Central Research Unit)
Scottish Office, 1980

COTTAM, J. F.
Farmhouse and self-catering accomodation on the farm. (Socio-economic Paper no. 5). (Booklet 2005)
ADAS, 1979

COTTAM, M. B.
The Highlands in transition: current aspects of social geography in a peripheral area, by M. B. Cottam, P. L. Knox, D. H. Hirsch. (North Sea Oil Panel Occasional Paper no. 6)
SSRC, 1981

COTTEN, J.
Assessing resistance to globodera pallida in potato varieties entered for national list testing. Report of a study tour
ADAS, 1982

COTTRELL, J.
Appeals by the prosecution against sentences and acquitals; a survey of the situation in some Commonwealth Countries, by A. Paliwala and J. Cottrell
Commonwealth Secretariat, 1982

COTTRILL, B. R.
Development of protein feeding systems for ruminants. Report of a study tour
ADAS, 1982

Ruminant physiology. Fifth international symposium, September 1979. Report of a visit to France
ADAS, 1979

COUSINS, J.
Working in the inner city; a case study (Inner Cities Research Programme, 8)
DoE, 1982

COUSINS, John
Efficiency dialogues in the tyre manufacturing industry. A document for discussion. Rubber Processing SWP
NEDO, 1980

The tyre industry; first conference of the Rubber Processing SWP. Report of the Birmingham conference, November 1978
NEDO, 1980

Tyre Industry SWP progress report 1980
NEDO, 1980

Tyres, the road ahead. Rubber processing SWP
NEDO, 1979

COX, P. D.
International congress on photobiology, 8th report
ADAS, 1981

CRAFT, Michael
Whole healthy or diseased disabled teeth? Phase 1. Results of pilot studies and controlled feasibility trials, by Michael Craft and others. (Monograph Series no. 4)
Health Education Council, 1981

CRAGG, Arnold
Qualitative research among homeworkers, by A. Cragg and T. Dawson. (Research Paper no. 21)
Employment Dept., 1981

CRAIG, Christine
Abolition and after: the Jute Wages Council. (Labour Studies Group, Dept. of Applied Economics, University of Cambridge, Research Paper no. 15)
Employment Dept., 1980

CRAIG, J.
Review of the government statistical services. Initial study of the Office of Population Censuses and Surveys, by S. Witzenfeld and J. Craig
Central Statistical Office, 1981

CRAIG, John
Population density and concentration in Great Britain, 1951, 1961 and 1971. (Studies on Medical and Population Subjects no. 42)
OPCS, 1980

Variations between small areas in some 1971 census variables. (Occ. Paper 17)
OPCS, 1981

CRASTER, O. E.
Hurst Castle. 2nd ed., 3rd impr.
DoE, 1982

CRAVEN, Edward
Inner city partnerships. (CSC Working Paper no. 15)
Civil Service College, 1979

CRAVEN, J. A.
An analysis of FMS costed farms, 1979–80, by S. J. Amies and J. A. Craven. (Farm Management Services Information Unit Report no. 24)
Milk Marketing Board, 1980

An analysis of FMS costed farms 1981–82, by S. J. Amies and J. A. Craven (Farm Management Service Report no. 33)
Milk Marketing Board, 1982

CRAVEN, T.
Productivity, by H. Campbell and T. Craven. (Research Paper no. 4)
Labour Relations Agency, 1981

CRAWSHAY, Lady Elizabeth
Borough of Aberconway. Review of district electoral arrangements draft proposals
Local Government Boundary Commission for Wales, 1982

Borough of Afan. Review of district electoral arrangements report and proposals
Local Government Boundary Commission for Wales, 1980

Borough of Arfon. Review of district electoral arrangements: draft proposals
Local Government Boundary Commission for Wales, 1981

Borough of Brecknock. Special community review: report and proposals
Local Government Boundary Commission for Wales, 1981

Borough of Colwyn. Review of district electoral arrangements draft proposals
Local Government Boundary Commission for Wales, 1982

Borough of Cynon Valley. Review of district electoral arrangements: draft proposals
Local Government Boundary Commission for Wales, 1981

Borough of Cynon Valley. Review of district electoral arrangements: report and proposals
Local Government Boundary Commission for Wales, 1982

Borough of Delyn. Special community review report and proposals
Local Government Boundary Commission for Wales, 1980

Borough of Islwyn. Review of district electoral arrangements
Local Government Boundary Commission for Wales, 1982

Borough of Merthyr Tydfil. Review of district electoral arrangements: draft proposals
Local Government Boundary Commission for Wales, 1981

Borough of Neath. Review of district electoral arrangements: draft proposals
Local Government Boundary Commission for Wales, 1981

Borough of Neath. Review of district electoral arrangements: report and proposals
Local Government Boundary Commission for Wales, 1982

Borough of Newport. Review of district electoral arrangements: draft proposals
Local Government Boundary Commission for Wales, 1981

CRAWSHAY, Lady Elizabeth *(continued)*
Borough of Newport. Review of district electoral arrangements: report and proposals
Local Government Boundary Commission for Wales, 1982

Borough of Ogwr. Review of district electoral arrangements draft proposals
Local Government Boundary Commission for Wales, 1982

Borough of Rhondda. Review of district electoral arrangements
Local Government Boundary Commission for Wales, 1982

Borough of Rhuddlaw. Review of district electoral arrangements: draft proposals
Local Government Boundary Commission for Wales, 1981

Borough of Rhuddlaw. Review of district electoral arrangements: report and proposals
Local Government Boundary Commission for Wales, 1982

Borough of Taff-Ely. Review of district electoral arrangements: draft proposals
Local Government Boundary Commission for Wales, 1982

Borough of Vale of Glamorgan. Review of district electoral arrangements: draft proposals
Local Government Boundary Commission for Wales, 1981

Borough of Wrexhan Maelor. Review of district electoral arrangements
Local Government Boundary Commission for Wales, 1982

Borough of Ynys Mon – Isle of Anglesey. Review of district electoral arrangements draft proposals
Local Government Boundary Commission for Wales, 1982

City of Cardiff. Review of district electoral arrangements: draft proposals
Local Government Boundary Commission for Wales, 1981

City of Swansea. Review of district electoral arrangements: draft proposals
Local Government Boundary Commission for Wales, 1982

City of Swansea. Review of district electoral arrangements: report and proposals
Local Government Boundary Commission for Wales, 1982

County of Dyfed and County of West Glamorgan, Borough of Dinefwr and Borough of Liw Valley boundary review: consequential electoral arrangements
Local Government Boundary Commission for Wales, 1979

District of Alyn and Deeside. Special community review and proposals
Local Government Boundary Commission for Wales, 1981

District of Ceredigion. Special community review: report and proposals
Local Government Boundary Commission for Wales, 1982

District of Dwyfor. Review of district electoral arrangements: draft proposals
Local Government Boundary Commission for Wales, 1982

District of Glyndwr. Review of district electoral arrangements: draft proposals
Local Government Boundary Commission for Wales, 1982

District of Meirionnydd. Review of district electoral arrangements: draft proposals
Local Government Boundary Commission for Wales, 1982

District of Preseli. Special community review: report and proposals
Local Government Boundary Commission for Wales, 1982

District of Radnor. Review of district electoral arrangements: draft proposals
Local Government Boundary Commission for Wales, 1981

District of Radnor. Review of district electoral arrangements: report and proposals
Local Government Boundary Commission for Wales, 1982

District of South Pembrokeshire. Report and proposals: special community review
Local Government Boundary Commission for Wales, 1981

CRESSER, C.
Building economics: cost analysis of livestock units
ADAS, 1981

CRESSWELL, M.
Technical supplement on the analysis of APU monitoring in mathematics, by B. Sexton and M. Cresswell. (APU (Stat) (81) 1)
DES, 1981

CRETNEY, S. M.
Family law: illegitimacy. Report of the working party. (Working Paper no. 74)
Law Commission, 1979

CRICKMORE, Maurice
Sewage sludge disposal in Liverpool Bay. Research into effects, 1975–77, part 1: general. Liverpool Bay working group of the standing committee on the disposal of sewage sludge. (Standing Technical Committee Reports no. 16)
National Water Council, 1979

CRINDLE, V. H.
Protected vegetable production. Report of a visit to Holland, May 1980, by V. H. Crindle and C. J. W. Talent
ADAS, 1980

CRISP, E. W.
Economics of sewage sludge disposal. Report of the sub-committee. (Standing Technical Committee Report no. 19)
National Water Council, 1981

CRITCHLEY, J. B.
Flight path deviations due to cumulo-nimbus activity in the U. K. controlled airspace, by J. B. Critchley and P. L. Congdon. (CAA Paper 79005)
Civil Aviation Authority, 1979

CROFT, John
Concerning crime. (Research Study no. 75)
Home Office, 1982

Crime and comparative research. (Research Study no. 57)
Home Office, 1979

Crime and the community. (Research Study no. 50)
Home Office, 1979

Managing criminologiceal research. (Research Study no. 69)
Home Office, 1981

Research and criminal policy. (Research Study no. 59)
Home Office, 1980

CROMACK, H. T. H.
Early potato production: report of a study tour undertaken in France and Spain, 2–7 May 1981
ADAS, 1982

CROMBIE, S.
Conflict in industry: an organisational perspective, by S. Crombie and M. O. Lundy. (Research Paper no. 1)
Labour Relations Agency, 1980

CROOKENDEN, S.
Footwear EDC progress report 1980
NEDO, 1980

CROOM, Sir John
Cancer services in Scotland. A report by the Cancer Programme Planning Group of the Scottish Health Service Planning Council
SHHD, 1982

CROOM-JOHNSON, David
Crown Agents. Tribunal appointed to inquire into certain issues arising out of the operations of the Crown Agents as financiers on own account in the years 1967–74. 1982
Session 1981–82 HC 364; HL 149

CROSS, Don
Some educational aspects of tourist guide training in the British Isles and parts of Europe
Air Transport and Travel Industry Training Board, 1980

CROSS, J. V.
Crop production in hardy nursery stock production. Report of a study tour by J. V. Cross and D. Hutchinson
ADAS, 1982

CROSS, M.
Unemployment and racial conflict in the inner city, by J. Rex and M. Cross. (Working Papers on Ethnic Relations no. 16)
SSRC, Research Unit on Ethnic Relations, 1982

CROUSAZ, Diane
Local authority community work, realities of practice, by C. Davies and D. Crousaz. (Research Report 9)
DHSS, 1982

CROWE, J.
Setting up a workshop. 5th ed
Crafts Council, 1982

CROWLEY, A. J.
WHO consultation on natural barriers of wildlife rabies in Europe. Report of a visit to Switzerland, October 1979, by A. J. Crowley and others
ADAS, 1979

WHO consultation on rabies prevention and control. Report of a visit to France, March 1980
ADAS, 1980

CROWTHER, P. C.
The processing of banana products for food use. (G122)
Tropical Products Institute, 1979

Tomato paste or puree: an industrial profile, by G. Flynn and P. C. Crowther. (G133)
Tropical Products Institute, 1980

CRUDEN, Stewart
Arbroath Abbey, by R. L. Mackie and S. Cruden
Scottish Development Dept., 1982

CULLEN, B.
Study of housing action areas; the case study reports, 1976–78, by S. Morgan and B. Cullen
Scottish Development Dept., 1981

CULLEN, G. A.
Fakieh farms. Taif, Saudi Arabia, 20–26 November 1981. Report of a visit
ADAS, 1982

Western poultry disease conference. Report of a visit to USA
ADAS, 1979

CULLEN, J. E.
The application of a behavioural regime to disturbed young offenders, by J. E. Cullen and J. W. Seddon. (DPS Report Series I, no. 15)
Home Office, 1980

The prediction and treatment of self-injury by female young offenders. (DPS Report Series I, no. 17)
Home Office, 1981

CULLINGWORTH, J. B.
Environmental planning, 1939–1969, vol. 3: new towns policy. (Peacetime History)
Cabinet Office, 1979

Environmental planning, vol. 4: land values, compensation and betterment. (Peacetime History)
Cabinet Office, 1981

CUMMINGS, J. H.
Nutritional aspects of bread and flour. Report of the panel on bread, flour and other cereal products; committee on

medical aspects of food policy, by Frank Young and J. H. Cummings. (Report on Health and Social Subjects 23)
DHSS, 1981

CUNINGHAME, K.
National Health Service treatment for foreign patients. (Research Note no. 63)
House of Commons, 1982

Naional Health Service treatment for foreign patients. 4th ed. (Research Note no. 63)
House of Commons, 1982

CURRAN, J. H.
Social enquiry reports in Scotland, pt. 1: social enquiry reports in two Scottish regions, by J. H. Curran, pt. 2: sheriffs' perspective, by G. A. Chambers
Scottish Office, 1982

CURRIE, B.
Fourth City and Commercial Investment Trust Ltd., Excelads Ltd., Systematic Tooling Ltd., Cambranain Ltd. Investigations under the Companies Act
Trade Dept., 1981

CURRIE, W. M.
The energy conservation demonstration projects scheme: what it is all about
Energy Technology Support Unit, 1981

CURTIS, Colin H.
Buses of London. 2nd ed
London Transport, 1979

CUTLER, D. P.
A fast response two-colour pyrometer. (Tech. Paper 5)
Health and Safety Laboratories, 1979

DADSON, R. J.
Handbook of EEC potato statistics including states applying for membership
Potato Marketing Board, 1982

DALE, G. C.
The CEGB and nuclear power. Questions and answers, ed. by G. C. Dale and written and researched by J. M. Bowerman
Central Electricity Generating Board, 1979

The CEGB and nuclear power: questions and answers
Central Electricity Generating Board, 1981

DALGLEISH, Mary
Children's residential accommodation: policies and user reaction. Sheffield development project for mentally handicapped people. (Mental Health Buildings Evaluation, Report S2)
DHSS, 1979

Community reaction to local buildings pilot study. Sheffield development project for mentally handicapped people. (Mental Health Buildings Evaluation, Report S3)
DHSS, 1979

Hospital day care for adults. Sheffield development project for mentally handicapped people. (Mental Health Buildings Evaluation, Report S6)
DHSS, 1980

Residential facilities for mentally handicapped children, by M. Dalgleish and R. Matthews. (Mental Health Buildings Evaluation Pamphlet 1)
DHSS, 1982

DANCEY, R. J.
International Farm Management Association congress 4th, Israel, 23–28 June 1980. Report by R. J. Dancey, P. D. Mills and P. J. James
ADAS, 1981

DARBY, John
The vocational aspirations and expectations of school leavers in Londonderry and Strabane, by D. Murray and J. Darby. (Research Paper 6)
Fair Employment Agency (Belfast), 1980

DAVIDGE, M. E.
Medicine workshop. Report of a visit to France, June 1979
ADAS, 1979

DAVIDSON, I.
WHO expert group on biological standardisation. Report of a visit to Switzerland, April 1980
ADAS, 1980

DAVIDSON, I. C.
A report on the feasibility of a national protocol testing centre
National Computing Centre, 1982

DAVIES, B.
Men whose income out of work was high compared with their income in work (DHSS Cohort Study of Unemployed Men Working Paper no.2)
DHSS, 1982

DAVIES, Carolyn
Local authority community work, realities of practice, by Carolyn Davies and Diane Crousaz. (Social Research Branch, Research Report no. 9)
London, HMSO for DHSS, 1982

DAVIES, D. A.
ADAS involvement with small groups (Extension Development Unit Report no.18)
ADAS, 1982

DAVIES, D. B.
International soil tillage conference, 8th. Report of a visit to West Germany, September, 1979
ADAS, 1979

DAVIES, E.
The pottery industry: a report by W. H. Holmes and E. Davies. (Energy Audit Series no. 7)
Energy Dept., 1979

DAVIES, E. T.
Veterinary problems in Botswana. Report of a visit to Botswana, 18 September – 2 October 1981
ADAS, 1982

DAVIES, G.
Symposium on veterinary epidemiology and economics. Report of a visit to Australia, May 1979, by A. J. Stevens and G. Davies
ADAS, 1979

Veterinary epidemiology and preventative medicine. Report of a visit to Australia and New Zealand, April/May 1979
ADAS, 1979

DAVIES, J.
European Grassland Federation, Zagreb, Yugoslavia: forage production under marginal conditions, 2–8 June 1980. Report on 8th general meeting
ADAS, 1981

DAVIES, J.
Norwest Holst Limited. Investigation under the Companies Act, 1948
Trade Dept., 1981

DAVIES, J. M. L.
Carnation production. Report of a study tour undertaken in Holland and France, September 1979, by D. E. Green and J. M. L. Davies
ADAS, 1979

Winter oil seed rape. Report on a visit by J. M. L. Davies and J. Macleod
ADAS, 1982

DAVIES, L. I. C.
Ground-roll noise modelling in the DORA noise and number index computer model, and measurements at Heathrow and Gatwick. (DORA Communication 8204)
Civil Aviation Authority, 1982

DAVIES, L. Myrrdin
Three Mile Island incident. (Atomic Energy Technical Unit)
UKAEA, 1979

DAVIES, R. L.
Retail employment change in Scotland with special reference to super-stores, by R. L. Davies and B. Wade. (Central Research Unit Papers)
Scottish Office, 1982

DAVIES, Stephen
The Treasury world economic prospects model. (Government Economic Service Working Paper no. 25)
Treasury, 1979

DAVIS, E. P.
The consumption function in macroeconomic models; a comparative study. (Discussion Papers, Technical Series no.1)
Bank of England, 1982

DAVIS, F. P.
Severn crossing working party report, by S. Godsell and F. P. Davis,
DTp, 1981

DAVISON, Ian Hay
Grays Building Society. Report of investigation under the Building Societies Act, 1962, by I. H. Davison and M. Stuart-Smith, May 1979
Session 1979–80 Cmnd. 7557

DAVISON, Robert
Transfer of employment (TOE) courses, a follow-up study
MSC, 1982

DAWKINS, M. E.
Report of an assessment of long handled reachers at Middlesborough General Hospital
DHSS, 1980

DAWSON, D.
The cheaper end of the owner-occupied housing market: an analysis for the city of Glasgow 1971–77: main report on a study carried out by D. Dawson, C. Jones, D. Maclennan and G. Wood for the Scottish Office
Scottish Economic Planning Dept., 1982

DAWSON, D. W.
Tetney outmarsh reclamation 1974–1980: final report, by A. M. Barker and D. W. Dawson. (Land Drainage Service: R & D report no. 10)
ADAS, 1981

DAWSON, J. K.
Wave energy, a review paper. (Energy Paper no. 42)
Energy Dept., 1979

DAWSON, P. M.
Impact of new technologies on publishing. Symposium, November 1979. Report of a visit to Luxembourg
ADAS, 1979

DAWSON, R. L
Special provision for disturbed pupils, a survey. (Research Studies)
Schools Council 1980

DAWSON, Tim
Qualitative research among homeworkers, by A. Cragg and T. Dawson. (Research Paper no. 21)
Employment Dept., 1981

DAY, G. V.
An analysis of the low energy strategy for the U.K. as proposed by the International Institute for Environment

DAY, G. V. *(continued)*
and Development, by G. V. Day and others. (UKAEA Energy Discussion Papers no. 1)
UKAEA, 1980

Long term prospects for electricity in industry. (UKAEA Energy Discussion Papers no. 2)
UKAEA, 1980

DAY, M. J. L.
Measurement of accessibility benefits in transport models. (LTRI Working Paper 10)
DTp, 1979

Partial matrices, empirical deterrence functions and ill defined results, by M. J. L. Day and A. F. Hawkins. (LTRI Working Paper 9)
DTp, 1979

DAYAL, Rajeshwar
Southern Rhodesia elections, February 1980. The report of the Commonwealth observer group on elections leading to independent Zimbabwe
Commonwealth Secretariat, 1980

DE LA MER, G.
Guide to British control equipment (Exports to Europe Branch)
Trade Dept., 1981

DE PEYER, D.
Advisory group on resource allocation. Report
DHSS, 1980

DEADMAN, N. M.
An evaluation of the IL508 Discrete Multichannel Electrolyte and Chemistry Analyser (Health and Social Work Dept)
Welsh Office, 1982

DEAKIN, Rose
Participation in local social services; an exploratory study, by R. Deakin and P. Willmott. (Studies in Participation 1)
Personal Social Services Council, 1979

DEAKINS, R. M.
Herbage seed production. Report of a visit to Holland, July 1979
ADAS, 1979

DEAN, K. J.
Microelectronics in F. E.; some personal perceptions
DES, 1982

DEAN, P.
Packet switches data networks. (Guides to Computing Standards no. 22.6). (NCC Standardization Office)
National Computing Centre, 1981

DEATON, D. R.
The determinants of bargaining structure: some large scale survey evidence for Britain, by D. R. Deaton and P. B. Beaumont. (Discussion Paper no. 15)
Industrial Relations Research Unit (SSRC), 1979

DELBRIDGE, Rosemary
Tendering for government contracts; advice for small firms, by R. Delbridge. (Small Firms Service Series)
Industry Dept., 1980

DENNIS, C. W.
Field drainage pipes and filters: report of a study tour undertaken in Canada and USA, 23 August–5 September 1981
MAFF, 1982

DENNY, William
Kina Holdings Ltd. Investigation under the Companies Act, 1948. Report by W. Denny and K. Webb
Trade Dept., 1981

DERMOTT, W.
International congress (12th) of soil science, New Delhi, February 1982 . Report by W. Dermott and P. Needham
ADAS, 1982

DERWENT, H. C. S.
Report on Rayner study of non-staff running costs in the Department of the Environment (central). Volume 1: Main report, by C. J. P. Joubert and H. C. S. Derwent. Volume 2: Annexes
DoE, 1981

DEVEREUX, R. J.
Employment changes in Scottish manufacturing industry (1954–1974). (Economics and Statistics Unit: Discussion Paper no. 12)
Scottish Economic Planning Dept., 1980

DEVON, S. J.
Mid-air collisions involving public transport and executive jet aircraft 1959–1978, worldwide. (CAA paper 80007).
Civil aviation authority, 1980.

DEWHURST, W.
Analyses of wind direction and speed for Calshot, 1960–1979. (Southampton Weather Centre memorandum no. 5A).
Meteorological Office, 1982.

DEXTER, E.
European seminar (5th) on extension education, West Germany, 30 August–6 September 1981.
ADAS, 1982.

DEXTER, K.
Policy review of the Agricultural Development and Advisory Service.
Report of the review group.
MAFF, 1979.

DHOOGE, Y.
Ethnic difference and industrial conflicts. (Research Unit of Ethnic Relations working papers on ethnic relations no. 13).
SSRC, 1981.

DIAMOND, John, Lord
Royal commission on the distribution of income and wealth.

4th report on the standing reference. (report no. 7), July 1979. Session 979–80 Cmnd. 7595.

5th report on the standing reference. (Report no. 8), October 979. Session 1979–80 Cmnd. 7679.

DICK, G. C.
Possible sites for a third London airport. Report of the study group on south east airports.
Trade Dept., 1979.

DICK, T. A.
The measurement of electrical conductivity and the laboratory determination of the pH value of natural, treated and waste waters 1978. Methods for the examination of waters and associated materials. (Standing committee of analysists).
DoE, 1979.

Standing commitee of analysts to review standard method for quality control of the water cycle: second report, February 1977–April 1979. (Standing technical committee report no. 23). National Water Council, 1981.

Swimming pool disinfection systems using chlorine gas; guidelines for design and operation. Report of the working party on the safe installation of disinfection systems for swimming pools.
DoE, 1979

DIBB, C.
International grassland congress (14th), U.S.A., June 1981, by A. H. Adamson and C. Dibb
ADAS, 1982

DICKEN, P.
Industrial change, local manufacturing firms in Manchester and Merseyside by P. Lloyd and P. Dicken. (Inner Cities Research Programme, 6)
DoE, 1982

DICKENS, F. J.
Rhone Poulenc symposium on Alliette, Munich, September/October 1980. Report
ADAS, 1980

DICKENS, J. S. W.
International Workshop on Seed Pathology, 17th, Zurich – Reckenholz, Switzerland, 17–22 May 1981. Report
ADAS, 1981

DICKENS, Linda
Disclosure of information to trade unions in Britain. (Industrial Relations Research Unit Discussion Paper)
SSRC, 1979

DICKINSON, J. C.
Furness Abbey, Lancashire
DoE, 1982

DICKINSON, Sheila
A framework for assessing the economic effects of a green pound devaluation, by S. Dickinson and J. Wildgoose. (Government Economic Service Working Paper no.23)
Treasury, 1979

DICKSON, G. R.
Urban fringe farming seminar. Report of proceedings. (Land service)
ADAS, 1979

DICKSON, R. J.
In-service training. Report of the working party on administrative and legislative aspects of reorganisation of secondary education
Dept. of Education for Northern Ireland, 1979

Preparatory and boarding departments. Reports of the working party on administrative and legislative aspects of reorganisation of secondary education
Dept. of Education for Northern Ireland, 1979

Staffing of secondary schools. Report of the working party on administrative and legislative reorganisation of secondary education
Dept. of Education for Northern Ireland, 1979

DIETSCH, J. F. W.
The role of the Animal Health Officer in West Germany: report of a visit to West Germany, September 1980
ADAS, 1981

DIGHT, R. J. W.
Open-cast coal restoration: report of a visit to the USA, 12–27 June 1980, by D. S. Stevens and R. J. W. Dight
ADAS, 1981

DIGHT, Susan
Undergraduate income and expenditure, a survey, by P. Bush and S. Dight
OPCS, 1979

DILLON, Thomas Michael
Burnholme and Forder Ltd. (in liquidation); Brayhead Ltd. (in liquidation). Investigation under the Companies Act, 1948. Report by T. M. Dillon and D. Garrett
Trade Dept., 1979

DIMBLEBY, G. W.
The scientific treatment of material from rescue excavations. A report by a working party of the committee for rescue archaeology of the Ancient Monuments Board for England
DoE, 1979

DINGWALL, R.
The development of ethnography in Britain, by R. Dingwall, G. Payne and J. Payne. (Centre for Socio-Legal Studies)
SSRC, 1980

DINWIDDY, Robert
The concept of personal income in the analysis of income distribution. (Government Economic Service Working Paper no. 30)
Treasury, 1980

DIPLOCK, Lord W. J. Kenneth
Interception of communications in G.B. Report
Session 1980–81 Cmnd. 8191

DIXON, David
Higher education – finding your way. A brief guide for school and college students
DES, 1979 and 1981

DIXON, T.
Large dairy herds. Report of a visit to USA, March 1979
ADAS, 1979

DOBBS, J.
Nurses working in the community, a survey, by K. Dunnell and J. Dobbs. (Social Survey 1141)
OPCS, 1982

DOBBY, John
Objective assessment by means of item banking, by John Dobby and Derek Duckworth. (Schools Council Examinations Bulletin 40)
Schools Council, 1979

DOBSON, P. H.
United Industrial Company Ltd. Investigation under the Companies Act, 1948. Report by G. J. K. Coles and P. H. Dobson
Trade Dept., 1981

DODD, P. A.
The electoral registration process in the United Kingdom, by J. E. Todd and P. A. Dodd (Social Survey Division, SS1171)
OPCS, 1982

DODGE, John D.
Marine dinoflagellates of the British Isles
MAFF, 1982

DOIG, Barbara
The nature and scale of aliment and financial provision on divorce in Scotland. (Central Research Unit papers)
Scottish Office, 1982

Debt recovery through the Scottish Sheriff Courts. (Research report for the Scottish Law Commission no. 3)
Scottish Office, 1980

Nature and scale of diligence. (Research report for the Scottish Law Commission no. 1)
Scottish Office, 1980

DONNAN, S. P. B.
Study of causes of death in firemen. (Joint Committee on Fire Research Report 20)
Home Office, 1982

DORLING, Jenny
'WOW' case record book. Material produced for use on the Wider Opportunities for Women course by Jenny Dorling, Kate Keenan and Jill Fairbairns. (Training Services Division Report no. DTP 12)
MSC, 1979

DORN, N.
Teaching decision-making skills about legal and illegal drugs
Health Education Council, 1982

DOUGHTY, G.
Heavy electrical machinery. Heavy electrical machinery sector working party
NEDO, 1980

DOUGLAS, I. J.
Audit of computer systems, by A. J. Thomas and I. J. Douglas
National Computing Centre, 1981

DOVE, A. R.
Some aspects of noise and hearing loss: notes on the problem of noise at work and report of the HSE working group on machinery noise
Health and Safety Executive, 1981

DOVE, Linda A.
Curriculum reforms in secondary schools. A commonwealth survey
Commonwealth Secretariat, 1980

DOVER, P. A.
Engineering section meeting, European Association for Potato Research, Wageningen, Holland, September 1980. Report
ADAS, 1981

DOYLE, P. J.
Glass industry: energy conservation and utilisation in the glass industry. A report by G. Perry and P. J. Doyle. (Energy Audit Ser. no. 5)
Energy Dept., 1979

DRAIN, G.
Energy and the paper and board industry. Report by the energy sub-committee of the Paper and Board S W P
NEDO, 1981

DRAKE, Madeline
Single and homeless
DoE, 1981

A study of the records of a national referral agency, by M. Drake and C. Francis. (Single and Homeless Working Paper, 1)
DoE, 1982

A study of an East End night shelter, by M. Drake and M. O'Brien. (Single and Homeless Working Paper, 2)
DoE, 1982

Six discussion groups of single homeless people, by T. Biebuyck and M. Drake (Single and Homeless Working Paper no. 4)
DoE, 1982

DRAKES, G. D.
Utilisation of reject heat in horticulture. Report of a visit to Romania, May 1979, by B. R. Smith and G. D. Drakes
ADAS, 1979

DREW Alan E.
Arrival runway capacity and arrival delays at London Heathrow Airport, summer 1980, by A. E. Drew and H. K. Logan. (CAA Paper 81014). (DORA Communication 8108)
Civil Aviation Authority, 1981

The effect of certain facilities on the runway capacity and aircraft delays at Gatwick Airport, 1981, by A. E. Drew and H. K. Logan. (CAA Paper 82019)
Civil Aviation Authority, 1982

The magnitude and causes of departure delays at London Heathrow airport, summer 1978, by R. A. G. Stamp and A. E. Drew. (CAA Paper 80006)
Civil Aviation Authority, 1980

The runway capacity at Aberdeen airport. (CAA Paper 80014)
Civil Aviation Authority, 1980

DREW, S. B.
9th international congress on animal production and artificial insemination – Madrid, Spain 16–20 June 1980. Report
ADAS, 1980

DRING, J. C.
European Association for Animal Production annual meeting, by J. C. Dring and G. Alderman
ADAS, 1982

International symposium on applied ethology: Hungary, 24–27 August 1981, by J. C. Dring, R. Moss and C. M. Hann
ADAS, 1982

DRIVER, Geoffrey
Beyond under-achievement: case studies of English, West Indian and Asian school leavers at 16 plus
Commission for Racial Equality, 1980

DRIVER, Rosalind
Science in schools. Age 15: report no. 1, by R. Driver (et al)(Assessment of Performance Unit)
DES, 1982

DRUMMOND, I. R.
Conservation and land drainage working party report
Water Space Amenity Commission, 1980

DUCKWORTH, Derek
Objective assessment by means of item banking, by John Dobby and Derek Duckworth. (Examination Bulletin 40)
Schools Council, 1979

DUFFIELD, Brian S.
Large scale recreation participation surveys: lessons for the future, by B. S. Duffield and J. A. Long. (WP16)
Countryside Commission 1979

DUFFIELD, M.
The theory of underdevelopment and the underdevelopment of theory: the pertinence of recent debate to the question of post-colonial immigration to Britain. (Research Unit on Ethnic Relations Working Papers on Ethnic Relations no. 15)
SSRC, 1982

DUNGATE, Michaela
Training workshops; the way they work in YOP. (Special Programmes Research and Development Series, no.8)
MSC, 1982

DUGUID, G.
Community service in Scotland: the first two years
Scottish Office, 1982

DUNBAR, J. G.
Dusntaffnage Castle
Scottish Development Dept., 1981

DUNLOP, Anne B.
Junior attendance centres. (Research Study no. 60)
Home Office, 1980

DUNN, B.
Regional strategy for water recreation. Report 5: zone 4 – the rivers Lee, Stort, Colne and associate waters including the Grand Union Canal. (B. Dunn, *ch*)
Eastern Council for Sport and Recreation, 1982

DUNNELL, Karen
Family formation 1976. A survey. (Social Survey 1080)
OPCS, 1979

Nurses working in the community: a survey, by K. Dunnell and J. Dobbs. (Social Survey 1141)
OPCS, 1982

DUNNING, E.
Soccer: the social origins of the sport and its development as a spectacle and profession. (A review for the SC/SSRC Joint Panel on Leisure and Recreation Research)
Sports Council, 1979

DUNSTER, H. J.
Carcinogens in the workplace: the views of the Health and Safety Executive on a strategy for control. (Technical Report no. 1)
Health and Safety Executive, 1981

DURHAM, K.
Sectoral report – food, drink and packaging machinery. Memorandum (NEDC (82) 58)
NEDO, 1982

DURWARD, L.
Elderly electricity consumers (Research report 4)
Elderly Consumers Council, 1981

Electricity and the disabled customer (Research report 9)
Electricity Consumers Council, 1982.

DUTHIE, R. B.
Orthopaedic services; waiting time for out-patient appointments and in-patient treatment. Report of a working party
DHSS, 1981

DUTTON, R. A.
Land reclamation in cities. A guide to methods of establishment of vegetation on urban waste land, by R. A. Dutton and A. D. Bradshaw
DoE, 1982

EAGLE, D. J.
Investigation of the current situation with regard to the use of methyl bromide in protected cropping, by J. T. Fletcher and D. J. Eagle. (Report of a visit to the Netherlands, May 1982)
ADAS, 1982

Report on 1) EWRS symposium, France, 8–9 December 1981, and 2) 11th Columa conference, France, 10–11 December 1981, by D. J. Eagle and S. A. Evans
ADAS, 1982

EAST, J. P. G.
Tramlines in cereals, Shropshire 1979
ADAS, 1980

ECCLES, J. D.
British Rail Hovercraft Ltd. and Hoverlloyd Ltd. A report on the proposed merger by the Monopolies and Mergers Commission
Session 1980–81 HC 374

Caledonian MacBrayne Ltd. A report on shipping services provided by the company, by the Monopolies and Mergers Commission, February 1983
Session 1982–83 Cmnd. 8805

Contraceptive sheaths. Report on the supply in the U.K., by the Monopolies and Mergers Commission, November 1982
Session 1982–83 Cmnd. 8689

Nabisco Brands Inc. and Huntley and Palmer Foods etc. Report by the Monopolies and Mergers Commission on the proposed merger
Session 1981–82 Cmnd. 8680

South Wales Argus (Holdings) Ltd. and Express Newspapers Ltd. A report on the proposed transfer of three newspapers, by the Monopolies and Mergers Commission, October 1981
Session 1980–81 Cmnd. 8385

ECCLESTONE, M. J.
Management of high yielding dairy herds. Report of a study tour in USA and Canada, by M. J. Ecclestone and J. I. Whipp
ADAS, 1979

ECKFORD, Jim
'Community participation in hospitals for the long-stay mentally handicapped'. Study day presented by management education and training division of the common services agency and 'one-to-one' in Scotland, November 1979. Report
Scottish Health Service, 1979

EDEN, E. N.
Pattern examination of weighing and measuring equipment. Report of the joint industry/departmental working party
Trade Dept., 1981

EDGAR, John R.
Box prefabricated structures in housing; a study of mobile homes and related improved products. (HDD Occasional Paper 2/78)
DoE, 1979

EDMUND-DAVIES, Lord
Police Committee of inquiry, 3rd report. Structure and role of police staff associations, July 1979
Sessions 1979–80 Cmnd. 7633

EDWARDS, A. J.
Farm management data: report of a study tour undertaken in West Germany, June 1980
ADAS, 1981

EDWARDS, C. A.
Study of the influence of pesticides on the natural ecosystem and different species of fauna and flora. Report of a visit to USSR, September 1979, by P. J. Bunyan and C. A. Edwards
ADAS, 1980

EDWARDS, D.
Economic aspects of small-scale fish canning, by D. Edwards and others. (G151)
Tropical Products Institute, 1981

EDWARDS, J. P.
International conference on the regulation of insect development and behaviour, 23–28 June 1980. Report by J. P. Edwards
ADAS, 1980

Project on insect endocrinology. Report of a visit to USA, ADAS, 1979 January/April 1979

EDWARDS, Joan M. B.
Immunofluorescence techniques in diagnostic microbiology. (Monograph Series 18)
Public Health Laboratory Service, 1982

EDWARDS, M.
The evaluation of some Phocion MX dyes for the dyeing of sisal, by M. Edwards and A. J. Canning. (L56)
Tropical Products Institute, 1981

EDWARDS, M.
Understanding urban land values: a review, by M. Edwards and D. Lovatt. (The Inner City in Context 1)
SSRC, 1980

EDWARDS, P. K.
The cross-sectional analysis of strike activity; some American evidence. (Industrial Relations Research Unit)
SSRC, 1980

EDWARDS, P. N.
Yield models for forest management, models prepared by J. M. Christie. (Booklet 48)
Forestry Commission, 1981

EDWIN, E. E.
International symposium on ruminant physiology, 7th. Report of a visit to France, September 1979
ADAS, 1979

EKBLOM, Paul
Police response to calls from the public, by P. Ekblom and K. Heal. (Research and Planning Unit Paper 9)
Home Office, 1982

ELBRA, Tony
Database for the small computer user
National Computing Centre, 1982

ELLENBY, Jean
Britain: four countries, one kingdom, by Jean Ellenby and Suzy Siddons
British Tourist Authority, 1980

ELLIOTT, D.
An introduction to steel selection: part 2, stainless steels, by D. Elliott and S. M. Tupholme. (Engineering Design Guides 43)
Design Council, 1981

ELLIOTT, David
Cluster analysis. (New Methodology Series no. NM4)
OPCS, 1980

ELLIOTT, Gordon
Geography of hunger: draught in the Sahel
Schools Council, 1980

Geography of hunger: teacher's guide. (History, Geography and Social Science 8–13)
Schools Council, 1980

Geography of hunger. Who is hungry? (History, Geography and Social Science 8–13)
Schools Council, 1980

ELLIOTT, M. J
Role of law in central-local relations
SSRC, 1982

ELLIS, C. G. J.
Plum production. Report of a study tour in France and Italy
ADAS, 1982

ELLIS, R. W.
The management of herring fisheries, by R. W. Ellis, K. Cormack and W. B. McKeller. (Fishery Economics Research Unit Occasional Paper Series no. 2, 1981)
White Fish Authority, 1981

ELLIS, S.
Sweden; materials handling equipment report. (British Embassy, Stockholm)
Foreign and Commonwealth Office, 1982

ELLISON, Gerald Alexander, Bp. London
Diocese in Europe measure. Report by the Ecclesiastical Committee, April 1980. (Ecclesiastical Committee 183rd report)
Session 1979–80 HC 558

ELLMAN, A.
Guide to technology transfer in East, Central and Southern Africa, compiled by A. Ellman, B. Mackay and T. Moody. (Food Production and Rural Development Div.)
Commonwealth Secretariat, 1981

ELSE, George
Conservation of bees and wasps
Nature Conservancy Council, 1979

ELSON, Martin J.
Countryside trip making. (State of the Art Review no. 12)
Sports Council, 1979

Leisure use of green belts and urban fringes
Sports Council, 1979

ELY, S. V.
Scanning electron microscope symposium. Report of a visit to USA, April 1978
ADAS, 1978

EMELEUS, C. H.
Field guide to the tertiary igneous rocks of Rhum, Inner Hebrides, by C. H. Emeleus and R. M. Forster. (Geology and Physiography section)
Nature Conservancy Council, 1979

EMERY, A. C.
Cornish beef, pt. 1, by A. C. Emery and J. M. Weeks
MAFF, 1979

EMMETT, B. J.
International symposium on insect control of tomorrow, Wagenlingen, Holland, 14–16 September 1981. Report
ADAS, 1981

EMPSON, D. W.
Cereal pests, 2nd ed., revised by R. Gair. (Reference Book 186)
ADAS, 1982

EMPSON, J. D.
U.K. dairy industry; statistical projections of prospects to 1983. (Statistics Sub-group of the Milk and Milk Products Sector Working Group)
NEDO, 1980

ENGLAND, Glyn
Backing Britain. (G1012)
Central Electricity Generating Board, 1981

CHP: from debate to practical progress? (G1033)
Central Electricity Generating Board, 1982

Challenges to management
Central Electricity Generating Board, 1982

Efficiency audit and public enterprise: problems and options
Central Electricity Generating Board, 1982

Electricity from coal, based on a talk to the Coal Industry Society in London on 2 November 1981
Central Electricity Generating Board, 1981

Electricity production and transmission in a changing world. (G1026)
Central Electricity Generating Board, 1982

Facing the challenge. (G1036)
Central Electricity Generating Board, 1982

Helping large power users. (G1027)
Central Electricity Generating Board, 1982

Managing for growth
Central Electricity Generating Board, 1981

Managing for low growth
Central Electricity Generating Board, 1981

Nuclear electricity; a progress report.
Central Electricity Generating Board, 1980

Nuclear power . . . its integration into a large utility. (G949) repr
Central Electricity Generating Board, 1980

Planning for uncertainty, by Glyn England. (G983)
Central Electricity Generating Board, 1981

Power in the wind
Central Electricity Generating Board, 1981

Responding to economic change
Central Electricity Generating Board, 1981

Tackling high costs
Central Electricity Generating Board, 1981

ENOCH, C. A.
The direction of causality between the exchange rate, prices and money. (Discussion Paper no. 7)
Bank of England, 1979

Two studies of commodity price behaviour: interrelationships between commodity prices, by J. L. Hedges and short-run pricing behaviour in commodity markets, by C. A. Enoch. (Discussion Paper no. 18)
Bank of England, 1981

EPSON, E.
Study of government noise insulation policies. Report by a working group
Noise Advisory Council, 1980

ERICSON, A. E.
Access to water recreation areas, by A. E. Ericson, *ch.* (Regional Strategy: Subject Report 3) (SCSR(81)69)
Southern Council for Sport and Recreation, 1981

ERRIDGE, Andrew
Decision-making in the European Community, an exercise
Civil Service College, 1980

ESSEN, J.
Continuities in childhood disadvantage by J. Essen and P. Wedge. (Studies in Deprivation and Disadvantage 6)
Heinemann for SSRC, 1982

ETCHELL, Lindsey
The neighbourhood
National Consumer Council, 1982

EVANS, Anthony H. M.
Orbit Holdings Limited. Report of investigation under the Companies Act 1948, by A. H. M. Evans and R. H. Morcom
Trade Dept., 1981

EVANS, D. J.
Man-made mineral fibres. Report of a working party to the advisory committee on toxic substances. (Discussion Document)
Health and Safety Commission, 1979

EVANS, D. H.
European Committee for Clinical Laboratory Standards seminar, 2nd. France, 25–27 November 1981
ADAS, 1982

EVANS, E. J.
International rapeseed conference, 5th. Report of a visit to Sweden
ADAS, 1980

EVANS, G. J.
The labour market for school leavers in Warrington, by G. J. Evans and P. Mitchell. (Manpower Intelligence and Planning)
MSC, 1981

EVANS, Mary
Disruptive pupils. (Programme 4: Individual Pupils)
Schools Council, 1981

Education of disturbed pupils, by M. D. Wilson and M. Evans. (Working Paper 65)
Schools Council, 1980

EVANS, P.
Pathway to success. Report by the Printing Machinery SWP
NEDO, 1981

Printing and Bookbinding Machinery SWP. Progress report 1980
NEDO, 1980

Printing machinery: what type of future?: a summary of the 1980 progress report from the Printing and Bookbinding Machinery SWP
NEDO, 1980

EVANS, S. A.
Report on 1) EWRS symposium, France, 8–9 December 1981, and 2) 11th Columa conference, France, 10–11 December 1981, by D. J. Eagle and S. A. Evans
ADAS, 1982

Symposium on the influence of different factors on the development and control of weeds. Report of a visit to West Germany, October 1979
ADAS, 1979

EVASON, E.
Just me and the kids
Equal Opportunities Commission for N.I., 1980

EVEREST, M. J.
Dialtech user manual, by B. A. Kingsmill and M. J. Everest
Technology Reports Centre, 1980

EVERLEY, Barry
What can do it now! (Ages 4–16): a report on some good practices in science, technology and crafts in schools, part 1
Equal Opportunities Commission, 1981

EVERSLEY, David
Changes in the resident populations of inner areas, by David Eversley and Lucy Bonnerjea. (The Inner City in Context 2)
SSRC, 1980

EXTON-SMITH, A. N.
Nutrition and health in old age. Report by the committee on medical aspects of food policy. (Reports on Health and Social Subjects 16)
DHSS, 1979

FAGANDINI, D. A. A.
Project finance for specialised organics; a growing and profitable sector. (Specialised Organics SWP)
NEDO, 1981

Specialised organics; your future in the industry. Specialised Organics SWP
NEDO, 1980

FAGIN, L.
Unemployment and health in families; case studies based on family interviews – a pilot study
DHSS, 1981

FAIRBARINS, Jill
Evaluation of wider opportunities for women (WOW) courses. Final report. (Report DTP14)
MSC, 1979

Expenses of using outward bound training as part of a youth opportunities programme. Training Services Division Report no. DTP25)
MSC, 1980

FAIRHEAD, Susan
Persistent petty offenders. (Research Study no. 66)
Home Office, 1981

FALKINGHAM, R. V.
Mechanised harvesting of willow rods for basket making. Report of a visit to Belgium to evaluate a self-propelled willow harvester, March 1979
ADAS, 1979

FARMER, P. E.
Jersey cows in Denmark; their breeding, feeding and milk quality. Report of a study tour by J. R. Mulholland and P. E. Farmer
ADAS, 1982

FARMER, P. J.
Hospital nursing trends in Scotland. (Occasional Paper 5)
Scottish Health Service, 1981

FARRAR, K.
A visit to research stations and farms in West Germany mainly in relation to fertiliser use, 29 June – 2 July 1980
ADAS, 1981

FARTHING, J. G.
Energy conservation and marketing of pot plants. Report of a visit to Germany
ADAS, 1982

FAULKNER, D. E. R.
Rank structure of the police. Report of the Joint Working Party part 2: ranks above chief superintendent. Police Advisory Boards of England and Wales, and of Scotland
Home Office, 1976

FAWCETT, R.
Edzell Castle
Scottish Development Dept., 1982

FELDMAN, Basil
Clothing '80; fight for success. Clothing EDC progress report.
NEDO, 1980

FELTHAM, R.
Psychological effects of social density – a study at Winson Green Prison. (DPS Reports Series I, no. 22)
Home Ofice, 1981

FENN, P.
The effect of ex-post compensation on absence from work. (Centre for Socio-legal Studies Working Paper no. 7)
SSRC, 1980

FENTON, P. H.
The case for exercise, by P. H. Fenton and E. J. Bassey. (Research Working Paper 8)
Sports Council, 1979

FERRIER, R. P.
Radiation effects in solids, including ion implantation: a summary of the conclusions of a review panel, 1980
SERC, 1981

FERRO, R. S. T.
The calculation of the twine area of a trawl net. (Scottish Fisheries Information Pamphlet no. 5)
Agriculture and Fisheries for Scotland Dept., 1981

Choosing the size of the Suberkrub trawl board to suit a pelagic-type four-panel trawl. (Scottish Fisheries Information Pamphlet no. 6)
Agriculture and Fisheries for Scotland Dept., 1981

FIDDICK, J.
The British Nationality Act 1981 and the Falkland Islanders. (Research Note no. 77)
House of Commons, 1982

Video piracy. (Research Note no. 78)
House of Commons, 1982

FIDGETT, Tony
Current trends in education, a staff handbook. (Library and Information Services nos. 8–13)
Engineering Industry Training Board, 1980–82

GCE and CSE examinations in computer studies/science 1975 to 1980
Engineering Industry Training Board, 1981

A guide to sources of local labour market information, by T. Fidgett and C. B. Moir. (Reference Paper RP/5/79)
Engineering Industry Training Board, 1979

Secondary school vocational education in engineering subjects. (Working Paper, WP/2/79)
Engineering Industry Training Board, 1979

A summary of information on the employment training and supply of technician engineers and technicians in the engineering industry. (RP/3/79)
Engineering Industry Training Board, 1979

A summary of information on the employment and training of clerical staff in the engineering industry. (Reference Paper RP/3/81)
Engineering Industry Training Board, 1981

FIELD, Julia
Safety and solid fuel; a survey among solid fuel users
Social and Community Planning Research for the Domestic Coal Consumers' Council, 1981

FIELD, M. J.
'So you want to farm?' by M. J. Field and S. W. W. Sutton. (Socio-economics Paper no. 12; Booklet 2012)
ADAS, 1979

FIELD, Simon
Public disorder: a review of research and a study in one inner city area. (Research study no. 72)
Home Office, 1982

FIELDER, R. J.
Toxicity review – benzene. (Toxicity Review 4)
Health and Safety Executive, 1982

Toxicity review – Pentachlorophenol. (Toxicity Review 5)
Health and Safety Executive, 1982

FIGG, C. D.
Retail meat cuts in Great Britain
Meat and Livestock Commission, 1980

FINCH, R. W.
Recruitment and training in the paper and board industry. Report of the Manpower Sub-committee of the Paper and Board SWP
NEDO, 1979

FINN, D.
Young people and the labour market: a case study, by G. Markall and D. Finn. (Inner Cities Research Programme 5)
DoE, 1981

FINNEY, J. B.
Bulk pasteurisation and spawning system for mushroom production. Report of a visit to Holland, February 1979, by J. B. Finney and L. S. Salter
ADAS, 1979

Reduced energy input in cultivation. Report of a visit to Yugoslavia, September 1979
ADAS, 1979

Symposium on economic and technological aspects of sugar beet production. Report of a visit to USSR, September 1979, by J. B. Finney and J. Smith
ADAS, 1979

FINNIGAN, M. J.
Agriculture and the countryside. Report of a visit to West Germany, March 1979, by R. B. Sayce and M. J. Finnigan
ADAS, 1979

FINNISTON, Montague
Engineering our future. Report of the committee of inquiry into the engineering profession, January 1980
Session 1979–80 Cmnd. 7794

FISH, S.
Silage unloaders and feeders, by G. E. Amos and S. Fish. Report of a study tour undertaken in France, 1979 series
ADAS, 1979

FISHER, S.
Planning and teaching world studies; an interim guide, by S. Fisher and D. Hicks. World Studies 8–13 Project.
Schools Council, 1982

Planning workshops and courses; a world studies in-service handbook, by S. Fisher and D. Hicks. World Studies 8–13 Project
Schools Council, 1982

FISHWICK, Frank
The introduction and extension of shiftworking, an outline of economic, technical and social considerations based on case studies in selected manufacturing industries. A report
NEDO, 1980

FITTON, Freda
Doctor/patient relationship: a study in general practice, by F. Fitton and H. W. K. Acheson
DHSS, 1979

FITZGERALD, R. S.
Liverpool road station, Manchester. An historical and architectural survey. (Royal Commission on Historical Monuments Supplementary Series 1)
Royal Commission on Historical Monuments, 1980

FLEMING, M. C.
Statistics collected by the Ministry of Works, 1941–76: Vol. 1 construction industry; Vol. 2 building materials production and prices
DoE, 1980

FLETCHER, J. T.
Investigation of the current situation with regard to the use of methyl bromide in protected cropping, by J. T. Fletcher and D. J. Eagle. (Report of a visit to the Netherlands, May 1982)
ADAS, 1982

FLETT, H.
The politics of dispersal in Birmingham. (Research Unit on Ethnic Relations; Working Papers on Ethnic Relations no. 14)
SSRC, 1981

FLOWERS, Lord.
Coal and the environment. (Commission on Energy and the Environment)
DoE, 1981

Commission on energy and the environment review of activities, 1978–79
DoE, 1979

London medical education, a new framework. Report by the Working Party on Medical and Dental Teaching Resources
University of London, 1980

FLUDGER, Neil
Ethnic minorities in borstal. (Directorate of Psychological Services Papers no. 1)
Home Office, 1981

FLURY-LEMBERG, Mechthild
Burial garments of Archbishop Ximenez de Rada and Sigismondo Malatesta, by Mechthild Flury-Lemberg. (Conservation Paper 1)
London, Crafts Advisory Committee, 1979

FLYNN, G.
Fermentation ethanol: an industrial profile, by M. R. Adams and G. Flynn. (Report G169)
Tropical Products Institute, 1982

Industrial profile of breadmaking by G. Flynn and A. W. James. (G147)
Tropical Products Institute, 1980

P. J. Manser. (G163)
Tropical Products Institute, 1982

An industrial profile of fibreboard panel processing, by G. Flynn and A. J. Hawkes. (G140)
Tropical Products Institute, 1980

Industrial profile of rice milling, by G. Flynn and P. A. Clarke. (G148)
Tropical Products Institute, 1980

An industrial profile of wood wool/cement slab manufacture, by G. Flynn and A. J. Hawkes. (G141)
Tropical Products Institute, 1980

Tomato paste or puree: an industrial profile by G. Flynn and P. C. Crowther. (G133)
Tropical Products Institute, 1980

FORBES, G. I.
Scottish pulmonary tuberculosis survey (SMR14): randomised health board data, by Dr. G. I. Forbes, V. K. Howie and J. Urquhart. (Working Party on Tuberculosis: Report no. 2 (supplement)) (Common Services Agency: Information Services Div.)
Scottish Health Service, 1980

Scottish pulmonary tuberculosis survey (SMR14): information on notifications recorded January to December 1978, by Dr. G. I. Forbes, V. K. Howie and J. Urquhart. (Working Party on Tuberculosis Report no. 3) (Common Services Agency: Information Services Div.)
Scottish Health Service, 1980

Scottish pulmonary tuberculosis survey (SMR14): clinical data on notifications recorded between January and December 1978, by V. K. Howie, Dr. G. I. Forbes and J. Urquhart. (Working Party on Tuberculosis Report no. 4) (Common Services Agency: Information Services Div.)
Scottish Health Service, 1980

Scottish pulmonary tuberculosis survey (SMR14): information and clinical data on notifications recorded between January and December 1979, by V. K. Howie, Dr. G. I. Forbes and J. Urquhart. (Working Party on Tuberculosis Report nos. 5 and 6) (Common Services Agency: Information Services Div.)
Scottish Health Service, 1981

FORBES, J. M.
Hormones and metabolism in ruminants. (Proceedings of a workshop held at Bodington Hall, University of Leeds, 22–24 September 1980)
Agricultural Research Council, 1981

FORBES, Jean
Intra-urban migration in greater Glasgow; a summary report
Scottish Office, 1979

FORD, J. A.
Policy on provision of facilities for cyclists
DTp, 1982

FORD, M. G.
Current practice in stock relegation in university libraries. A report presented by M. G. Ford, to the UGC steering group on library research
DES, 1979

FORDHAM, Paul
Participation, learning and change; commonwealth approaches to non-formal education. An edited version of papers prepared for the Commonwealth conference on non-formal education for development
Commonwealth Secretariat, 1980

FORREST, G. M.
Defining public examination standards, by T. Christie and G. M. Forrest
Schools Council, 1981

FORREST, R.
Housing market processes and the inner city, by A. Murie and R. Forrest. (The Inner City in Context 10)
SSRC, 1980

FORSTER, R. M.
Field guide to the tertiary igneous rocks of Rhum, Inner Hebrides, by C. H. Emeleus and R. M. Forster
Nature Conservancy Council, 1979

FORSYTH, Alastair
Buildings for the age: new building types 1900–1939
Royal Commission on Historical Monuments, 1982

FORSYTH, David J. C.
The choice of manufacturing technology in sugar production in less developed countries
Min. of Overseas Development, 1979

FORSYTHE, Diana
Urban-rural migration, change and conflict in an Orkney Island community. (North Sea Oil Panel Occasional Paper no. 14)
SSRC, 1982

FORSYTHE, Victor
Science communication in the Caribbean. Report of a workshop
Commonwealth Science Council, 1978

FORTE, A. D. M.
Insurance law: comments and recommendations on law commission working paper 73
Scottish Consumer Council, 1980

FOSTER, J. A.
Choice of a non-asbestos fire blanket for operational use by the fire service (Scientific Advisory Branch Report 1/81)
Home Office, 1981

General fireground lighting equipment for first attendance fire appliances, by J. A. Foster and P. L. Parsons. (Central Fire Brigades Advisory Councils for England and Wales, and Scotland Joint Committee on Fire Research, Research Report no. 13)
Home Office, 1979

FOULGER, R. J.
Programming embedded microprocessors; a high-level language solution
National Computing Centre, 1982

FOULKES, George
Adult literacy in Scotland. Report by the Scottish Adult Literacy Agency's management committee on the work of the Agency, 1976–79
Scottish Education Dept., 1980

FOWLER, J. A.
The fluid power equipment industry. Fluid power sector working party progress report 1978
NEDO, 1980

FOX, A. J.
Longitudinal study: socio-demographic mortality differentials. A first report on mortality in 1971–75. (Series LS no. 1)
OPCS, 1982

FOX, J.
Access to built facilities for sport. (Regional Strategy: Subject Report 1) (SCSR(81)66)
Southern Council for Sport and Recreation, 1981

FRANCE, G. H.
National administrative training scheme: the first twenty-five years, 1956–81
Scottish Health Service, 1981

'Scottish Health Authorities priorities for the eighties' and its implementation
Scottish Health Service, 1981

European Association of Animal Production. 30th annual meeting, July 1979. Report of a visit to Harrogate
ADAS, 1979

FRANCIS, Christine
A study of the records of a national referral agency, by M. Drake and C. Francis (Single and Homeless Working Paper no.1)
DoE, 1982

FRANCIS, J.
The Risley bail project: a study of remand decisions. (DPS report Series I, no. 20)
Home Office, 1980

FRANCIS, R. J.
Prospects for improved fuel economy and fuel flexibility in road vehicles. Report by R. J. Francis and P. N. Woollacott. (Energy Paper no. 45)
Energy Dept., 1981

FRANKS of Headington, Lord Oliver S.
Disclosure and the law. (CSC Working Paper no. 5)
Civil Service College, 1979

FRASER, R.
A critical view on Edward Brathwaite's 'Masks'. (Nexus Books 04)
Rex Collings for British Council, 1981

FREEMAN, David John
AEG – Telefunken (UK) Ltd., Chasgift Ltd. Investigations under the Companies Act, 1948. Report by D. J. Freeman and P. J. Oliver
Trade Dept., 1979

FRENCH, W. M.
Potato varieties and variety testing in Denmark, France, West Germany and the Netherlands. (James E. Rennie Awards Report no. 9)
Potato Marketing Board, 1980

FRERICHS, G. N.
International congress (17th) of the International Association of Biological Standardisation, Lyon, December 1981. Report
ADAS, 1982

FRESHWATER, Michael R.
Basic skills checklist and matrix. (Training Services Division Report no. DTP21)
MSC, 1980

The basic skills questionnaire – a tool for solving some teacher problems? (Training Services Division Report no. DTP17)
MSC, 1979

Basic skills reference manual. (Training Services Division Report no. DTP 20)
MSC, 1980

'Can-do' cards and profiles; tools for self-assessment, by M. R. Freshwater and N. Oates
MSC, 1982

Making the most of training workshop opportunities using a basic skills checklist, 2 vols. (Training Services Division Report no. DTP 22)
MSC, 1980

FRIMAN, R.
Automatic slurry handling and treatment processes, and hygiene in livestock buildings. Report of a study tour in Holland, January 1982, by S. C. M. Adams and R. Friman
ADAS, 1982

FRODSHAM, A. F.
Machine Tools EDC. Progress report 1980
NEDO, 1980

FRY, B. M.
American Daffodil Society convention and visits to narcissus growers – U.S.A., March 1981. Report
ADAS, 1981

FRY, M. J.
Financial intermediation in small island developing economies (Commonwealth Economic Papers, no.16)
Commonwealth Secretariat, 1981

FRY, Plantagenet Somerset
Fountains Abbey, North Yorkshire
DoE, 1981

FUHR, M. J.
Rayner project. Energy conservation on the government estate, by M. J. Fuhr. (Property Services Agency Study no. 2)
Property Services Agency, 1979

FULLER, D. J.
International Society for Horticultural Science meeting of the council and executive committee, Antibes, France, 25–28 September 1981. Report
ADAS, 1981

FULLER, J. R.
Alcohol abuse and the treatment of young offenders – a progress report. (DPS Report Series I, no. 13)
Home Office, 1979

GAFFNEY, Maurice
Setting up a new business. (Small Firms Service Series)
Industry Dept., 1980

Setting up a new business. (Small Firms Service)
Industry Dept., 1981 (reprinted 1982)

GAIGER, F.
Machine mouldings and coremaker operator training guide book
Foundry Industry Training Committee, 1979

GAIR, R.
Cereal pests by D. W. Empson, 2nd ed., revised by R. Gair. (MAFF Reference Book 186)
ADAS, 1982

GALLAGHER, E. M.
Services for blind and partially sighted people. Report of the sub-committee on personal social services for the blind, partially sighted and hearing impaired people
DHSS for N.I., 1980

GALSWORTHY, Sir John
Report on the election in El Salvador on 28 March 1982, by Sir John Galsworthy and Prof. Derek W. Bowett, May 1982
Session 1981–82 Cmnd. 8553

GANGULI, S.
Pulping characteristics of *Pinus caribaea* grown in Sri Lanka, by E. R. Palmer and S. Ganguli. (L57)
Tropical Products Institute, 1982

GARBUTT, Douglas
Computer assisted accountancy training and education research project at Dundee College of Technology, 1979–80. Final report
MSC, 1981

GARLAND, R.
Planning for change: a study of the way five foundries introduced changed moulding methods. (Foundries ECD)
NEDO, 1980

GARRETT, Dennis
Burnholme and Forder Ltd. (in liquidation), Brayhead Ltd. (in liquidation). Investigation under the Companies Act, 1948. Report by T. M. Dillon and D. Garrett
Trade Dept., 1979

GARSIDE, C. A.
Distribution and marketing of nursery stock and pot plants: report of a study tour undertaken in Belgium, 18–22 May 1981
ADAS, 1982

Protected vegetable cropping. Report of a visit to Holland, May 1979, by C. A. Garside and J. R. Smith
ADAS, 1979

GARSIDE, W. R.
Measurement of unemployment: methods and sources in G. B., 1850–1979
Blackwell for the SSRC, 1980

GASKIN, M.
Building materials: export opportunities and import substitution. Trade performance advisory group. Building and Civil Engineering EDC's
NEDO, 1980

GASKIN, Maxwell
Employment in insurance, banking and finance in Scotland. Report of a study. (ESU Research Papers no. 2)
Scottish Economic Planning Dept., 1980

GAULD, W. W.
Working party on the future of state funded plant breeding and crop research in Scotland
Agriculture and Fisheries for Scotland Dept., 1981

GAZE, R. H.
Seminar given by the Mushroom Growers Association of the U.K. in Eire, 24–25 April 1980. Report of a visit to Eire
ADAS, 1980

GEDDES, Reay
COID proposals for some possible new initiatives for British aid; the Ministry of Overseas Development's reply; and its paper on local costs. (Council on International Development Occasional Paper)
Ministry of Overseas Development, 1979

GELARDI, Anne
A survey of tenants' attitudes to recently completed estates, by E. Levy and A. Gelardi. (HDD Occasional Paper 2/81)
DoE, 1981

GEMMILL, R.
Arrest, charge and summons; current practice and resource implications, by R. Gemmill and R. F. Morgan-Giles. (Research Study no. 9)
Royal Commission on Criminal Procedure, 1980

GEORGE, K. S.
Integrated control in agriculture and forestry. Symposium, October 1979. Report of a visit to Austria, by K. S. George and P. W. Carden
ADAS, 1979

IOBS/WPRS group meeting: 'Integrated control in cereals'. Report of a visit to France, November 24–26 1981
ADAS, 1982

GIBB, G. D.
Towards better dental health: guidelines for the future: the report of the Dental Strategy Review Group
DHSS, 1981

GIBBON, Michael
Afan. Review of district electoral arrangements. Draft proposals
Local Government Boundary Commission for Wales, 1979

Borough of Aberconway. Special community review report and proposals
Local Government Boundary Commission for Wales, 1980

Borough of Arfon. Special community review report and proposals
Local Government Boundary Commission for Wales, 1979

Borough of Colwyn. Special community review report and proposals
Local Government Boundary Commission for Wales, 1979

Borough of Islwyn. Special community review report and proposals
Local Government Boundary Commission for Wales, 1979

Borough of Llanelli. Special community review report and proposals
Local Government Boundary Commission for Wales, 1980

Borough of Merthyr Tydfil. Special community review report and proposals
Local Government Boundary Commission for Wales, 1979

Borough of Neath. Special community review report and proposals
Local Government Boundary Commission for Wales, 1979

Borough of Rhondda. Special community review report and proposals
Local Government Boundary Commission for Wales, 1979

Borough of Rhuddlan. Special community review report and proposals
Local Government Boundary Commission for Wales, 1979

GIBBON, Michael *(continued)*
Borough of Taff-Ely. Special community review report and proposals
Local Government Boundary Commission for Wales, 1980

Borough of Vale of Glamorgan. Special community review report and proposals
Local Government Boundary Commission for Wales, 1979

Borough of Wrexham Maelor. Special community review report and proposals
Local Government Boundary Commission for Wales, 1980

City of Cardiff. Special community review report and proposals
Local Government Boundary Commission for Wales, 1979

District of Dwyfor. Special community review report and proposals
Local Government Boundary Commission for Wales, 1979

District of Glyndwr. Special community review report and proposals
Local Government Boundary Commission for Wales, 1980

District of Merionnydd. Special community review report and proposals
Local Government Boundary Commission for Wales, 1980

District of Radnor. Special community review report and proposals
Local Government Boundary Commission for Wales, 1980

Islwyn special community review draft proposals
Local Government Boundary Commission for Wales, 1979

Rhymney Valley special community review draft proposals
Local Government Boundary Commission for Wales, 1979

Torfaen special community review draft proposals
Local Government Boundary Commission for Wales, 1979

GIBBS, J. N.
Verticillium wilt. (Arboricultural Leaflet 9)
Forestry Commission, 1981

GIBBS, Stephen
The plastic industry's view of manpower and efficiency. Report of the plastics processing sector working party
NEDO, 1979

Plastics Processing SWP. Progress report 1980
NEDO, 1980

Putting plastic into shape. Plastics Processing SWP
NEDO, 1979

GIBSON, Keith
Wormwood Scrubs. Home Office statement on the background, circumstances and action subsequently taken relative to the disturbances at 'D' wing at H. M. Prison Wormwood Scrubs on 31 August 1979; together with the report of an inquiry by the direction of the South East Region and the Prison Department.Home Office
Session 1981–82 HC 199

GIBSON, Marion
The role of social work in the rehabilitation of traumatic onset disability. (Personal Social Services in N.I. no. 18)
DHSS for N.I., 1982

GIBSON, Ralph
Breach of confidence. (Law Com. no. 110)
Session 1980–81 Cmnd. 8388

Property law: rights of reverter. (Law Com. no. 111)
Session 1980–81 Cmnd. 8410

Family law: the financial consequences of divorce. (Law Com. no. 112)
Session 1981–82 HC 68

Classification of limitation in private international law. (Law Com. no. 114)
Session 1981–82 Cmnd. 8570

Property law: the implications of Williams and Glyn's Bank Ltd. *vs* Boland. (Law Com. no. 115)
Session 1981–82 Cmnd. 8636

Family law. Time restrictions on presentation of divorce and nullity petitions. (Law Com. no. 116)
Session 1981–82 HC 513

Family law. Financial relief after foreign divorce. (Law Com. no. 117)
Session 1981–82 HC 514

Family law. Illegitimacy. (Law Com. no. 118)
Session 1982–83 HC 98

Law Commission. 17th annual report, 1981–82. (Law Com. no. 119)
Session 1982–83 HC 203

GILBERT, B. K.
Appraisal of development options in the National Health Service, by A. Burchell and B. K. Gilbert. (Review of Capricode working paper)
DHSS, 1982

GILBERT, J.
Housing investment strategies for difficult-to-let public sector housing estates, by J. Gilbert and L. Rosenburg. (Central Research Unit)
Scottish Office, 1981

GILBERT, J.
Housing investment strategies for difficult to let public sector housing estates, by J. Gilbert and L. Rosenburg
Scottish Development Dept., 1980

GILBERT, S.
Planning for the use of bulk foam stocks. (Joint Committee on Fire Research. Research Report no. 12)
Home Office, 1979

GILLESPIE, A. E.
Transport and the inner city. (The Inner City in Context 3)
SSRC, 1980

GILLIE, C.
The urban programme. (Reference Sheet no. 82/9)
House of Commons, 1981

GILYARD-BEER, R.
The County Hall, Abingdon
DoE, 1981

Gisborough Priory
DoE, 1981

White Ladies Priory, 6th printing
DoE, 1982

GINSELL, L. V.
Hetty Pegler's Tump, 3rd impression
DoE, 1982

GLADSTONE, F. J.
Co-ordinating crime prevention efforts. (Research Study no. 62)
Home Office, 1980

GLADWELL, G. L.
Computerised labour and machinery planning methods for field work. Report of a study tour in Holland
ADAS, 1982

Symposium of the labour and labour management commission of the International Society of Horticultural Science, Yugoslavia, September 1980. Report
ADAS, 1981

GLEW, G.
Meat fresh and frozen: food quality standards for the caterer. A practical guide to assist the caterer in his ordering and handling of fresh and frozen meat. (Food Quality Standards Committee)
NEDO, 1980

GLIDEWELL, I. D. L.
Fourth terminal, Heathrow and associated road access. Report of the public inquiry, May – December 1978
DoE, 1979

GLYPTIS, Sue
Providing for movement and dance: activities and facilities in the Bedford area, by E. M. Stokes and S. Glyptis. (Research Working Paper, 16)
Sports Council, 1979

GOACHER, David
Opportunities and constraints in community use of education facilities. The cases of Avon and Somerset; from a study. (Research Working Paper, 15)
Sports Council, 1979

GODDARD, J. B.
Technological change and the inner city, by J. B. Goddard and A. T. Thwaites. (The Inner City in Context 4)
SSRC, 1980

GODDARD, Sam
The role of nuclear power. (First of 6 articles reprinted from the East Anglian Daily Times)
Central Electricity Generating Board, 1981

How a nuclear power station works. (Second of 6 articles reprinted from the East Anglian Daily Times)
Central Electricity Generating Board, 1981

Radiation – a fact of life. (Third of 6 articles reprinted from the East Anglian Daily Times)
Central Electricity Generating Board, 1981

Why Britain needs the option of the pressurised water reactor. (Fourth of 6 articles reprinted from the East Anglian Daily Times)
Central Electricity Generating Board, 1981

The search for renewable energy resources. (Fifth of 6 articles reprinted from the East Anglian Daily Times)
Central Electricity Generating Board, 1981

Nuclear safety and the CEGB. (Sixth of 6 articles reprinted from the East Anglian Daily Times)
Central Electricity Generating Board, 1981

GODFREY, G. M.
Saint Piran Ltd. Interim report of investigation under the Companies Act, by G. M. Godfrey and A. J. Hardcastle
Trade Dept., 1980

Saint Piran Ltd. Investigation under section 165(b) and section 172 of the Companies Act 1948. Final report, by G. M. Godfrey and A. J. Hardcastle
Trade Dept., 1981

GODLEY, W. A. H.
The arguments for and against protectionism. Papers by M. Fg. Scott and W. A. H. Godley. (Papers Presented to the Panel of Academic Consultants no. 10)
Bank of England, 1980

GODSELL, S.
Severn crossing working party report, by S. Godsell and F. P. Davis
DTp, 1981

GOEL, K. M.
A nutrition survey of immigrant children in Glasgow, 1974–76. (Scottish Health Service Studies no. 40)
SHHD, 1979

GOLDBERG, A.
Whooping cough. Reports from the Committee on Safety of Medicines and the Joint Committee on Vaccination and Immunisation
DHSS, 1981

GOLDBLATT, P. O.
Longitudinal study: socio-demographic mortality differentials. A first report on mortality in 1971–75. (Series LS no. 1)
OPCS, 1982

GOLDMAN, H.
Research into the provision of information on hazardous substances: Hazfile. (Joint Committee on Fire Research, Research Report no. 14)
Home Office, 1980

GOLDSMITH, Michael
Register of research on central-local government relationships in Britain
SSRC, 1982

GOLLOP, C.
Developing a questionnaire to help prepare young people for work experience. (Training Services Division Report no. DTP28)
MSC, 1980

GOLTZ, M.
Plascon greenhouse. Report of a visit to Switzerland, by M. Goltz and G. Rose
ADAS, 1980

GOODE, D. A.
Lead poisoning in swans. Report of the working group, 1981
Nature Conservancy Council, 1981

GOODLASS, G.
The use of computers for data storage and manipulation, with particular reference to soil analytical data: report of a study tour undertaken in France, 9–14 November 1981
ADAS, 1982

GOOSE, J. M.
Recruitment into the police service of members of the ethnic minorities. Report of a study group
Home Office, 1982

GORDON, A.
Manpower in machine tools – employment and training in the metal-working machine tools industry. (Reference Paper RP/2/81)
Engineering Industry Training Board, 1981

GORDON, A. G.
Seed manual for ornamental trees and shrubs, by A. G. Gordon and D. C. F. Rowe. (Bulletin 59)
Forestry Commission, 1982

GORDON, Alex
Employment and training in industrial plant and steelwork manufacture. (Reference Paper RP/2/80)
Engineering Industry Training Board, 1980

GORMAN, T. P.
Language performance in schools, secondary survey report no. 1, by T. P. Gorman (et al)
Dept. Education and Science, Assessment of Performance Unit, 1982

GORONWY-ROBERTS, Goronwy Owen, Lord
Gilbert Islands constitutional conference report, February 1979
Session 1978–79 Cmnd. 7445

GOSS, R. O.
A comparative study of seaport management and administration (with) appendices. 2 vols
Industry Dept., 1979

GOSSOP, D.
Overseas visits programme; overall report on visits to Japanese companies. Food, Drink and Packaging Machinery SWP
NEDO, 1982

GOULD, H. J.
IOBS/WPRS study group meeting on integrated control in oilseed rape: report of a visit to Denmark, 20–22 April 1982
ADAS, 1982

Integrated crop protection: report on a symposium, Valance, France, June 1980, by P. W. Carden and H. J. Gould
MAFF, 1980

Meeting of working group on integrated control in glasshouses. Report of a visit to Finland, June 1979
ADAS, 1979

GOULD, P.
Variable direction signs to car parks – Truro experiment, by P. Gould and P. J. Kinsey
DTp, 1981

GOWER, L. C. B.
Review of investor protection, a discussion document
Trade Dept., 1982

GRAHAM, Barbara
New Horizons: opportunities for students discontinuing study at Scottish universities
Scottish Education Dept., 1979

GRAHAM, C.
Rayner scrutiny: DHSS activities in support of health care experts: report by Scrutiny Team. (C. Graham and Miss E. Shiells)
DHSS, 1980

GRAHAM, Finlay
The effectiveness of an anti-vandalism programme at Low Newton Remand Centre. Report. (DPS Report Series I, no. 16)
Home Office, 1980

Young persons remanded in custody: can the numbers safely be reduced? (DPS Report Series I, no. 14)
Home Office, 1979

GRAHAM, Hilary
The first months of motherhood. Summary report of a survey of women's experiences of pregnancy, childbirth and the first 6 months after birth, by H. Graham and L. McKee. (Monograph Series no. 3)
Health Education Council, 1980

GRAHAM, Hilary
Guide to school health education, compiled by J. Lee and H. Graham
Health Education Council, 1982

GRAHAM, J.
Study of returnable and non-returnable containers. (Waste Management Advisory Council Packaging and Containers Working Party)
DoE, 1981

GRAHAM, J. D. P.
Effects of cannabis use – report of the Expert Group. (Advisory Council of the Misuse of Drugs)
Home Office, 1982

GRAHAM, S.
The multi-purpose claim form trial in Brighton, by S. Graham and F. Brasier
DHSS, 1979

GRANT, Colin D.
Energy conservation in the chemical and process industries.
Chemical and Allied Products I. T. B. and Institution of Chemical Engineers, 1979

GRANT, M. H.
Forms under control. Review of administrative forms: report on control
Management and Personnel Office, 1982

GRANT, N.
Survey of visitors to the Scottish national museums and galleries
Scottish Office, 1981

GRATWICK, J.
People make clothing: a study of factors affecting employment in twenty companies in the clothing industry. (Clothing Employment Steering group)
NEDO, 1980

GRAYSON, A. J.
Investment appraisal in forestry with particular reference to conifers in Britain, by R. J. N. Busby and A. J. Grayson. (Booklet 47)
Forestry Commission, 1981

GRAYSON, David
Unlocking the facts: a review of prison psychologists research which has had a bearing on managerial decisions
Home Office, 1979

GRAYSON, R.
Salthill Quarry geology trail
Nature Conservancy Council, 1981

GREAVES, J. H.
International theriological congress, Report (3rd), by W. A. Rees and H. J. H. Greaves
ADAS, 1982

GREEN, D. D.
Industrial review: inorganic chemicals. (Chemicals EDC: Inorganics Sector Group)
NEDO, 1981

GREEN, D. E.
Carnation production. Report of a study tour undertaken in Holland and France, September 1979, by D. E. Green and J. M. L. Davies
ADAS, 1979

Tour with West Sussex carnation growers. Report of a visit to Israel, February 1979
ADAS, 1979

GREEN Diana
Managing industrial change? French policies to promote industrial adjustment
Industry Dept., 1981

GREEN, S.
Minorities in the market place; a study of south Asian and West Indian shoppers in Bradford, by Ramindar Singh and S. Green
National Consumer Council, 1982

GREENBOROUGH, John Hedley
Languages and export performance. A conference held at the Royal Society of Arts, October 1979
British Overseas Trade Board, 1979

GREENHALGH, Peter
The market for culinary herbs. (G121)
Tropical Products Institute, 1979

The markets for mint oils and methol. (G126)
Tropical Products Institute, 1979

The markets for selected herbaceous essential oils, by S. R. J. Robbins and P. Greenhalgh. (G120)
Tropical Products Institute, 1979

GREENHILL, Basil
The Royal dockyards; a unique survival. Report prepared by a panel of the Ancient Monuments Board for England
DoE, 1981

GREENOUGH, G. K.
Dust helmet in mining: a review of experience and possible future developments, by G. K. Greenough and B. Bancroft. (Research paper 12)
Health and Safety Executive, 1980

GREER, D. S.
Small claims procedure in Northern Ireland. Report by D. S. Greer and L. Leonard
Northern Ireland Consumer Council, 1980

GREGORY, C.
Training of medical physics and physiological measurement technicians within the TEC system. Final draft report and appendix. (Report of a DHSS Working Party). 2 vols.
DHSS, 1979

GREGORY, Janet
Survey of defenders in debt actions in Scotland. (Research Report for the Scottish Law Commission no. 6; SS1124)
OPCS, 1981

GREGSON, Lord John
Trade statistics and the industrial strategy. Report of the proceedings of the NEDO/Customs and Excise seminars, July 1978. (M. Griffin and Lord Gregson, chairmen)
NEDO, 1980

GRIBBIN, J. D.
The role of competition in the 1977 Price Commission Act. (Government Economic Service Working Paper no. 21)
Price Commission, 1979

GRIBBLE, C. D.
Potential for a large coastal quarry in Scotland. Preliminary research report, by C. I. Wilson and C. D. Gribble. (Planning Services)
Scottish Development Dept., 1980

GRICE, S. Le
FDEU sites for 1978. A progress report. (Technical Report 97/3; Reference Book 340)
ADAS, 1980

GRIEVE, Lord William Robertson
Administration of Sheriffdoms. Report of the committee, June 1982
Session 1981–82 Cmnd. 8548

GRIFFIN, G. W.
Investigation of the crop disease *colletrotricnum acutatum*. Report of a visit to Holland, August 1979
ADAS, 1979

GRIFFIN, M.
Trade statistics and the industrial strategy. Report of the proceedings of the NEDO/Customs and Excise seminars, July 1978. (M. Griffin and Lord Gregson, chairmen)
NEDO, 1980

GRIFFIN, M. J.
International post-graduate course on fungicide resistance in crop protection, Wageningen, Holland, 12–21 August 1980. Report
ADAS, 1981

GRIFFIN, M. J.
Vibration injuries of the hand and arm: their occurance and the evolution of standards and limits. (HSE Research Paper 9)
Health and Safety Executive, 1980

GRIFFIN, R. M.
Northampton fire priority demonstration scheme, by R. M. Griffin and P. G. Bennett. (Technical Paper 19)
DTp, 1979

GRIFFITH, E. M. W.
Arable crops and forage board. Final report
Agricultural Research Council, 1980

GRIFFITHS, D.
Experimental investigation of the operating efficiencies of two different types of fume cupboard. (Research Paper 13)
Health and Safety Executive, 1980

GRIFFITHS, J. T.
Electronic consumer goods industry. Report of the second stage of the Electronics Consumer SWP's strategy
NEDO, 1982

Electronic Consumer Goods Sector Working Party. Progress report, 1979
NEDO, 1979

Electronic Consumer Goods SWP. Progress report, 1980
NEDO, 1980

Sectoral report – the electronic consumer goods industry. Memorandum. (NEDC (82) 27)
NEDO, 1982

GRIFFITHS, W. J.
The distribution of resources to health authorities in Wales. 4th report of the steering committee, December 1979
Welsh Office, 1979

GRIMBLE, Ian
Highland man
Highlands and Islands Development Board, 1980

GRIMES, W. F.
Capel Garmon Burial Chamber, Gwynedd
Welsh Office, June 1980

GRIMSHAW, John
Study of disused railways in England and Wales: potential cycle routes. A study for the Department of Transport, by John Grimshaw and associates
DTp, 1982

GRINSELL, L. V.
Early man: archaeological sites on Exmoor to 1066
Exmoor National Park Authority, 1982

Stoney Littleton long barrow, 3rd ed
DoE, 1982

GROOM, C. M.
1) Jubilee symposium on 'The World's Poultry Production'; 2) 5th symposium on quality of poultry meat; 3) 1st symposium on egg quality: The Netherlands, 17–23 May 1981, by C. M. Groom, N. D. Overfield and F. H. Whaley
ADAS, 1982

GROOMBRIDGE, Brian
World checklist of endangered amphibians and reptiles
Nature Conservancy Council, 1981

GRYLLS, Michael
National Enterprise Board: a case for euthanasia, by M. Grylls and J. Redwood
National Enterprise Board, 1980

GUEST, David
Job design and the psychology of boredom. (Work Research Unit Occasional Paper no. 13)
Employment Dept., 1979

GUNN, J. S.
Conference (8th triennial) of the European Association for Potato Research, Munich, August/September 1981. Report
ADAS, 1982

Potato harvesting, handling, storage and marketing in USA. Report of a study tour undertaken in USA, September/October 1979, by J. S. Gunn and R. C. Balls
ADAS, 1979

GUNNELL, Clive
Somerset and North Devon coast path. (Long-distance Footpath Guide no. 10)
Countryside Commission, 1981

GURNELL, John
Woodland mice. (Forest Record no. 118)
Forestry Commission, 1979

GWILLIAM, Sue
If the village shop closes . . . a handbook on community shops
Development Commission, 1981

GWYNNE, D. C.
Latest developments at Limbourgerhof, BASF station and farm trials in the surrounding area. Report of a visit to West Germany, July – August 1979, by J. F. Roebuck and D. C. Gwynne
ADAS, 1979

HADLEY, Roger
Research on the voluntary sector: some proposals for exploring alternative patterns of welfare provision. A report to the SSRC sociology and social administration committee, by R. Hadley and S. Hatch
SSRC, 1980

HAGENBUCH, P.
Breeding herd results – year ending December 1981. (Pig Improvement Services Data Sheet 82/1)
Meat and Livestock Commission, 1982

Feeding herd results – year ending December 1981. (Pig Improvement Services Data Sheet 82/3)
Meat and Livestock Commission, 1982

Rearing herd results – year ending December 1981. (Pig Improvement Services Data Sheet 82/2)
Meat and Livestock Commission, 1982

HAGUE, D. B.
Gwydir Uchaf Chapel, Gwynedd
Welsh Office, 1980

HAINES, C. P.
Insects and arachnids from stored products; a report on specimens received by the Tropical Stored Products Centre, 1973–77. (Report L54)
Tropical Products Institute, 1981

HAIRE, T. H.
Adult dental health survey Northern Ireland 1979, by J. R. Rhodes and T. H. Haire
DHSS for N.I., 1981

HAKIM, Catherine
Occupational segregation. A comparative study of the degree and pattern of the differentiation between men and women's work in Britain, the USA and other countries. (Research Paper no. 9)
Employment Dept., 1979

HALE, David
Psychology laboratory computing, by D. Hale and others
SSRC, 1981

HALES, A. W.
Horticultural economics, 6th symposium. Report of a visit to Belgium, September 1979
ADAS, 1979

HALL, A.
Radio ignition hazards at St. Fergus, Scotland. Report of a working group
Health and Safety Executive, 1979

HALL, P. G.
Environmental education in urban areas. Report by a working party of the Environmental Board
DoE, 1979

HALL, P. J.
Mushroom training course. Report of a visit to Holland, June 1980
ADAS, 1980

HALLAM, David
Econometric forecasting in the U.K. egg market
Eggs Authority, 1981

HALLIDAY, J. M.
Review of arrangements for the sale of Robroyston Hospital. Report
SHHD, 1981

HALSTEAD, D. G. H.
Entomology. Report on 16th international congress, Kyoto, Japan, August 1980, by C. R. B. Baker and D. G. H. Halstead
ADAS, 1980

HALSTEAD, R.
Knitting sector working party progress report, 1980
NEDO, 1980

Manpower and productivity. Knitting SWP
NEDO, 1980

HAMBLYN, E. L.
The collection of fisheries statistics using photography, January 1979. (Amended 10.8.82)
Overseas Development Administration, 1982

HAMILL, L.
Wives as sole and joint breadwinners. (Government Economic Service Working Paper 13)
Civil Service Dept., 1979

HAMILTON, G. J.
Thinning control in British woodlands; metric revision by G. J. Hamilton and J. M. Christie. (Booklet no. 32, 2nd impr.)
Forestry Commission, 1982

HAMILTON, Sir James
Management review of the DES. Report of a steering committee
DES, 1979

HAMILTON, N.
Svensk form: a conference about Swedish design
Design Council, 1981

HAMILTON, V.
Impact of indirect taxes on households, by D. Todd and V. Hamilton (Government Economic Service Working Paper, 44)
Treasury, 1981

HAMMOND, E. A.
Electronic Components SWP. Progress report, 1980
NEDO, 1980

Electronic Components SWP. Progress report
NEDO, 1981

HAMMOND, P. J.
Die casting operator training guide book
Foundry Industry Training Committee, 1979

HAMMOND, V. J.
Women in the oil industry; attitude to work survey, by C. A. Carnall and V. J. Hammond
Petroleum Industry Training Board, 1979

HAMPSON, S. F.
Recent trends in the Scottish energy market, by S. F. Hampson and L. H. Thomson. (ESU Discussion Paper no. 1)
Scottish Economic Planning Dept., 1979

HAMPTON, William
Byker community development project, 1974–78. A report, by W. Hampton and I. Walkland. (Newcastle upon Tyne Council for Voluntary Service)
Home Office, 1980

HANBURY-TRACY, D. A. J.
Land restoration following mineral working with particular reference to the Polder method of restoration. Report of a study tour undertaken in West Germany, June 1979, by W. M. Waller and D. A. J. Hanbury-Tracy
ADAS, 1979

HANN, C. M.
Meeting of the poultry welfare working group (working group IX) of the European federation of the world's poultry science association at Koge, Denmark. Report of a visit to Denmark, March 1980
ADAS, 1980

Poultry breeding and genetics (working group 3) of the European federation of the world's poultry science association. Meeting at Jouy-en-Josas, September 1979. Report of a visit to France
ADAS, 1979

HANNAH, Leslie
New horizons for business history?
SSRC, 1981

HANNON, V.
Ending sex-stereotyping in schools: a source-book for school-based teacher workshops, rev. ed
Equal Opportunities Commission, 1981

HANS-KLAU, C.
Planning research in Germany
SSRC, 1982

HANSELL, J. R. F.
Transmigration settlements in central Sumatra: identification, evaluation and physical planning. (Land Resource Study 33)
Land Resources Development Centre, 1981

HARDCASTLE, A. J.
Saint Piran Ltd. Interim report of investigation under the Companies Act, by G. M. Godfrey and A. J. Hardcastle
Trade Dept., 1980

Saint Piran Ltd. Investigation under section 165(b) and section 172 of the Companies Act 1948. Final report by G. M. Godfrey and A. J. Hardcastle
Trade Dept., 1981

HARDIE, C. J. M.
Anglian Water Authority, North West Water Authority. A report on the sewerage functions of the two authorities, November 1982. Monopolies and Mergers Commission
Session 1981–82 Cmnd. 8726

Benham Newspapers Ltd., St. Regis International Ltd. and Reed International plc. Report of the Monopolies and Mergers Commission, June 1982
Session 1981–82 HC 402

Ensearch Corp. and Davy Corp. Ltd. Report on the proposed merger by the Monopolies and Mergers Commission 1981
Session 1980–81 Cmnd. 8360

London Electricity Board. A report by the Monopolies and Mergers Commission, March 1983
Session 1982–83 Cmnd. 8812

HARDY, A. R.
International training seminar on research and control of vertebrate pests in Santo Domingo, Dominican Republic, November 1979
ADAS, 1979

HARDY, R. P.
Flexible joints for gravity sewers. (Occasional Technical Paper no. 3)
National Water Council, 1979

HARKER, A. P.
The production of charcoal in a portable metal kiln, by A. R. Paddon and A. P. Harker. (G119)
Tropical Products Institute, 1979

Utilization of waste heat produced during the manufacture of coconut shell charcoal for the centralised production of copra, by G. R. Breag and A. P. Harker. (G127)
Tropical Products Institute, 1980

HARLEY, R. F. M.
Heating, Ventilating, Air Conditioning and Refrigeration Equipment SWP. Progress report 1980
NEDO, 1980

Heating, Ventilating, Air Conditioning and Refrigeration Equipment SWP. Progress report, 1981
NEDO, 1981

A participative approach to efficiency improvement. Heating, Ventilating, Air Conditioning and Refrigeration Equipment SWP
NEDO, 1979

HARRIS, Harry
The Commonwealth casebook for school administrators
Commonwealth Secretariat, 1982

HARRIS, M.
Psychology theses register: a register commissioned by the Psychology Committee
SSRC, 1982

HARRIS, P. S.
The brewing industry; energy consumption and conservation in the brewing industry. (Energy Audit Series no. 8)
Energy Dept., 1979

HARRIS, S. M.
English static self-catering accommodation occupancy survey 1980
English Tourist Board, 1981

HARRISON, A.
Review of graded tests. (Examinations Bulletin 14)
Methuen for Schools Council, 1982

HARRISON, Alan
Distribution of wealth in ten countries. (Background Paper 7)
Royal Commission on the Distribution of Income and Wealth, 1979

HARRISON, I. B.
Groundwater potential of the old red sandstone formations of East Berwickshire: a report. (Applied Research and Development Report no. ARD10)(Civil Engineering and Water Services)
Scottish Development Dept., 1981

HART, C.
Values enquiry in practice. (Occasional Paper no. 3) (Geography 16–19 Curriculum Development)
London University for Schools Council, 1982

HARTLAND, J. R.
Mechanical egg collection and associated husbandry practice on breeder farms. Report of a study tour undertaken in West Germany, October 1979
ADAS, 1979

HARVEY, B. H.
Framing noise legislation. Report by the Industrial Health Advisory Sub-committee on Noise
Health and Safety Executive, 1980

HARVEY, J. J.
Sugar beet. Report on a visit to Belgium, June 1979
ADAS, 1979

HARVEY, Juliet
Young people on YOP, by T. Bedeman and J. Harvey (Special Programmes Research and Development Series no. 3)
MSC, 1981

HARVEY, N.
Effective writing in advisory work, by G. Cherry and N. Harvey
ADAS, 1981

HASLAM, S. M.
Vegetation in British rivers: vol. I – text; vol. II – river maps. Nature Conservancy Council, 1982

HATCH, Stephen
Research on the voluntary sector; some proposals for exploring alternative patterns of welfare provision. A report to the SSRC sociology and social administration committee, by R. Hadley and S. Hatch
SSRC, 1980

HATTON, Neville
Explanations and explaining, by G. Brown and N. Hatton. (DES Teacher Education Project)
Macmillan for DES, 1982

HAWES, W. R.
Patterns of representation of the parties in unfair dismissal cases: a review of the evidence, by W. R. Hawes and G. Smith. (Research Paper no. 22)
Employment Dept., 1981

HAWKES, A. J.
An industrial profile of fibreboard panel processing, by G. Flynn and A. J. Hawkes. (G140)
Tropical Products Institute, 1980

An industrial profile of wood wool/cement slab manufacture, by G. Flynn and A. J. Hawkes. (G141)
Tropical Products Institute, 1980

HAWKINGS, Francis
House of Lords reform, 1850–1970, 2nd ed. (Factsheet no. 1)
House of Lords, 1979

HAWKINS, A.
Trends in leisure, 1919–1939, by A. Hawkins and J. Lowerson. (A Review for SC/SSRC Joint Panel on Leisure and Recreation Research)
Sports Council, 1979

HAWKINS, A. F.
Partial matrices, empirical deterrence functions and ill defined results, by M. J. L. Day and A. F. Hawkins. (LTR Working Paper 9)
DTp, 1979

HAWTHORNE, R. S.
East Tyrone area plan public inquiry. Report and recommendations by Planning Appeals Commission
DoE for N.I., 1979

HAWTHORNE, Sir William R.
Advisory Council on Energy Conservation. Report to the Secretary of State for Energy. (Energy Paper no. 40)
Energy Dept., 1979

HAY, J.
Room utilisation in educational institutions, by W. T. Beveridge and J. Hay
Scottish Education Dept., 1979

HAYES, C.
Foundation training issues, by C. Hayes and others. A report for the MSC (Institute of Manpower Studies Report 39)
MSC, 1982

HAYES, E.
Directory of libraries in Northern Ireland government departments.
Library Advisory Council of Northern Ireland, 1980

HAYFIELD, C. P.
The geographical stability of a typical trip generation model, by C. P. Hayfield and R. B. Stoker. (LTR1 Working Paper 11)
DTp, 1979

A method for forecasting car ownership in local areas using national travel survey data. (LTR1 Working Paper 12)
DTp, 1979

HAYWARD, Richard
New towns staff commission, 1976–1978, the first report
DoE, 1979

HEAD, J. M.
Site investigation manual, by A. J. Weltman and J. M. Head. (PSA Civil Engineering Technical Guide, no. 35)
PSA, 1982

HEADY, Patrick
Labour mobility in the construction industry. Survey of manual workers conducted for the Construction Industry Manpower Board and the DoE. Final report, by A. Marsh and P. Heady
OPCS, 1980

HEAL, Kevin
Crime control and the police: a review of research by P. Morris and K. Heal. (Home Office Research Study no. 67)
Home Office, 1981

Police response to calls from the public, by P. Ekblom and K. Heal (Research and Planning Unit Paper no. 9)
Home Office, 1982

HEALD, D.
The Monopolies and Mergers Commission's verdict on the CEGB's investment appraisals. (Occasional Paper no. 5)
Electricity Consumers' Council, 1982

HEALY, P. R.
Piling in 'boulder clay' and other glacial tills, by A. J. Weltman and P. R. Healey. (Report PGS)
Property Services Agency, Piling Development Group, 1978.

Piling in chalk, by N. B. Hobbs and P. R. Healy. (DOE and CIRIA piling development group report PG6) (PSA Civil Engineering Technical Guide 24)
Property Services Agency, 1979

Survey of problems associated with the installation of displacement piles, by P. R. Healey and A. J. Weltman. (Report PG8; Civil Engineering Technical Guide 26)
Property Services Agency, 1980

HEANEY, Henry
Union Catalogues. Report of the British Library ad hoc working party
British Library, 1982

HEATH, A. G. D.
Seminar on viticulture: report of a visit to the Mosel-Saar-Ruwer district of West Germany, 6–14 September 1981
ADAS, 1982

HEATH, John B.
Management in nationalised industries. (NICG Occasional Paper no. 2)
Nationalised Industries' Chairmen's Group, 1980

HEATHCOTE, G.
Curriculum styles and strategies: a project repocrt, by G. Heathcote, R. Kempa and I. Roberts. (Further Education Unit)
DES (FEU), 1982

HEBBERT, M.
The inner city problem in historical context. (The Inner city in Context 5)
SSRC, 1980

HEBBLETHWAITE, R. J.
Unit trust accounts. Joint working party report by the unit trust association and the companies division of the Dept. of Trade
Trade Dept., 1981

HEBERT, C. N.
Council of Europe – European Pharmacopoeis Commission. 41st meeting of a group of experts on 15V. Report of a visit to Belgium, June 1980
ADAS, 1980

HEDGES, J. L.
Two studies of commodity price behaviour: interrelationships between commodity prices by J. L. Hedges and short-run pricing behaviour in commodity markets, by C. A. Enoch. (Discussion Paper no. 18)
Bank of England, 1981

HEGARTY, S.
Stretching the system; FE and related responses to students with special needs, by J. Bradley and S. Hegarty
DES, 1982

Students with special needs in further education: a review of current and completed research relating to young people in the 14–19 age range with special educational needs, by J. Bradley and S. Hegarty. (Further Education Curriculum Review and Development Unit: Project Report 12)
DES, 1981

HELME, R. W.
Study tour with NFU. Report of a visit to Holland, May 1979
ADAS, 1979

HENDERSON, D. S.
The 1973 Scottish input-output tables: some definitional issues. (Economics and Statistics Unit: Discussion Paper no. 8)
Scottish Economic Planning Dept., 1980

Consumers' expenditure in Scotland 1962 to 1977. (Economics and Statistics Unit: Discussion Paper no. 9)
Scottish Economic Planning Dept., 1980

The revised index of industrial production for Scotland for the period 1958 to 1970, by A. M. Burnside and D. S. Henderson
(Economics and Statistics Unit: Discussion Paper no. 6)
Scottish Economic Planning Dept., 1980

HENDERSON, H.
Building societies – valuations and surveys
Scottish Consumer Council, 1981

HENDERSON, R. A.
Employment performance of established manufacturing industry in the Scottish new towns. (ESU Discussion Paper, 16)
Scottish Economic Planning Dept., 1982

HENDRY, L. B.
Adolescents and leisure. (Review for the Joint Sports Council/SSRC Panel on Leisure and Recreation Research)
Sports Council, 1981

HENLEY, Alix
Asians in Britain. Caring for Muslims and their families; religious aspects of care. (King Edward's Hospital Fund for London)
DHSS, 1982

HENNESSY, P. J.
Families, funerals and finances. A study of funeral expenses and how they are paid. (Statistics and Research Division Research Report no. 6)
DHSS, 1980

HENSTRIDGE, John
Industrial relations in the civil service. A training document issued by the Civil Service College Working Party on Industrial Relations Training
Civil Service Department, 1980

HEPBURN, A. C.
Employment and religion in Belfast, 1901–1971
Fair Employment Agency, 1982

HEPPER, F. Nigel
Royal Botanic Gardens Kew: gardens for science and pleasure
Royal Botanic Gardens Kew, 1982

HERBERT, David
Simulations, by David Herbert and Gill Sturtridge (ELT Guide 2)
British Council, 1979

HERRING, D.
Research and advisory methods, socio-economics and tourism; technical development in buildings and related topics. Report of a visit to the Republic of Ireland. (FR6840)
ADAS, 1982

HERRON, Frank
Post Industry Act (1972) industrial movement into, and expansion in, the assisted areas of Great Britain; some survey findings (Government Economic Service Working Paper no. 46)
Industry Dept., 1981

HERSLEB, Anton
The supply and demand for computer related manpower to 1985. Final report of the Manpower Sub-committee of the Electronic Computers SWP and computer manpower in the '80's, by A. Anderson and A. Hersleb
NEDO, 1980

HESELTINE, Michael
Speeding the planning process
DoE, 1980

HESSELMAN, Linda
Macro-economic role of relative price change in the U.K. and U.S. (Economic Working Paper no.3)
NEDO 1981

Non-price factors in the U.K. washing machine market; a hedonic approach. (Economic Working Paper no. 1)
NEDO, 1981

Trends in European industrial innovation. (Economic Working Paper no. 7)
NEDO, 1982

HEWGILL, D.
Land capability classification. Report of a study tour undertaken in Canada and USA, June/July 1980
ADAS, 1980

HICKLIN, J.
Competitiveness and manufactured exports; some tests of the Treasury model specification by A. Ritchie and J. Hicklin. (Government Economic Service Working Paper 51)
Treasury, 1981

HICKS, D.
Planning and teaching world studies; an interim guide by S. Fisher and D. Hicks. World Studies, 8–13, Project
Schools Council, 1982

Planning workshops and courses; a world studies in-service handbook, by S. Fisher and D. Hicks. World Studies, 8–13, Project
Schools Council, 1982

HIDER, A. T.
A school facing change: a case study in staff development. (Programme 1: Purpose and Planning in Schools: Activity 1)
Schools Council, 1981

HIGGINS, P. B.
Molten metal and water explosions. Joint Standing Committee on Health, Safety and Welfare in Foundries; sixth report of the Sub-Committee on Molten Metal and Water Hazards
Health and Safety Executive, 1979

Safety during semi-continuous casting of copper and copper-based alloys. Joint Standing Committee on Health, Safety and Welfare in Foundries; 5th report of the Sub-committee on Molten Metal and Water Hazards
Health and Safety Executive, 1979

HILGENDORF, Linden
Learning at work; the Tavistock guide, by L. Hilgendorf and R. Welchman (Special Programmes Research and Development Series no. 9)
MSC, 1982

Police interrogation; the psychological approach, by B. Irving and L. Hilgendorf. (Research Study no. 1)
Royal Commission on Criminal Procedure, 1980

Social workers and solicitors in child care cases
DHSS, 1981

Tied houses in British forestry, by B. L. Irving and E. L. Hilgendorf. (Research and Development Paper no. 117)
Forestry Commission, 1979

HILL, A. R. C.
Pesticide residue analysis: report of a study tour undertaken in Denmark and Holland, October 1980
ADAS, 1981

HILL, G. A.
Symposium on agriculture and tourism June 1982. Report of a visit to Mariehamina, Finland
ADAS, 1982

HILL, S. A.
Fruit tree virus diseases (11th international symposium) and small fruit virus diseases (2nd international symposium). Report of a visit to Hungary, July 1979, by S. A. Hill and R. A. C. Jones
ADAS, 1979

Potato viruses in tubers. Report of a study tour undertaken in West Germany and Switzerland, September 1979
ADAS, 1979

HILLIARD, B. C.
The Bank of England small monetary model; recent developments and simulations properties. (Discussion Paper no. 13)
Bank of England, 1980

Exchange flows and the guilt-edged security market, a causality study. (Discussion Paper no. 2)
Bank of England, 1979

HILLYER, John Selby
Scotia Investments Ltd. Report of investigations under the Companies Act, 1948, by L. Bromeley and J. S. Hillyer
Trade Dept., 1980

HIMSWORTH, K. H.
Review of areas of outstanding natural beauty. (CCP140)
Countryside Commission, 1980

HINCHCLIFFE, M. P. R.
Residual flows to estuaries
Central Water Planning Unit, 1979

HINDE, Joe E.
Make ready for success; the characteristics of successful firms in the UK printing industry
NEDO, 1981

Manufacturing efficiency checklists, by J. Hinde and N. Raine. (Manufacturing efficiency action team; Printing Machinery SWP)
NEDO, 1980

Press ahead into the 1980's. A summary of the 1979 progress report from the Printing and Bookbinding Machinery SWP
NEDO, 1979

Why do research and development? Printing Machinery Sector Working Party
NEDO, 1980

HINTON-MEAD, T.
International horticultural fair. Report of a visit to Austria
ADAS, 1979

HITCHCOCK, G. D.
ENT services in the North Thames regions. (London Health Planning Consortium. Report of the Study Group)
DHSS, 1980

HOARE, J.
National health service; the recruitment and career development of administrators. A report by the National Staff Committee for Administrative and Clerical Staff. Working party of the Training of Administrators
DHSS, 1979

HOBBS, N. B.
Piling in chalk (full version), by N. B. Hobbs and P. R. Healy. (DOE and CIRIA Piling Development Group, Report PG6; PSA Civil Engineering Technical Guide 24)
Property Services Agency, 1979

HOBROW, H. A.
Tool making craftsmen. Gauge and tool SWP
NEDO, 1981

HODGE, A. W.
Laboratory design. Interim report of the joint DHSS-LIU working party. (Laboratory Investigation Unit)
DES, 1979

HODGES, R. J.
A review of the biology and control of the rice moth *corcyra cephalonica stainton* (lepidoptera: Gallerniinae). (G125)
Tropical Products Institute, 1979

HODGETTS, B.
Aspects of poultry production. ADAS study tour programme, 1980–81, by B. Hodgetts and D. Spackman
MAFF, 1980

HODGSON, Jenny
Fire (open science)
Schools Council, 1979

HOEY, P. O'N.
Investigation of scientific and technical information systems related to agriculture in the USSR. Report of a visit to the USSR, October 1979
ADAS, 1979

HOFFMAN, J. M.
Quarterly small monetary model of the UK economy: preliminary estimation and simulation results. (Discussion Paper no. 14)
Bank of England, 1980

HOLDEN, A. V.
Control of pine beauty moth by fenitrothion in Scotland, 1978, edited by A. V. Holden and D. Bevan
Forestry Commission, 1979

HOLDGATE, M. W.
Review of the scientific civil service, 1980. Report of a working group of the management committee for the science group (CSD), September 1980
Session 1979–80 Cmnd. 8032

HOLLIDAY, F. G. T.
Nature conservation and the Clyde estuary. Report of a symposium held at Paisley College of Technology, November 1979. (South West Scotland Region)
Nature Conservancy Council, 1980

HOLMES, Martin
The crown jewels at the Tower of London
DoE, 1981

HOLMES, Peter
Handbook for co-ordinators. (Schools Council Project on Statistical Education)
Schools Council, 1981

HOLMES, W. H.
The pottery industry; a report by W. H. Holmes and E. Davies. (Energy Audit Series no. 7)
Energy Dept., 1979

HOLTERMAN, S.
The costs of alcohol misuse, by S. Holterman and A. Burchell. (Government Economic Service Working Paper no. 37)
DHSS, 1981

HOMAN, J. R. S.
Electronic Computers SWP. Progress report, 1980
NEDO, 1980

Man-made Fibre Production Sector Working Party. Progress report
NEDO, 1979

The man-made fibres industry and the future. Summary of sector working party progress report
NEDO, 1980

Mining Machinery SWP code of good practice for improving performance
NEDO, 1979

Mining Machinery Sector Working Party. Progress report, 1979
NEDO, 1979

Mining Machinery SWP. Progress report, 1980
NEDO, 1980

Survey of processors' views of the competitiveness of UK plastics materials. Petrochemicals SWP
NEDO, 1981

Telecommunications Sector Working Party. Progress report
NEDO, 1979

HONEYMAN, H. L.
Dunstanburgh Castle, by C. H. H. Blair and H. L. Honeyman. 3rd ed.
DoE, 1982

Warkworth Castle, Northumberland, by C. H. H. Blair and H. L. Honeyman
DoE, 1982

Warkworth Hermitage
DoE, 1981

HOOD, Neil
European development strategies of US-owned manufacturing companies located in Scotland, by N. Hood and S. Young.
Scottish Economic Planning Council, 1980

HOOD, R. E.
Report on the training of portering staff. (NHS National Staff Committee (Accommodation, Catering and other Support Services))
DHSS, 1981

HOOPER, A. J.
Seminar on remote sensing applications and technology transfer for international development and 13th international symposium on remote sending of the environment. Report of a visit to USA, April 1979
ADAS, 1979

HOOPER, Brian Michael
North Devon Railway Co. Ltd.; Words in Action Co. Ltd. Investigations under the Companies Act, 1948. Reports by B. M. Hooper and J. M. Buttimer
Trade Dept., 1979

HOPE, Tim
Burglary in schools; the prospects of prevention. (Research and Planning Unit Paper 11)
Home Office, 1982

HOPKINS, B. P.
A comparison of dairy farming in Brittany and England and Wales. (Report no. 21)
Milk Marketing Board, 1979

HOPKINSON, E. G.
Mineral assessment, evaluation and calculation. Report of the regional workshop, Bangalore, March/April 1979. Vol. 1: Proceedings. (Report CGLO SLR3)
Commonwealth Geological Liaison Office, 1980

HOPSON, A. J.
Lake Turkana. Report on the findings of the Lake Turkana Project, 1972–75. 6 vols
Overseas Development Administration, 1982

HORNSTEIN, Zmira
The economics of the labour market. Proceedings of a conference on the labour market, sponsored by Her Majesty's Treasury, the Department of Employment and the Manpower Services Commission. Edited by Z. Hornstein, J. Grice and A. Webb
Treasury, 1981

HOSSAIN, Kamal
Law and policy in petroleum development; changing relations between transnationals and governments
Commonwealth Secretariat, 1979

HOUGH, J. M.
Uniformed police work and management technology. (Research Unit Paper 1)
Home Office, 1980

HOUGH, M.
Crime and public housing, ed. by M. Hough and P. Mayhew. (Research and Planning Unit: Paper 6)
Home Office, 1982

HOUGHTON, S.
Adaptation of the soya bean to cooler regions of Europe: report of a visit to Switzerland, 3–4 August 1981
ADAS, 1982

HOUSEMAN, Alex R.
Gauge and Tool SWP. Progress report
NEDO, 1980

Toolmaking; a comparison of UK and West German companies. (Gauge and Tool Sector Working Party)
NEDO, 1981

HOUSEMAN, C. I.
Videotext system for farmers; the green thumb box. Report of a study tour in the USA
ADAS, 1980

HOWARTH, G.
Members' pay and allowances. (Factsheet no. 17)
House of Commons, 1982

HOWBROW, H. A.
Tool making craftsmen. Gauge and Tool SWP
NEDO, 1981

HOWE, P. M.
CULV 2.0: programme for the automatic design and detailing of rectangular reinforced concrete box culverts. (HECB/4)
DTp, 1981

HOWELL, Dennis G.
The inter-relationship within the commonwealth between animal production and animal health. Report on a commonwealth foundation lecture tour. (Occasional Paper no. XLVII)
Commonwealth Foundation, 1979

HOWIE, E.
Mathematical requirements of commerce; an investigation. Consultative Committee on the Curriculum
Scottish Education Dept., 1981

HOWSON, S. K.
Portfolio model of domestic and external financial markets, by C. B. Briault and S. K. Howson. (Discussion Paper no. 20)
Bank of England, 1982

HUBBARD, A. W.
Survey of arsenic in food. The eighth report of the Steering Group on Food Surveillance. The Working Party on the Monitoring of Foodstuffs for Heavy Metals. (Food Surveillance Paper no. 8)
MAFF, 1982

HUBBUCK, J
Half a chance; report on job discrimination against young blacks in Nottingham, by J. Hubbuck and S. Carter
Commission for Racial Equality, 1980

HUCKER, T. W. G.
Sub-committee on the disposal of sewage sludge to land. Report (Standing Technical Committee Reports no. 20)
National Water Council, 1981

HUGHES, Lord
Royal commission on Legal Services in Scotland: report and appendices. 2 vols. in 3, May 1980
Session 1979–80 Cmnd. 7846

HUGHES, A.
Issues in language testing, ed. by J. C. Alderson and A. Hughes. (ELT Documents 111)
British Council, 1981

HUGHES, A. A.
Scottish crafts now. (Crafts Consultative Committee)
Scottish Development Agency, 1980

HUGHES, D. F.
Ventilation: high velocity inlet system
ADAS, 1981

HUGHES, Eryl Rothwell
Conceptual powers of children: an approach through mathematics and science. (Schools Council Research Studies)
Schools Council, 1979

HUGHES, H.
An evaluation of the Innotron Hydragomma 16 gamma counter, by H. Hughes and G. H. Beastall
Welsh Office, 1982

HUGHES, Hilary M.
Strawberries, 9th ed. (Reference book 95)
ADAS, 1980

HUGHES, J.
Mastitis control. ADAS study tour programme 1980/81, by G. Jackson and J. Hughes
ADAS, 1980

HUGHES, Sir Jack W.
Planning gain. Report by the Property Advisory Group
DoE, 1981

Structure and activity of the development industry. Report of the Property Advisory Group
DoE, 1980

HUGHES, Katherine
Survey of rail users on the Merthyr-Cardiff line
Welsh Consumer Council, 1979

What's where in Gwynedd
Welsh Consumer Council, 1979

HUGHES, M. G.
Leaders in the management of education; handbook for educational supervisors. Revised by M. G. Hughes
Commonwealth Secretariat, 1981

HUGHES, R. G.
CIBA-GEIGY pesticide briefing. (Report of a visit to West Germany, 11–14 June 1981)
ADAS, 1982

International congress of plant protection, 9th. Report of a visit to the USA, August 1979, by R. G. Hughes and others
ADAS, 1979

HUGILL, J.
The actions of the authorities and agencies relating to Darryn James Clarke. Report of the committee of inquiry, November 1979
Session 1979–80 Cmnd. 7730

HULLS, R. H.
Farmers use of the ADAS booklet 'The Use of Fungicides and Insecticides in Cereals 1980' (Extension Development Unit Report no. 17)
ADAS, 1982

International seminar on extension education, 4th. Report of a visit to Eire
ADAS, 1979

Visitors at two ADAS events in 1981. (Extension Development Unit Report no. 19)
ADAS, 1982

HULSE, Simon
Microprocessors and the small business. (Small Firms Service Series)
Industry Dept., 1980

HUMPHREY, David H.
A review of evidence on the economic costs and benefits of trade protection. (Economic Working Paper no. 2)
NEDO, 1981

HUMPHRIES, Alan P.
Aveley Laboratories Limited. Report by A. J. D. McCowan and A. P. Humphries
Trade Dept., 1981

Electerminations Ltd. (in liquidation) (formerly known as APT Electronic Industries Ltd.). Report of investigations under the Companies Act, by A. J. D. McCowan and A. P. Humphries
Trade Dept., 1979

HUNT OF TANWORTH, John J. B., Baron
Report of the inquiry into cable expansion and broadcasting policy, October 1982
Session 1981–82 Cmnd. 8679

HUNT, A. W.
Role of the social services in the care of the deaf of all ages. Report of a Sub-committee of the Advisory Committee on Services for Hearing-impaired People
DHSS, 1978

HUNT, G. J.
Radioactivity in surface and coastal waters of the British Isles, 1978. (Aquatic Environment Monitoring Report no. 4)
MAFF, 1980

Radioactivity in surface and coastal waters of the British Isles, 1979. (Aquatic Environment Monitoring Report no. 6)
MAFF, 1981

HUNT, T. J.
Full time/part time PSV driver accident study. Complete report
DTp, 1978

HUNTER, J. O. M., Lord
Report of inquiry into the whole circumstances of the murder of Mrs Rachel Ross at Ayr in July 1969, and the action taken by the Police, the Crown Office, and the Scottish Home and Health Department relating to that case before and after the trial of Mr. Patrick Meehan. 4 vols
Session 1981–82 HC 444

Scottish Law Commission. 13th annual report, 1977–78. (Scottish Law Commission no. 55). 1979
Session 1978–79 HC 157

Scottish Law Commission. 14th annual report, 1978–79. (Scottish Law Commission no. 56). December 1979
Session 1979–80 HC 276

Lost and abandoned property. Report by the Scottish Law Commission. (Scottish Law Commission no. 57). 1980
Session 1979–80 HC 346

The consolidation of certain enactments relating to education in Scotland. Report. Education (Scotland) Bill. (Scottish Law Commission no. 58). April 1980
Session 1979–80 Cmnd. 7688

Scottish Law Commission report on powers of judicial factors, July 1980. (Scottish Law Commission no. 59)
Session 1979–80 Cmnd. 7904

Report on occupancy rights in the matrimonial home and domestic violence. (Scottish Law Commission no. 60). 1980
Session 1979–80 HC 676

Scottish Law Commission. 15th annual report, 1979–80. (Scottish Law Commission no. 61). December 1980
Session 1980–81 HC 17

Judicial pensions bill. (Law Commission no. 105; Scottish Law Commission no. 62). November 1980
Session 1980–81 Cmnd. 8097

Statute law revision, 10th report. Draft statute law (repeals) bill. (Law Commission no. 106; Scottish Law Commission no. 63). December 1980
Session 1980–81 Cmnd. 8089

Trustee savings banks bill. Report on consolidation. (Law Commission no. 108; Scottish Law Commission no. 65). 1981.
Session 1981–82 Cmnd. 8257

Family law. Report on aliment and financial provision. (Scottish Law Commission no. 67). 1981
Session 1981–82 HC 2

Bankruptcy and related aspects of insolvency and liquidation. Report. (Scottish Law Commission no. 68). 1982
Session 1981–82 HC 176

Law of incest in Scotland. (Scottish Law Commission no. 69). 1981
Session 1981–82 Cmnd. 8422

HUNTER, J. O. M., Lord *(continued)*
Scottish Law Commission. 16th annual report, 1980–81. (Scottish Law Commission no. 70). 1981
Session 1981–82 HC 38

HUNTER OF NEWINGTON, Lord Robert Brockie
Developments in tobacco products and the possibility of 'lower-risk' cigarettes. (Second Report of the Independent Scientific Committee on Smoking and Health)
DHSS, 1979

HUNTER, R. D.
The development of obstacle clearance criteria for ILS operations at civil airports. (CAA Paper 80009)
Civil Aviation Authority, 1980

HUTCHINSON, D.
Crop production in hardy nursery stock production. Report of a study tour by J. V. Cross and D. Hutchinson
ADAS, 1982

Tree and shrub protection. Report of a study tour undertaken in Holland, August 1979
ADAS, 1979

HUTSON, Susan
A review of the role of clubs and voluntary associations based on a study of two areas in Swansea
Sports Council, 1979

HUWS, Ursula
New technology and women's employment: case studies from West Yorkshire. (Leeds Trade Union and Community Resource and Information Centre)
Equal Opportunities Commission, 1982

HYDER, Masood
Parliament and defence affairs; a critique of the major decisions approach. (CSC Working Paper no. 11)
Civil Service College, 1979

IMBER, Valerie
Public expenditure 1978–79: outturn compared with plan. (Government Economic Service Working Paper no. 31)
Treasury, 1980

Public expenditure 1979–80; outturn compared with plan. (Government Economic Service Working Paper, 40)
Treasury, 1981

INCE, Roy
Tenant participation in the repair and maintenance of council houses
DoE, 1982

INGHAM, P. C.
Computer aided design in FE. Further Education Unit
DES, 1982

INGLIS, I. R.
International symposium on the integrated study of bird population. Report of a visit to Holland, September 1979
ADAS, 1979

INGOLDBY, M. J. R.
Forest fire fighting with foam, by M. J. R. Ingoldby and R. O. Smith (Leaflet 80)
Forestry Commission, 1982

INGRAM, Collingwood William Malcolm
Dunlop Holdings Ltd. Interim report of investigation under the Companies Act, 1948, by C. W. M. Ingram and F. H. Pulling
Trade Dept., 1981

INSALL, Donald W.
Conservation in action: Chester's Bridgegate. (Aspects of Conservation Series)
DoE, 1982

IRETON, B. R.
Review of government statistical services: ODA departmental study
Overseas Development Administration, 1981

IRVING, Barrie L.
Police interrogation; a case study of current practice. (Research Study no. 2)
Royal Commission on Criminal Procedure, 1980

Police interrogation; the psychological approach, by B. Irving and L. Hilgendorf. (Research Study no. 1)
Royal Commission on Criminal Procedure, 1980

Tied houses in British forestry, by B. L. Irving and E. L. Hilgendorf. (Research and Development Report no. 117)
Forestry Commission, 1979

IRVING, H.
Structure plan monitoring. Report of a joint working party
Scottish Development Dept., 1979

ISON, J.
Ports '82: guide to the nineteen ports
Charter Pubns. for British Transport Docks Board, 1982

JACKMAN, Brian
Dorset coast path. (Long-distance Footpath Guide no. 8)
Countryside commission, 1979

JACKSON, Anthony
Way of life and identity. (North Sea Oil Panel Occasional Paper no. 4)
SSRC, 1981

Way of life: dominant ideologies and local communities, ed. by A. Jackson. (North Sea Oil Panel Occasional Paper no. 11)
SSRC, 1982

Way of life: integration and immigration. (North Sea Oil Panel Occasional Paper 12)
SSRC, 1982

Way of life: negative aspects of community. (North Sea Oil Panel Occasional Paper no. 8)
SSRC, 1981

JACKSON, G.
Mastitis control. ADAS study tour programme 1980–81, by G. Jackson and J. Hughes
ADAS, 1980

JACKSON, H.
Play it safe! A guide to preventing children's accidents
Health Education Council, 1982

JACKSON, J. McG.
Educational guidance for adults in Northern Ireland. Report of an inquiry, November 1979
Dept. of Education for N.I., 1979

JACKSON, Joseph
Ferguson and General Investments Ltd.; C.S.T. Investments, Ltd. Report of investigations under the Companies Act, 1948, by J. Jackson and K. L. Young
Trade Dept., 1979

JACKSON, M. V.
Zero grazing. (Grassland Practice no. 3) (Booklet 2043)
MAFF, 1979

JACOBY, H. G.
Increasing your profits in overseas clothing markets. A report on a study of successful exports. (Export Advisory Group)
NEDO, 1979

JAMES, A. W.
Industrial profile of breadmaking, by G. Flynn and A. W. James. (G147)
Tropical Products Institute, 1980

JAMES, Jeremy
Students with special needs in FE: a review of current and completed research relating to young people in the 14–19 age range with special educational needs. (Further Education Curriculum Review and Development Unit P.R. 12)
DES, 1981

JAMIESON, I.
Schools and industry, by I. Jamieson and M. Lightfoot. (Working Paper 73)
Methuen Educational for Schools Council, 1982

JAMIESON, M.
Mechanisation and microbiological aspects of chemical treatment of forage: report of a study tour undertaken in West Germany, Denmark and Norway, October 1980, by M. Jamieson and C. L. Benham
ADAS, 1981

JARVIS, Richard
The Welsh social accounts, 1968: a labour dimension, by P. Sadler and R. Jarvis
Welsh Council, 1979

JAY, Peggy
Mental handicap nursing and care. Report of the committee of enquiry. March 1979, 2 vols
Session 1978–79 Cmnd. 7468–I, II

A summary of the Jay report, by members of the Committee of Enquiry into Mental Handicap Nursing and Care
DHSS, 1980

JEFFERSON, C. W.
The cost of living in Northern Ireland. A report prepared by C. W. Jefferson and J. V. Simpson
Northern Ireland Consumer Council, 1980

JELLICOE, George P. J. R., 2nd Earl Jellicoe
Review of the operation of the Prevention of Terrorism (Temporary Provisions) Act 1976
Session 1982–83 Cmnd. 8803

JENKINS, D.
The Ford Bridgend report: labour market effects of the Ford Motor Company's new Bridgend plant. (Manpower Intelligence and Planning)
MSC, 1981

JENKINS, David
Work reform in France; a ten year record of continuous progress. (WRU Occasional Paper 15)
Employment Dept., Work Research Unit, 1981

JENKINS, J. E. E.
Institut technique des cereales et des fourrages. Report of a visit to France
ADAS, 1982

JENKINS, Janet
Correspondence institutions in the Commonwealth, 1980. A report
Commonwealth Secretariat, 1981

JENKINS, R.
Managers: recruitment procedures and black workers. (Research Unit on Ethnic Relations; Working Papers on Ethnic Relations no. 18)
SSRC, 1982

JENKINS, R. P.
Selective detection assessment – South Kensington, London, by R. P. Jenkins and H. S. Moseley. (Traffic Advisory Unit)
DTp, 1981

JENKINSON, Andrew M.
Explore your local countryside; guided walks in the West Midlands. A report. (CCP 135)
Countryside Commission, 1980

JENKINSON, N. H.
Investment, profitability and the valuation ratio. (Discussion Paper no. 17)
Bank of England, 1981

JENNETT, Sean
Official guide to the Royal parks of London
DoE, 1979

JENSON, A. G.
Proofing of buildings against rats, mice and other pests. (GB1)
ADAS, 1979

JOBLING, J.
Establishment of trees on regraded colliery spoil heaps: a review of problems and practice, by J. Jobling and F. R. W. Stevens. (Occasional Paper no. 7)
Forestry Commission, 1980

JOHN, Brian
Milford Haven Waterway. (Pembrokeshire Coast National Park Area Guide)
Pembrokeshire Coast National Park, 1981

Presely hills. (Pembrokeshire Coast National Park Area Guide)
Pembrokeshire Coast National Park, 1981

JOHN, Geraint
Handbook of sports and recreational building design. 4 vols
Sports Council, 1981

JOHNSON, A. L.
Notes on the behaviour of roe deer (capreolus capreolus L.) at Chedington, Dorset 1970–1980 (Research and Development Paper, 130)
Forestry Commission, 1982

JOHNSON, E. W.
Symposium 'substrates in horticulute other than soils in situ' held in France, August/September 1981. Report
ADAS, 1982

JOHNSTON, D. R.
The formulation of research programmes, by D. R. Johnston. Prepared for the eleventh Commonwealth Forestry Conference, Trinidad, September 1980. (R & D Paper 126)
Forestry Commission, 1980

JOHNSTON, Dan
Design protection: a guide to the law on plagiarism for manufacturers and designers
Design Council, 1979

JOHNSTON, Edward
The draft of the social security benefits uprating (amendment) order 1979. Report by the Government Actuary. October 1979
Session 1979–80 Cmnd. 7736

Occupational pension schemes. Review of certain contracting-out terms. Reports by the Government Actuary
Session 1981–82 Cmnd. 8516

Social security benefits. Up-rating order, 1979. Report by the Government Actuary on the draft. July 1979
Session 1979–80 Cmnd. 7606

Social security benefits up-rating (amendment) order, 1979. Report on the draft order, by the Government Actuary. October 1979
Session 1979–80 Cmnd. 7736

Social Security benefits up-rating order, 1982. Report by the Government Actuary on the draft. June 1982
Session 1981–82 Cmnd. 8588

Social Security (Contributions) Bill, 1981. Report by the Government Actuary on the financial provisions of the bill
Session 1981–82 Cmnd. 8443

Social security (contributions, re-rating) order, 1979. Report on the draft by the Government Actuary. November 1979
Session 1979–80 Cmnd. 7771

Social security (contributions, re-rating) order, 1982. Report on the draft by the Government Actuary
Session 1981–82 Cmnd. 8742

Teachers' superannuation scheme, England and Wales. Report, 1971–76. January 1979
Session 1978–79 HC 136

The teachers' superannuation scheme (Scotland) 1971–1976. Report, May 1980. (Teachers' superannuation (Scotland) regulations 1977 to 1980)
Session 1979–80 HC 565

JOHNSTON, R. B.
Banks' international lending decisions and the determination of spreads on syndicated medium-term euro-credits. (Discussion Paper no. 12)
Bank of England, 1980

JOHNSTON, S. M.
Pilot course for Euronet users in the agricultural sector and related fields. Report of a visit to West Germany, December 1979
ADAS, 1979

International MEDLARS workshop, Cologne, Federal Republic of Germany, 10–11 November 1981. Report
ADAS, 1982

JOHNSTONE, A. I.
Guidelines for the management of major projects in the process industries. Project Guidelines Group of the Engineering Construction EDC
NEDO, 1982

JOHNSTONE, J. S.
Integration in the social subjects in SII (third term). Report of the steering group of the Scottish Committee on Social Subjects (occasional paper)
Consultative Committee on the Curriculum, 1981

JOLLANS, W. M.
Standing technical committee on water treatment. First biennial report 1976–78. (Standing Technical Committee Report no. 15)
National Water Council, 1979

JOLLY, J.
Age as a factor in employment. (Unit for Manpower Studies, Research Paper no. 11)
Employment Dept., 1980

JONES, Chris
Structures. (Open science)
Schools Council, 1979

JONES, Clement
Race and the media: thirty years' misunderstanding. (Occasional Paper Series no. 1)
Commission for Racial Equality, 1982

JONES, D. J. H.
Pre-assembly for process plant construction. (Process Plant EDC and Engineering Construction EDC)
NEDO, 1981

JONES, D. R.
Developments in poultry breeding and embryology. Report of a visit to the USSR, June 1979
ADAS, 1979

JONES, E.
Consultation of the European co-operative research network on trace elements. Report of a visit to Belgium, April 1979
ADAS, 1979

JONES, G. W.
Central-local government relationships. Report of an SSRC Panel
SSRC, 1979

New approaches to the study of central-local government relationships
SSRC, 1980

JONES, Huw R.
Recent migration in northern Scotland: pattern process, impact. (North Sea Oil Panel Occasional Paper no. 13)
SSRC, 1982

Review of Scottish population migration studies. (North Sea Oil Panel Occasional Paper no. 15)
SSRC, 1982

JONES, Katherine
Getting primary care on the NHS, by K. Jones and P. Woods.
Welsh Consumer Council, 1979

JONES, M. G. Stuart
International scientific congress in fur animal production, 2nd. Report of a visit to Denmark
ADAS, 1980

JONES, P. Hope
Seabird movement at coastal sites around Great Britain and Ireland, 1978–1980
Nature Conservancy Council, 1982

JONES, P. R.
Vietnamese refugees; a study of their reception and resettlement in the United Kingdom (Research and Planning Unit Paper 13)
Home Office, 1982

JONES, R. A. C.
Fruit tree virus diseases (11th international symposium) and small fruit virus diseases (2nd international symposium). Report of a visit to Hungary, July 1979, by S. A. Hill and R. A. C. Jones
ADAS 1979

International potato centre (CIP): report of a visit to the Middle East (Egypt, Jordan and Syria) April 1980
MAFF, 1980

Research for the potato in the year 2000. Report on the congress at Lima, Peru, 1982
ADAS, 1982

JONES, Reginald
Local government audit law
DoE, 1981

JONES, Sheila
Design of instruction. (Training Information Paper)
MSC, 1979

JONES, Stephen F.
The world market for desicated coconut. (G129)
Tropical Products Institute, 1979

JORDAN, J.
Work facts for young workers, rev. ed.
MSC, 1981

JOUBERT, C. J. P.
Report on Rayner study of non-staff running costs in the Department of the Environment (central). Volume 1: Main report, by C. J. P. Joubert and H. C. S. Derwent. Volume 2: Annexes
DoE, 1981

JOYNER, L. P.
Chemotherapy of protozoal infections of veterinary importance. Report of a visit to USA, June 1980
ADAS, 1980

JUDGE, G.
Survey of knee mechanisms for artificial legs
DHSS, 1980

JULLIEN, E. T.
Improvement grant administration. An investigation into the interpretation of, and procedural matters relating to part VII of the Housing Act, 1974. A report. (Report 759, Project no. H6/123)
National Building Agency, 1979

JUTSUM, Carolyn
Public expenditure 1977–78: outturn compared with plan, by Carolyn Jutsum and Graeme Walker. (Government Economic Service Working Paper no. 28)
Treasury, 1979

KARAS, G. Christopher
In-house moulder: his skills and attitudes.
Science Research Council, 1980

KARIS, I. G.
Commonwealth regional programme on standardization and quality control. Report of the second meeting of the steering committee, July 1979, Blantyre, Malawi
Commonwealth Science Council, 1979

KASASIAN, L.
British overseas aid: agricultural research (crop and soil sciences) 1974–1978, compiled by L. Kasasian and H. A. Turner (Overseas Research Publication no. 26)
Overseas Development Administration, 1980

KAUFMANN, M.
Implications of the SPRU study on the use of skills within the injection moulding sector of the plastics industry
Science Research Council, 1980

KAY, Brian
Assessment – the American experience, by C. Burstall and B. Kay
Dept. Education and Science, 1979

KAY, Daisy E.
Food legumes. (TPI Crop and Product Digest no. 3)
Tropical Products Institute, 1979

KAYE, David R.
Organisational implications of change. (Research Paper no. 12)
Royal Commission on Criminal Procedure, 1980

KEDDIE, Vincent
Industry and employment in the inner city, by A. McIntosh and V. Keddie. (Inner Cities Research Programme no. 1)
DoE, 1979

KEITH-LUCAS, David
Design education at secondary level. A Design Council report
Design Council, 1980

KELLETT, A. J.
Gravel filled mole channels; a technical and economic assessment. (Tech. Report 79/2; Reference Booklet 388)
ADAS, 1980

Sedimentation of drain pipes; results of a national investigation (DW14). Preliminary report by A. J. Kellett and A. C. Armstrong. (Land Drainage Service R & D Report no. 2)
ADAS, 1980

KELLY, C. M.
Scottish output in sub-sectors of manufacturing industry: modelling in relation to expenditure aggregates. (Economics and Statistics Unit: Discussion Paper no. 7)
Scottish Economic Planning Dept., 1980

KELLY, T. J.
Trends in Dutch and British dairying, 1975–1978. (Report no. 18)
Milk Marketing Board, 1979

KEMP, Brian Allen
Ozalid Holdings Ltd. Report of investigation under the Companies Act, 1948, by N. Butter and B. A. Kemp
Trade Dept., 1980

KEMPSON, E.
Computer benefits?: guidelines for local information and advice centres, by P. Ottley and E. Kempson
National Consumer Council, 1982

KEMSLEY, W. F. F.
Family expenditure survey handbook: sampling, fieldwork, coding procedures and related methodological experiments, by W. F. F. Kemsley and others. (Social Survey Division)
OPCS, 1980

KENNEDY, H. P.
Public inquiry into the proposed permanent use of Lisnevin School, Newtownards as a training school/remand home under the Children and Young Persons Act (Northern Ireland), 1968. Report
Northern Ireland Office, 1979

KENNETT, Stephen
The inner city in the context of the urban system. (The Inner City in Context 7)
SSRC, 1980

Local government fiscal problems: a context for inner areas (Inner City in Context 6)
SSRC, 1980

KENNY, A. W.
'The control of radioactive wastes'; a review of Cmnd. 884. A report by an expert group made to the Radioactive Waste Management Committee
DoE, 1979

Private water supplies in the U.K. (1982). Report of the sub-committee of the standing technical advisory committee on water quality
DoE, 1982

Standing technical advisory committee on water quality. 2nd biennial report, 1977–1979. (Standing Technical Committee Reports no. 22)
National Water Council, 1979

KENT, Prince Edward George Nicholas Patrick, Duke of Kent
Foreign languages for overseas trade. A report by a study group
British Overseas Trade Board, 1979

KEOHANE, K. W.
Proposals for a certificate of extended education. Report of a study group established to consider the Schools Council's proposals for a certificate of extended education (CEE) in relation to other courses and examinations for those for whom the CEE is intended. December 1979
Session 1979–80. Cmnd. 7755

KERNEY, Michael
The conservation of snails, slugs and freshwater mussels, by M. Kerney and A. Stubbs
Nature Conservancy Council, 1980

KERR, J. Y. K.
Oral practice in the language laboratory. (ELT Guide 3)
British Council, 1980

KERR, Michael
The consolidation of certain enactments relating to justices of the peace (including stipendiary magistrates) justices' clerks and the administrative and financial arrangements for magistrates' courts, and to matters connected therewith. Report, June 1979. Justices of the Peace Bill. (Law Commission no. 94)
Session 1979–80 Cmnd. 7583

Law of Contract: implied terms in contracts for the supply of goods. (Law Commission no. 95). July 1979
Session 1979–80 HC 142

Criminal law. Offences relating to interference with the course of justice. Law Commission report. (Law Commission no. 96). November 1979
Session 1979–80 HC 213

Law Commission, 14th annual report, 1978–79. (Law Commission no. 97)
Session 1979–80 HC 322

Reserve Forces Bill. The consolidation of certain enactments relating to the reserve and auxillary forces. Law Commission report. (Law Commission no. 98). November 1979
Session 1979–80 Cmnd. 7757

Family Law: orders for sale of property under the matrimonial causes act, 1979. (The Law Commission). (Law Commission no. 99). 1979
Session 1979–80 HC 369

Highways bill. Report on the consolidation of the highways acts 1959 to 1971 and related enactments, February 1980. (Law Commission no. 100)
Session 1979–80 Cmnd. 7828

Magistrates' courts bill. Report on the consolidation of certain enactments relating to the jurisdiction of, and the practice and procedure before, magistrates' courts and the functions of justices' clerks, and to matters connected therewith, April 1980. (Law Commission no. 101)
Session 1979–80 Cmnd. 7887

Criminal law: attempt, and impossibility in relating to attempt, conspiracy and incitement, June 1980. (Law Commission no. 102)
Session 1979–80 HC 646

Family Law. Financial consequences of divorce: the basic policy. A discussion paper. (Law Commission no. 103)
Session 1979–80 Cmnd. 8041

Insurance law: non disclosure and breach of warranty. (Law Commission no. 104). Law Commission, October 1980
Session 1979–80 Cmnd. 8064

Judicial pensions bill. (Law Commission no. 105; Scottish Law Commission no. 62). November 1980
Session 1980–81 Cmnd. 8097

Statute law revision, 10th report. Draft statute law (repeals) bill. (Law Commission no. 106; Scottish Law Commission no. 63). 1980
Session 1980–81 Cmnd. 8089

Law Commission 15th annual report, 1979–80. (Law Commission no. 107)
Session 1980–81 HC 161

Trustee savings banks bill. Report on consolidation. (Law Commission no 108; Scottish Law Commission no. 65). 1981
Session 1980–81 Cmnd. 8157

Offences against religion and public worship. (Working Paper 79)
Law Commission, 1981

KERRY, Trevor
Effective questioning . . . (DES Teacher Education Project Focus Books)
Macmillan for DES, 1982

Handling classroom groups, by Trevor Kerry and Margaret Sands. (DES Teacher Education Project Focus Books)
Macmillan for DES, 1982

KERRY, Trevor *(continued)*
Mixed ability teaching in the early years of the secondary school, by Trevor Kerry and Margaret Sands. (DES Teacher Education Project Focus Books)
Macmillan for DES, 1982

The new teacher: examining in-school provision for student teachers and probationers. (DES Teacher Education Project Focus Books)
Macmillan for DES, 1982

Teaching slow learners in mixed ability classes, by P. Bell and T. Kerry. (DES Teacher Education Project)
Macmillan for DES, 1982

KERSHAW, D. T.
Small craft foundries – their present role and future prospects. Report of a Working Party of the Foundries EDC
NEDO, 1979

Small craft foundries: some pointers to survival. (Foundries EDC)
NEDO, 1982

KESSEL, W. I. Neil
Advisory committee on alcoholism. Report on education and training for professional staff and voluntary workers in the field.
DHSS, 1979

The pattern and range of services for problem drinkers. Report by the Advisory Committee on Alcoholism
DHSS, 1979

KETCHIN, A. C.
Evaluation of cereal production in the Schleswig Holstein area. Report of a visit
ADAS, 1982

KEW, Stephen
Ethnic groups and leisure. (A Review for the SC/SSRC Joint Panel on Leisure and Recreation Research)
Sports Council, 1979

KEYMER, I. F.
British Veterinary Zoological Society and international study group meeting, Blijdorp Zoo, Rotterdam. Report
ADAS, 1982

KHAN-FREUND, Otto
Labour law and politics in the Weimar Republic. (Warwick Studies in Industrial Relations)
SSRC, 1981

KIDWELL, Raymond Mcledon
Peachey Property Corporation Ltd. Report of investigation under the Companies Act, 1948, by R. I. Kidwell and S. D. Samwell
Trade Dept., 1979

KILKENNY, J. B.
Pedigree beef cattle averages 1979–81. (Beef Improvement Services Data Sheet 81/7)
Meat and Livestock Commission, 1981

Results from grassland recording scheme – 1979 grazing season. (Sheep Improvement Services Data Sheet 80/4)
Meat and Livestock Commission, 1980

Results for recorded commercial flocks selling finished lambs, winter 1979-spring 1980. (Sheep Improvement Services Data Sheet 80/3)
Meat and Livestock Commission, 1980

Results for store lamb finishing enterprise 1979–80. (Sheep Improvement Services Data Sheet 80/2)
Meat and Livestock Commission, 1980

KILPATRICK, J. S.
A future for foundries. (Foundries EDC)
NEDO, 1980

KILPATRICK, R.
Review of the safety for use in the UK of the herbicide 2,4,5–T, March 1979. (Advisory Committee on Pesticides)
MAFF, 1979

KILPATRICK, T. S.
A future for foundries. (Foundries EDC)
NEDO, 1980

KING, John
Golden Gatwick: 50 years of aviation, by John King and Geoff Tait
British Airprorts Authority, 1980

KING, P.
Holiday entitlement and (long) holiday taking 1973–1980
English Tourist Board, 1981

KING, Patrick
A guide to the economics of dehydration of vegetables in developing countries. (G131)
Tropical Products Institute, 1980

The market for aubergines and courgettes in selected western European countries. (G113)
Tropical Products Institute, 1979

KINGSMILL, B. A.
Dialtech user manual, by B. A. Kingsmill and M. J. Everest
Technology Reports Centre, 1980

KINSEY, P. J.
Variable direction signs to car parks – Truro experiment, by P. Gould and P. J. Kinsey
DTp, 1981

KIRBY, Celia
Hormone weedkillers, a short history of their discovery and development
British Crop Protection Council, 1980

KIRBY, Keith
An investigation of difficult to let housing. Vol. 2: case studies of post-war estates, by Sheena Wilson and Keith Kirby. (HDD Occasional Paper 4/80)
DoE, 1981

An investigation of difficult to let housing. Vol. 3: case studies of pre-war estates, by Sheena Wilson and Keith Kirby. (HDD Occasional Paper 5/80)
DoE, 1981

KIRBY, Norman G.
Field surgery pocket book edited by Major General N. G. Kirby and G. Blackburn
Defence Min., 1981

KIRBY, R. W.
The recruitment, training and development of Health Education Officers: a report
National Staff Committee for Administrative and Clerical Staff, 1981

KIRKPATRICK, T. S.
Non-ferrous foundries; interfirm comparison
NEDO, 1980

KIRWAN, R.
The inner city in the United States. (The Inner City in Context 8)
SSRC, 1980

KITCHING, Robert J.
Evaluation of the MSC Training Services Division's essay in management development through action learning, by A. I. Thomas and R. J. Kitching. (Training Services Division Report no. 15)
MSC, 1979

KITCHING, Robert J. *(continued)*
Evaluation of the structured work experience programme run by Vauxhall Mawar School. (Training Services Division Report no. DTP18)
MSC, 1979

KLEEMAN, H.
British plastics; the next ten years. Sectoral Prospects Steering Group. Plastics Processing S W P
NEDO 1982

KNASEL, Edward G.
The benefit of experience; individual guidance and support within the YOP, by E. G. Knasel, A. G. Watts and J. M. Kidd (Special Programmes Research and Development Series no. 5)
MSC, 1982

Experience is not enough
MSC, 1982

KNIGHT, Ian B.
Company organisation and worker participation. A survey of attitudes and practices in industrial democracy. (Social Survey Division Report SS1082)
OPCS, 1979

Family finances: a methodology report on a survey of low income families and their financial circumstances with a brief descriptive summary of results. (Social Survey Division Occasional Paper 26)
OPCS, 1981

The feasibility of conducting a national wealth survey in Great Britain. (New Methodology Series no. NM6)
OPCS, 1980

Scottish licensing laws, a survey . . . by I. Knight and P. Wilson. (SS1094)
OPCS, 1980

KNIGHT, Jeremy K.
Bronllys Castle, Powys
Welsh Office, 1981

Grosmont Castle, Gwent
Welsh Office, 1980

KNIGHT, Peter
Population projections, Scotland, 1977 based. (Occasional Paper 4)
Scottish Health Service, 1981

KNIGHTS, Peter
Birds of the Pembrokeshire coast. (Subject Guide no. 3)
Pembrokeshire Coast National Park, 1979

KORNBERG, Hans
Royal Commission on Environmental Pollution, 7th report: agriculture and pollution. September 1979
Session 1979–80 Cmnd. 7644

Royal Commission on Environmental Pollution, 8th report: oil pollution of the sea
Session 1980–81 Cmnd. 8358

KORNER, E.
Health Services Information Steering Group. (First report on the collection and use of information about hospital clinical activity in the National Health Service)
DHSS, 1982

KOURIS, George J.
The price sensitivity of petrol consumption and some policy implications: the case of EEC
SSRC, 1979

KRUYS, Ivan
Butterflies of Pembrokeshire. (Pembrokeshire Coast National Park Subject Guide)
Pembrokeshire Coast National Park, 1981

LAIDLAW, C. J.
Women in engineering, by P. Brayshaw and C. J. Laidlaw. (Reference Paper RP/4/79)
Engineering Industry Training Board, 1979

Young people in engineering, by P. Brayshaw and C. J. Laidlaw. (Reference Paper RP/4/82)
Engineering Industry Training Board, 1982

LAMB, R. G.
Archaeological sites and monuments of Sanday and North Ronaldsay, Orkney; an archaeological survey of two of the north isles of Orkney
Royal Commission on the Ancient and Historical Monuments of Scotland, 1980

LANCUCKI, L. B.
Previous convictions, sentence and reconviction; a statistical study. (Research Study no. 53)
Home. Office, 1979

LANE, David
Cottrell and Rothon estate agent. Report of a formal investigation
Commission for Racial Equality, 1980

LANE, J. E.
Choosing programmes for micro-computers
National Computing Centre, 1980

Communicating with microcomputers
National Computing Centre, 1981

Computing in the '80's.
National Computing Centre, 1981

Graphics on microcomputers
National Computing Centre, 1981

LANG, J.
World rabbit science congress, 2nd. Report of a visit to Spain
ADAS, 1980

LANGDON, Janet
SRC co-operative awards in science and engineering: a study
Science Research Council, 1979

LANGFORD, Vicky
Assessing managerial effectiveness: a guide
MSC, 1981

LANGMUIR, E.
Mountain leadership. Official handbook of the Mountain Leadership Training Boards of G.B. and N.I. Reprinted
Scottish Sport Council, 1980

LANTIN, B.
Service please: services and the law: a consumer view, by B. Lantin and G. Woodroffe
National Consumer Council, 1981

LAPPIN, L. A. W.
Spearhead Germany; increasing exports of U.K. knitwear to the Federal Republic of Germany. Report of the export sub-group of the Knitting S W P
NEDO, 1982

LARGE, Peter
'Can disabled people go where you go?' Report by the silver jubilee committee on improving access for disabled people
DHSS, 1979

LATHAM, G.
Roller skating in the eastern region
Eastern Council for Sport and Recreation, 1982

LAUENER, P. R.
Labour supply in Scotland. (ESU Discussion Paper no. 13)
Scottish Economic Planning Dept., 1982

LAWRENCE, N. G.
The storage feeding of grass silage to bull beef: report of a study tour undertaken in Denmark, 11–18 July 1981
ADAS, 1981

LAWSON, G.
Manpower and training in the electronics industry, by P. Brayshaw and G. Lawson (Reference Paper RP/5/82)
Engineering Industry Training Board, 1982

LAWSON, Nigel
Speech on energy policy. (Energy Paper no. 5)
Energy Dept., 1982

LAWTHER, P. J.
Lead and health: report of a DHSS Working Party on Lead in the Environment
DHSS, 1980

LAWTON, Lord Justice
Sexual offences. Criminal law revision committee working paper
Home Office, 1980

Offences against the person. Criminal Law Revision Committee, 14th report, March 1980
Session 1979–80 Cmnd. 7844

Working paper on offences relating to prostitution and allied offences. (Criminal Law Revision Committee)
Home Office, 1982

LAYFIELD, Frank
Constructional Steelwork Sector Working Party. Progress Report, 1978
NEDO, 1980

Construction Steelwork SWP. Progress report, 1980
NEDO 1980

Constructional Steelwork SWP. Progress report
NEDO, 1981

Sizewell B public enquiry. Transcript of proceedings, 26 July 1982
Central Electricity Generating Board, 1982

LE QUESNE, Sir Godfray
Bristol Omnibus Co. Ltd.; Cheltenham District Traction Co.; City of Cardiff District Council; Trent Motor Traction Co. Ltd.; and West Midland Passenger Transport Executive. A report on stage carriage services
Session 1981–82 HC 442

Bicycles. Report on the application by T. I. Raleigh Industries Ltd. . . . of certain criteria for determining whether to supply bicycles to retail outlets, by Monopolies and Mergers Commission
Session 1981–82 HC 67

BTR Ltd. and Serck Ltd. A report on the merger, by the Monopolies and Mergers Commission
Session 1981–82 HC 392

Car Parts. A report on the matter of the existence of a complex monopoly situation in relation to the wholesale supply of motor car parts in the UK, by the Monopolies and Mergers Commission
Session 1981–82 HC 318

Charter Consolidated Plc. and Anderson Strathclyde Plc. Report by the Monopolies and Mergers Commission on the proposed merger. December 1982
Session 1982–83 Cmnd. 8771

Concrete roofing tiles. Report by the Monopolies and Mergers Commission. November 1981
Session 1981–82 HC 12

The General Electric Company Ltd. and Averys Ltd. A report on the proposed merger by the Monopolies and Mergers Commission. September 1979
Session 1979–80 Cmnd. 7653

European Ferries Ltd., Sealink Ltd. A report by the Monopolies and Mergers Commission, December 1981
Session 1981–82 HC 65

The inner London letter post. A report on the letter post service in the area comprising the numbered London postal districts, March 1980. (The Monopolies and Mergers Commission)
Session 1979–80 HC 515

Insulated electric wires and cables. A report on the supply in the UK and the export from the UK of insulated electric wires and cables. Report of the Monopolies and Mergers Commission. March 1979
Session 1978–79 HC 243

Lonrho Ltd. and House of Fraser Ltd. A report by the Monopolies and Mergers Commission on the proposed merger. December 1981
Session 1981–82 HC 73

Lonrho Ltd. and Scottish and Universal Investments and House of Fraser Ltd. A report on the proposed merger and the resulting merger situation between Lonrho and House of Fraser Ltd. Monopolies and Mergers Commission, March 1979
Session 1978–79 HC 261

The Observer and George Outram and Co. Ltd. A report on the proposed transfer, by the Monopolies and Mergers Commission
Session 1980–81 HC 378

Petrol. A report on the supply of petrol in the UK by wholesale. Report of the Monopolies and Mergers Commission. January 1979
Session 1978–79 Cmnd. 7433

Ready mixed concrete. A report on the supply. Monopolies and Mergers Commission 1981
Session 1980–81 Cmnd. 8354

Roadside advertising services. A report on the supply, by the Monopolies and Mergers Commission
Session 1980–81 Cmnd. 8365

Trading check franchise and financial services. Report of the Monopolies and Mergers Commission, December 1981
Session 1981–82 HC 62

LEACH, C.
Study of recruitment, training and retention of skilled workers. (Constructional Steelwork SWP Manpower Subcommittee)
NEDO, 1980

LEACH, Peter
Kirby Hall, Northamptonshire, 3rd ed. by G. H. Chettle, rev. and expanded by P. Leach
DoE, 1980

St. Mary's Church Studley Royal
DoE, 1981

LEAPER, Robert
Setting a target date. Report of a study group
Personal Social Services Council, 1980

LEATHER, D. S.
Adults' attitudes towards drinking and smoking among young people in Scotland. Vol.IV
SHHD, 1981

LEE, D. F.
Control of pesticide residues in foodstuffs: report of a visit to Hungary, 13–25 October 1980
ADAS, 1981

LEE, David
Flight from the Middle East. A history of the Royal Air Force in the Arabian peninsula and adjacent territories, 1945–1972. (Air Historical Branch)
Defence Min., 1980

LEE, J.
A guide to school health education, compiled by J. Lee and H. Graham
Health Education Council, 1982

LEE, L.
North Atlantic MNPS airspace operations manual, ed. by H. Sweetman and L. Lee
Civil Aviation Authority, 1979

LEECH, Roger
Early industrial housing: the Trinity area of Frome. (Supplementary Series 3)
Royal Commission on Historical Manuscripts, 1981

LEEN, Jentina
Problems and ethics of textile conservation. (Conservation Paper 2.)
Crafts Advisory Committee, 1979

LEES, D. S.
Extension of title to invalid care allowance to non-relatives. Report of the National Insurance Advisory Committee, June 1980
Session 1979–80 Cmnd. 7905

Household duties test for non-contributory invalidity pension for married women. Report of the National Insurance Advisory Committee, July 1980
Session 1979–80 Cmnd. 7955

Mobility Allowance Amendment Regulations, 1979. Report of the National Insurance Advisory Committee, February 1979
Session 1978–79 Cmnd. 7491

Social Security Benefit (Dependency) Amendment Regulations 1980. (S.I. 1980 no. 585). Report of the National Insurance Advisory Committee, May 1980
Session 1979–80 Cmnd. 7896

Social Security Benefit (Married Women and Widows Special Provisions) Amendment Regulations 1980. Report of the National Insurance Advisory Committee, July 1980
Session 1979–80 Cmnd. 7970

Social Security (Categorisation of Earners) Amendment Regulations 1978. Report of the National Insurance Advisory Committee, October 1978
Session 1977–78 Cmnd. 7393

Social Security (Categorisation of Earners) Amendment Regulations 1980. Report of the National Insurance Advisory Committee, November 1980
Session 1980–81 Cmnd. 8082

Social Security (Claims and Payments) Amendment (No. 2) Regulations. Report of the National Insurance Advisory Committee, October 1979
Session 1979–80 Cmnd. 7680

Social Security (Determination of Claims and Questions) Amendment Regulations 1979. Report of the National Insurance Advisory Committee, September 1979
Session 1979–80 Cmnd. 7669

Social Security (Earnings-Related Addition to Widow's Allowance) (Special Provisions) Regulations 1979. Report of the National Insurance Advisory Committee, October 1979
Session 1979–80 Cmnd. 7699

Social Security (Overcharging Benefits) Amendment Regulations 1980. Report of the National Insurance Advisory Committee, December 1980
Session 1980–81 Cmnd. 8116

Social Security (Unemployment, Sickness and Invalidity Benefit) Amendment (No. 2) Regulations. Report of the National Insurance Advisory Committee, July 1979
Session 1979–80 Cmnd. 7622

Unemployment benefit for students. Report of the National Insurance Advisory Committee, July 1979
Session 1979–80 Cmnd. 7613

LEES, P. D.
Culinary and medicinal herbs. rev. ed. (Reference Book 325)
ADAS, 1980

LEESON, R. C.
Dairy cows: advisory drawings: 1, layouts
ADAS, 1981

Design data: commercial vehicles on the farm
ADAS, 1981

Ventilation of cattle buildings: 4, building details
ADAS, 1981

LEETE, Richard
Changing patterns of family formation and dissolution in England and Wales 1964–76. (Studies on Medical and Population Subjects no. 39)
OPCS, 1981

LEGGATT, Andrew
Trade union recruitment activities. Report of inquiry, October 1979
Session 1979–80 Cmnd. 7706

LEITCH, Sir George
Forecasting traffic on trunk roads; a report on the regional highway traffic model project. Standing Advisory Committee on Trunk Road Assessment
DTp, 1979

Trunk road proposals – a comprehensive framework for appraisal. (Standing Advisory Committee on Trunk Road Assessment)
DTp, 1980

LELLIOTT, R. A.
National work conference on microbial collections of major importance to agriculture. Report of a visit to USA, March 1980
ADAS, 1980

LEMAY, G. D.
Brussel sprouts; production, harvesting and marketing of brussel sprouts for the fresh market and for processing. (Reference Book 323)
ADAS, 1979

LENTON, E. J.
Otter survey of England 1977–1979
Nature Conservancy Council, 1980

LEONARD, L.
Small claims procedure in Northern Ireland. Report by D. S. Greer and L. Leonard
Northern Ireland Consumer Council, 1980

LESLIE, Peter J.
Employing a designer. A management guide to the selection, employment and payment of staff and consultant industrial designers.
Design Council, 1980

LEVI, M.
Commonwealth frauds; problems and remedies in the judicial process.
Commonwealth Secretariat, 1982

LEVY, Elliot
A survey of tenants' attitudes to recently completed estates, by E. Levy and A. Gelardi. (HDD Occasional Paper 2/81)
DoE, 1981

LEWIS, A. Fenton
Linking of birth notification and birth registration data
DHSS, 1979

LEWIS, D. R.
Characteristics required in tomorrow's public servants. (CSC Working Paper no. 20)
Civil Service College, 1980

LEWIS, David
Aftermath of tribunal reinstatement and re-engagement, by K. Williams and D. Lewis. (Research Paper 23)
Employment Dept., 1981

LEWIS, R.
Using role play; an introductory guide, by R. Lewis and J. Mee
MSC, 1981

LIGHTFOOT, M.
Schools and industry, by I. Jamieson and M. Lightfoot. (Working Paper 73)
Methuen Educational for Schools Council, 1982

LIKIERMAN, Andrew
Cash limits and external financing limits, by A. Likierman. (Civil Service College Handbook no. 22)
Civil Service Dept., 1981

The reports and accounts of nationalised industries; a user's guide. (Civil Service College Handbook no. 20)
Civil Service Dept., 1979

LILLEY, G. M.
The third London airport. Report by a working group
Noise Advisory Council, 1980

LINDFIELD, A. G.
Assisting the vision of firemen in smoke: the development and trial of a thermal imaging system, by A. G. Lindfield and A. C. Wells. (Research Report no. 17; Central Fire Brigades Advisory Councils for England and Wales and for Scotland: Joint Committee on Fire Research)
Home Office, 1981

LINDLEY, P. D.
Regional services of government; general introduction
Civil Service College, 1982

LITTLE, A.
Loading the law: a study of transmitted deprivation, ethnic minorities and affirmative action, by A. Little and D. Robbins. (Summary)
Commission for Racial Equality, 1982

LITTLE Alan
Multi-ethnic education: the way forward, by A. Little and R. Willey. (Schools Council Pamphlet 18)
Schools Council, 1981

LITTLE, R. C.
International congress of soil science, 11th. Report of a visit to Canada by R. C. Little and T. H. Caldwell
ADAS, 1978

Investigation of work on organic farming systems and furtherance of Anglo-Netherlands cooperation in research and development, by R. C. Little and M. Barker
ADAS, 1982

LITTLE, T. W. A.
European association of animal production. 30th annual meeting, July 1979. Report of a visit to Harrogate. (Veterinary Service Report)
ADAS, 1979

Leptospirosis and other bacterial diseases of farm animals: report of a visit to Bulgaria, 26 October – 10 November 1981
ADAS, 1982

Meeting of European leptospira workers, 2nd. Report of a visit to France, September 1979, by T. W. A. Little and J. H. Morgan
ADAS, 1979

LITTLEWOOD, Judith
Families in flats, by J. Littlewood and A. Tinker
DoE, 1981

LLOYD, L. M.
Cardiothoracic services in Wales; the study team's report on the Welsh Medical Committee's working party report
Welsh Office, 1982

LLOYD, M.
Results from grassland recording scheme – 1979 grazing season. (Sheep Improvement Services Data Sheet 80/4)
Meat and Livestock Commission, 1980

LLOYD, P.
Industrial change, local manufacturing firms in Manchester and Merseyside by P. Lloyd and P. Dicken (Inner Cities Research Programme, 6)
DoE, 1982

LLOYD, Selwyn
European assembly constituencies. Report of the Boundary Commission for Scotland
Session 1978–79 Cmnd. 7336

LLOYD JONES, D.
Three international conventions on hijacking and offences on board aircraft; explanatory documentation for Commonwealth jurisdictions
Commonwealth Secretariat, 1980

LOCKE, T.
International course on fungicide resistance in crop protection, 2nd, and a symposium on fungicide resistance at Wageningen, The Netherlands, 27 July – 7 August 1981. Report
ADAS, 1981

LOCKHART, G. W.
How to start exporting; a guide for small firms, by A. Wilson and G. W. Lockhart. (Small Firms Service Series)
Industry Dept., 1980

LOCKWOOD, Baroness Betty
Health and safety legislation, should we distinguish between men and women? Report and recommendations by the working party
Equal Opportunities Commission, 1979

LODSMORE, F. A.
Curriculum and assessment in Wales; an exploratory study
Schools Council, Committee for Wales, 1981

LOGAN, H. K.
Arrival runway capacity and arrival delays at London Heathrow Airport, summer 1980. (CAA Paper 81014)
Civil Aviation Authority, 1981

Effect of certain facilities on the runway capacity and aircraft delays at Gatwick Airport, 1981, by A. E. Drew and H. K. Logan (CAA Paper 82019)
Civil Aviation Authority, 1982

Runway capacity and aircraft delays at Gatwick Airport, by I. M. Reay and H. K. Logan (CAA Paper 81002)
Civil Aviation Authority, 1981

LOGAN, W. P. D.
Cancer mortality by occupation and social class, 1851–1971. (IARC Scientific Publications 36; Studies on Medical and Population Subjects no. 44)
OPCS, 1982

LOMAX, M. A.
Hormones and metabolism in ruminants. (Proceedings of a workshop held at Bodington Hall, University of Leeds, 22–24 September 1980)
Agricultural Research Council, 1981

LONG, Jonathan A.
Large scale recreation participation surveys: lessons for the future, by B. S. Duffield and J. A. Long. (WP16)
Countryside Commission, 1979

Leisure and the over 50's, by J. A. Long and E. Wimbush. (A Review for the SC/SSRC Joint Panel on Leisure and Recreation Research)
Sports Council, 1979

LONGSTAFF, J.
New Zealand apple and pear industry. Report of a visit
ADAS, 1982

LONGWORTH, G.
Standards in programming: methods and procedures
National Computing Centre, 1981

LONSDALE, Susan
Long term psychiatric patients; a study in community care, by S. Lonsdale and others
Personal Social Services Council, 1980

LOOSMORE, F. A.
Curriculum and assessment in Wales; an exploratory study
Schools Council, Committee for Wales, 1981

LOTT, B. M.
A survey of British services relevant to the teaching of English as a foreign or second language.
British Council, 1979

LOURIE, J.
Social security benefit upratings. (Research Note no. 62)
House of Commons, 1982

LOVATT, D.
Understanding urban land values: a review, by M. Edwards and D. Lovatt. (The Inner City in Context 1)
SSRC, 1980

LOVELL, R. B.
Study of information services on training matters in the NHS. Report by J. Brophy and R. B. Lovell
National Training Council for the National Health Service, 1980

LOVETT, J. F.
24th annual meeting of the collaborative international pesticides analytical council and the FAO panel of experts on specifications – Spain 21–30 May 1980. Report by R. H. Thompson and J. F. Lovett
ADAS, 1981

Annual meeting of CIPAC and meeting of the FAO panel of experts on pesticide specifications. Report of a visit to USA, May–June 1979, by R. H. Thompson and J. F. Lovett
ADAS, 1979

Collaborative international pesticides analytical council. Report on the 26th annual meeting, Italy, May 1982, S. Bailey and J. F. Lovett
ADAS, 1982

FAO panel of experts on pesticide specifications, registration requirements and applications standards. (Report of a visit to Italy, 5–9 October 1981)
ADAS, 1982

International symposium organised by the International Union of Pure and Applied Chemistry. (Report of a visit to Finland, 20–21 August 1981)
ADAS, 1982

LOW, Colin
Participation in services for the handicapped; two contrasting models, by C. Low and others. (Studies in Participation 2)
Personal Social Services Council, 1979

LOW, J. C.
Real-time softwood research and development in the U.K. A survey and recommendations for action. Electronics Capital Equipment S W P
NEDO, 1982

LOWE, C. R.
Asbestos-related diseases without asbestosis. Report by the Industrial Injuries Advisory Council, November 1982
Session 1982–83 Cmnd. 8750

Industrial diseases: a review of the schedule and the question of individual proof. Report by the Industrial Injuries Advisory Council, August 1981
Session 1980–81 Cmnd. 8393

Occupational deafness. Report by the Industrial Injuries Advisory Council, November 1982
Session 1982–83 Cmnd. 8749

Vibration white finger. Report by the Industrial Injuries Advisory Council, September 1981
Session 1980–81 Cmnd. 8350

LOWE, N. K.
Development and production of school science equipment: some alternative approaches, by E. Apea and N. K. Lowe
Commonwealth Secretariat

LOWERSON, J.
Trends in leisure, 1919–1939, by A. Hawkins and J. Lowerson. (A Review for the SC/SSRC Joint Panel on Leisure and Recreation Research)
Sports Council, 1979

LOWRY, J. P.
Contract cleaning industry. (Report no. 20)
Advisory, Conciliation and Arbitration Service, 1980

LOWRY, W. S. B.
The future development of health education in Northern Ireland. Report by the Advisory Committee on Health Education
Health and Social Services for Northern Ireland Dept, 1980

LUND, Robert T.
Microprocessor applications; cases and observations
Industry Dept., 1979

LUNDY, M. O.
Conflict in industry: an organisational perspective, by S. Crombie and M. O. Lundy. (Research Paper no. 1)
Labour Relations Agency, 1980

LUNZER, Eric
Reading for learning in science, by Eric Lunzer, Florence Davies and Terry Greene. (Schools Council Project: Reading for Learning in the Secondary School)
Schools Council, 1980

LYNDON, G. S.
Power press safety. Standards prepared by the Joint Standing Committee on Safety in the Use of Power Presses.
Health and Safety Executive, 1979

LYONS, J.
Industrial trucks and the future. Industrial trucks SWP
NEDO, 1979

McBARNET, Doreen J.
Conviction: law, the state and the construction of justice
SSRC, 1981

MACBETH, Alistair
Scottish school councils: policy making, participation or irrelevance. Report by A. Macbeth and others
Scottish Education Dept., 1980

McCALLUM, J. D.
Distribution and transport in the Highlands and Islands Report by J. G. L. Adams and J. D. McCallum
HIDB, 1982

McCALMONT, T.
Allocation and transfer of council houses. Report by a sub-committee of the Scottish Housing Advisory Committee
Scottish Development Dept., 1980

McCARTHY, Lady Margaret
Industrial relations training. 1st progress report
National Training Council for the National Health Service, 1978

McCLEAN, David
The Hague conventions on the service of process, the taking of evidence and legislation. Explanatory document-ation prepared for Commonwealth jurisdictions
Commonwealth Secretariat, 1979

International conventions concerning applications for and awards of maintenance; explanatory documentation for Commonwealth jurisdiction
Commonwealth Secretariat, 1981

McCLEMENTS, L. D.
Some experiments with the Singh Nagar method of estima-ting equivalence scales. (Government Economic Service Working Paper no. 20)
DHSS, 1979

McCONVILLE, Michael
Confession in Crown Court trials, by J. Baldwin and M. McConville. (Research Study no. 5)
Royal Commission on Criminal Procedure, 1980

McCOWAN, Anthony James Denys
Aveley Laboratories Limited. Report by A. J. D. McCowan and A. P. Humphries
Trade Dept., 1981

Electerminations Limited (in liquidation) formerly known as APT Electronic Industries Ltd. Investigation under section 165(b) of the Companies Act, 1948. Report by Anthony James Denys McCowan and Alan Peter Humphries
Trade Dept., 1979

McCOY, K. F.
Child care trends: a review of statistical returns 1970–1979. (Personal Social Services in Northern Ireland no. 14)
DHSS for N.I., 1982

Elderly people in hospitals and residential homes (Personal Social Services in Northern Ireland, no. 16)
DHSS for N.I., 1982

Health and social services for the very old at home (Personal social services in Northern Ireland, no. 15)
DHSS for N.I., 1982

Other people's children; some aspects of childminding in Northern Ireland. (Social Work Advisory Group Paper no. 9)
DHSS for N.I., 1980

McCUTCHEON, W. A.
The industrial archaeology of Northern Ireland
DoE for N.I., 1980

MacDERMOTT, John
Northern Ireland Review Committee on Mental Health Legislation
DHSS for N.I., 1981

MACDONALD, A.
Hand in your writing. Scottish Committee on Language Arts in the Primary School
Consultative Committee on the Curriculum, 1982

Mr. Togs the tailor; a context for writing. Scottish Committee on Language Arts in the Primary School
Consultative Committee on the Curriculum, 1982

MACDONALD, Elizabeth
Changing patterns of care. Report on services for the elderly in Scotland
SHHD, 1980

McDOUGALL, Cynthia
Prisoners' problems as viewed by prisoners and probation officers at Acklington prison. (DPS Report Series I, no. 18)
Home Office, 1980

McEWEN, J.
Health education in the workplace; report of a workshop organised and sponsored by Health Education Council, February 1980, by J. Randell and J. McEwen
Health Education Council, 1980

MACEY, R. D.
Job generation in British manufacturing industry: employ-ment change by size of establishment and by region. (Government Economic Service Working Paper no. 55; DI Regional Research Series no. 4)
Industry Dept., 1982

McFARLANE, G.
Social change in Dunrossness; a Shetland study, by R. Byron and G. McFarlane. (North Sea Oil Panel Occasional Paper no. 1)
SSRC, 1980

MACFARLANE, N.
Education for 16–19 year olds. A review undertaken for the government and the local authority associations.
Dept. Education and Science, 1980

McGAHEY, Michael
Strategy for tourism in the west country. Tourism develop-ment advisory panel
West Country Tourist Board, 1980

McGILL, D.
Tyne labour market: health service recruitment on Tyne-side, by K. Walsh and D. McGill. (Manpower Planning Series 6)
DHSS, 1982

McGILL, J. D.
The use of chironomid pupal exuviae for biological surveil-lance of water quality, by R. S. Wilson and J. D. McGill. (Technical Memorandum no. 18)
Water Data Unit, 1979

MACGREGOR, William G.
The development of a real-time flood forecasting model for the south west of England
Central Water Planning Unit, 1979

McGURK, B. J.
An abortive attempt to examine the institutional climates of twenty-three British prisons, by B. J. McGurk and others. (DPS Report Series I, no. 19)
Home Office, 1980

McINTOSH, Andrew
Industry and employment in the inner city, by A. McIntosh and V. Keddie. (Inner Cities Research Programme no. 1)
DoE, 1979

MACINTYRE, D. G.
Social priority schools. Report of a working party.
Department of Education for N.I., 1980

MACIVOR, Iain
Blackness Castle
Scottish Development Dept., 1982

MACK, T. A.
Multi-purpose non-turf surfaces. Report of a seminar held at Redhill Leisure Centre, Nottingham, May 1979. (Surfaces for Outdoor Sport, Seminar 2. Technical Bulletin no. 6)
Sports Council, East Midland region, 1979

MACKAY, G. A.
Ferry services for the Scottish islands: a discussion paper prepared by the SCC
Scottish Consumer Council, 1981

North Sea oil and the Aberdeen economy, by G. A. Mackay and Anne C. Moir. (North Sea Oil Panel Occasional Paper no. 3)
SSRC, 1981

Rural Scotland price survey: Spring 1981
Scottish Consumer Council, 1981

McKEE, Lorna
The first months of motherhood. Summary report of a survey of women's experience of pregnancy, childbirth and the first 6 months after birth, by H. Graham and L. McKee. (Monograph Series no. 3)
Health Education Council, 1980

MacKELLAR, D. J.
Dairy farming in Denmark. (Farm Management Services Information Unit, Report no. 31)
Milk Marketing Board, 1982

McKENZIE, John
The commonwealth: well what do you know?
Commonwealth Institute, 1979

MacKERRON, G.
Nuclear power and the economic interests of consumers. (Research Report no. 6)
Electricity Consumers' Council, 1982

MACKIE, R. L.
Arbroath Abbey, by R. L. Mackie and S. Cruden
Scottish Development Dept., 1982

McKILLOP, I. G.
Rabbit research and rabbit control: report of a visit to New Zealand, July-August 1981
ADAS, 1982

MACKINTOSH, H. B.
Elgin cathedral; the cathedral kirk of Moray. History by H. B. Mackintosh, description by J. S. Richardson. 2nd ed.
Scottish Development Dept., 1980

McKIRDY, A. P.
Severn tidal power: potential effects on barrage construction and operation on sites of earth science interest
Nature Conservancy Council, 1981

MacLARAN, Morag
The establishment and development of local health councils, by D. Bochel and M. MacLaran. (Scottish Health Service Studies no. 41)
SHHD, 1979

MACLEAN, A. D.
1980 chemical incidents survey: statistical analysis. (Fire Research Report 4/81)
Home Office, 1981

Domestic fire fatalities; whan can be done? (Scientific Advisory Branch fire research report 12/80)
Home Office, 1980

McLEAN, K. A.
Sugar beet transplanting in the Republic of Ireland. Report by R. Wickens and K. A. McLean
ADAS, 1982

MACLENNAN, D. N.
Hydrodynamic characteristics of trawl warps. (Scottish Fisheries Research Report no. 16)
Agriculture and Fisheries for Scotland Dept., 1979

The theory of solid spheres as sonar calibration targets. (Scottish Fisheries Research Report no. 22)
Agriculture and Fisheries for Scotland Dept., 1981

MacLENNON, W. D.
Hospital dental services in Scotland: a report by the National Dental Consultative Committee
Scottish Health Service Planning Council, 1981

McLEOD, Donald
Follow up of the administration trainee entry: the first two years of work, 1971–72 competitions. (Recruitment Research Unit Report no. 3)
Civil Service Commission, 1979

Short-term follow up of direct entry principal recruitment (1973–74) competitions), by D. McLeod and R. Bayne. (Recruitment Research Unit Report no. 7)
Civil Service Commission, 1979

MacLEOD, J.
Suckler cow workers meeting, Grange, Dunsany, Republic of Ireland, 9–12 June 1981. Report by J. R. Noble and J. Macleod
ADAS, 1981

Winter oil seed rape. Report of a visit by J. M. L. Davies and J. Macleod
ADAS, 1982

MacLEOD, J. R. M.
National approvals authority working group report. Heating, Ventilating, Air-conditioning and Refrigeration Equipment SWP
NEDO, 1979

MacLEOD, S.
Towards a policy for science in Scottish primary schools.
Committee on Primary Education
Consultative Committee on the Curriculum, 1981

MACMILLAN, M.
The recognition of private English language schools. Report of the working party
British Council, 1981

McNABB, Robert
Unemployment in West Cornwall, by R. McNabb and Nicholas Woodward (Research Paper no. 8)
Employment Dept., 1979

McNEILL, T. E.
Carrickfergus Castle. (Northern Ireland Archaeological Monographs, no. 1)
DoE for N.I., 1981

MacNICOLL, A. D.
FEBS advanced course on the biochemistry of blood coagulation – Holland, November 1980. Report by A. D. MacNicoll
ADAS, 1981

MACOWAN, K. J.
Expert consultation on mycoplasmoses in small ruminants. Report of a visit to Sudan, December 1979
ADAS, 1979

MacPHAIL, I. D.
Law of evidence of Scotland, a research paper
Scottish Law Commission, 1979

McQUEENEY, John
Company take-overs, management organization and industrial relations, by N. Millward and J. McQueeney. (Manpower Papers no. 16)
Employment Dept., 1981

MADGE, N.
Despite the welfare state: a report on the SSRC/DHSS Programme of Research into Transmitted Deprivation, by M. Brown and N. Madge. (Studies in Deprivation and Disadvantage)
Heinemann for SSRC, 1982

MAHMUD, I.
Commonwealth regional rural technology programme. Report on the first meeting of the steering committee, New Delhi, November 1978
Commonwealth Science Council, 1979

MAIN, J.
A study of the fish capture process in a bottom trawl by direct observations from a towed underwater vehicle, by J. Main and G. I. Sangster. (Scottish Fisheries Research Report no. 23)
Agriculture and Fisheries for Scotland Dept., 1981

MAINWARING, Rosamund
Starter homes: a report of a DoE survey of new small houses and flats for sale, by Rosamund Mainwaring and Elizabeth Young. (HDD Occasional Paper 2/80)
DoE, 1980

MAIR, G.
Abstracts of race relations research, ed. by G. Mair and P. Stevens. (Research and Planning Unit Paper, 7)
Home Office, 1982

MAKEHAM, Peter
Economic aspects of the employment of older workers. (Research Paper no. 14)
Employment Dept., 1980

Evaluation of the job release scheme, by P. Makeham and P. Morgan. (Research Paper no. 13)
Employment Dept., 1980

Youth unemployment, an examination of evidence on youth unemployment using national statistics. (Research Paper no. 10)
Employment Dept., 1980

MALKIN, L. S.
Cement industry. Energy consumption and conservation in the cement industry. (Energy Audit Series no. 11)
Energy Dept., 1980

MALLETT, G. P.
Damage to low bridges. Bridge height gauges. Report of the working party
DTp, 1982

MALUNGA, L. B.
Medical-legal issues. Report of a combined medical-legal workshop, Malawi, October 1979
Commonwealth Secretariat, 1979

MANN, Michael
Vale of Belvoir coalfield inquiry report
DoE, 1981

MANN, R. E.
Paris machinery show. Report of a visit to France, March 1979
ADAS, 1979

MANNERS, A. J.
Extending the electoral register – 2: two surveys of public acceptability, by A. J. Manners and I. Rauta. (Occasional Paper 21)
OPCS, 1981

MANSELL, J. W.
Basis for choice. Report of a study group on post–16 pre-employment courses. 2nd ed. Further Education Unit
DES, 1982

Who cares? A curriculum policy for caring courses at the initial level. Further Education Unit
DES, 1982

MANSER, P. J.
Industrial profile of cotton ginning, by G. Flynn and P. J. Manser. (G163)
Tropical Products Institute, 1982

MAPSTONE, E.
Assessment of children; a follow up survey, interim report, by E. Mapstone and M. Buist
Scottish Education Dept., 1980

MARAIS, D. A. J.
Method of quantifying companies relative strength. (Discussion Paper no. 4)
Bank of England, 1979

MARES, Penny
The Vietnamese in Britain; a handbook for health workers
Health Education Council, 1982

MARKALL, G.
Young people and the labour market: a case study, by G. Markall and D. Finn. (Inner Cities Research Programme 5)
DoE, 1981

MARKING, Henry
Standards in catering and transport. Report on a conference held in London, December 1979
British Tourist Authority, 1980

Tourism growth and London accommodation. Report on a conference, London, 5 December 1978
British Tourist Authority, 1979

MARKS, I. M.
Nurse therapy in general practice; epidemiology and efficacy. Two year interim report to the DHSS, Nov. 1978 – Oct. 1980, by I. M. Marks, P. Lindley and H. M. Waters
DHSS, 1981

MARKS, M. J.
Early analysis of apple fruits. Report of a visit to Belgium, February 1979
ADAS, 1979

Orchard systems: report of a study tour undertaken in Holland and Belgium, 16–21 August 1981, by J. Turnbull and M. J. Marks
ADAS, 1982

MARLAND, M.
English in the 1980's: a programme of support for teachers. A review of progress and a programme for future research and development from the English committee. (Working Paper 63)
Methuen for Schools Council, 1979

MARQUAND, Judith
Measuring the effects and costs of regional incentives. (Government Economic Service Working Paper no. 32)
Industry Dept., 1980

MARRE, Lady
Hospital services for children with cancer in the north western region. Report of the group appointed to examine the decision to develop a new regional department at the Christie Hospital for the treatment of children with cancer and to recommend whether the development should proceed
DHSS for N.I., 1979

MARREN, Peter
Muir of Dinnet; portrait of a national nature reserve
Nature Conservancy Council (North-East Scotland Region), 1980

MARSDEN, David
A six-country comparison of the distribution of industrial earnings in the 1970's, by C. Saunders and D. Marsden. (Background Paper no. 8)
Royal Commission on the Distribution of Income and Wealth, 1979

MARSH, Alan
Labour mobility in the construction industry, by A. Marsh and P. Heady. (Social survey 1121)
OPCS, 1981

Labour mobility in the construction industry. A survey of manual workers conducted for the Construction Industry Manpower Board and the Department of the Environment. Final report
OPCS, 1980

Women and shiftwork. The protective legislation survey carried out for the Equal Opportunities Commission
OPCS, 1979

MARSHALL, J. H.
The International Dairy Federation symposium on bacteriological quality of raw milk, West Germany, 8–10 September 1981
ADAS, 1982

MARSHALL, W.
Combined heat and electrical power generation in the United Kingdom. Report prepared by the combined heat and power group. (Energy Paper 23)
Energy Dept., 1979

MARTIN, A. B.
Safety in demolition work. Report of the Sub-committee of the Joint Advisory Committee on Safety and Health in Construction Industries
Health and Safety Executive, 1979

MARTIN, A. D.
Human health aspects to accidental chemical exposure of dioxins - strategy for environmental reclamation and community protection: report of a visit to USA, October 4–7 1981
ADAS, 1982

MARTIN, G. S.
Notes on the production of herbage seed
ADAS, 1980

MARTIN, J. S. B.
Internal scrutiny of the advisory and monitoring junctions of the SDD with respect to planning authorities
Scottish Office, 1980

MARTIN, John D.
Health education for Commonwealth youth. A commissioned study report.
Commonwealth Secretariat, 1981

MARTIN, N.
Writing and learning across the curriculum 11–16, by N. Martin, P. D'Arcy, B. Newton and R. Parker. (SC Writing Across the Curriculum Project, repr.)
Ward Lock for the Schools Council, 1981

MARTIN, W. E.
The economics of the profits crisis. Papers and proceedings of the seminar on profits held in London on 1 April 1980
Industry Dept., 1981

MARTIN, W. H.
Broad patterns of leisure expenditure, a state of the art review, by W. H. Martin and S. Mason
Sports Council, 1979

MARTINE, Roderick
Clanlands of Scotland. A guide to territories and locations of historic interest connected with the clans and major families of Scotland
Spur Books for the British Tourist Authority, 1981

MARTYN, E. H. B.
Planning control to protect agricultural land. Report of a study tour in the Netherlands by E. H. B. Martyn and M. P. Samuel
ADAS, 1982

MASLEN, N. R.
Conifer lachnids in Britain, by C. I. Carter and N. R. Maslen. (Bulletin 58)
Forestry Commission, 1982

Broad patterns of leisure expenditure, a state of the art review, by W. H. Martin and S. Mason.
Sports Council, 1979

MASON, Val
Empty housing in England. A report on the 1977 vacant property survey carried out on behalf of the Department of the Environment, by M. Bone and V. Mason. (Social Survey Division)
OPCS, 1980

MASTER, N. R.
Conifer lachnids in Britain, by C. I. Carter and N. R. Master. (Bulletin 58)
Forestry Commission, 1982

MASTERMAN, E. P.
The first community councils; the formation and election of councils throughout Scotland; a report, by E. P. Masterman and M. P. Masterson
Scottish Office, 1981

MASTERSON, M. P.
Community councils in Tayside and Fife regions, 1976–1979
Scottish Office, 1980

The first community councils; the formation and election of councils throughout Scotland, by M. P. Masterson and E. P. Masterman
Scottish Office, 1981

Participation in planning; the role of Scottish community councils
Scottish Development Dept., 1980

MATHIAS, P. L.
Aspects of plant nematology: report of a study tour undertaken in France, June 1980
ADAS, 1981

MATHIESON, A.
Staple Edge geology teaching trail
Nature Conservancy Council, 1981

MATTERSHAW, I. A.
Improving management performance; a guide to 'SWOT' anaylsis: strengths, weaknesses, opportunities, threats
Chemical and Allied Products ITB, 1980

MATTHEWS, Alison
Management cooperatives: the early stages
DoE, 1981

MATTHEWS, B. J.
The pattern of energy use in the UK – 1976, by R. P. Bush and B. J. Matthews. (ETSU R7)
Energy Technology Support Unit, 1981

MATTHEWS, Rowan
Residential facilities for mentally handicapped children, by M. Dalgleish and R. Matthews. (Mental Health Buildings Evaluation Pamphlet 1). 2nd ed.
DHSS, 1982

Community reaction to local buildings pilot study. Sheffield development project for mentally handicapped people. (Mental Health Buildings Evaluation. Report S3)
DHSS, 1979

MATTHEWS, R. R.
Notes on the contingency arrangements for irradiated fuel flask incidents
Central Electricity Generating Board, 1980

MATTHEWS, W. A.
Techniques used for isolating functional insect enzyme preparations. Report of a study tour in the USA, August 1980
ADAS, 1980

MAULE, Jeremy
The House of Lords and the European Communities. 3rd ed. (Factsheets no. 2)
House of Lords, 1979

MAUNDER, W. F.
International Chamber of Commerce conference 'Energy – a challenge for business': Portugal, November 1980
ADAS, 1981

MAXWELL, Peter, Lord
Further programme of consolidation and statute law revision. (Scottish Law Commission no. 71). October 1982
Session 1981–82 HC 516

Scottish Law Commission. 17th annual report, 1981–82. (Scottish Law Commission no. 73). December 1982
Session 1982–83 HC 60

Prescription and the limitation of actions. Report on personal injuries actions and private international law questions. (Scottish Law Commission no. 74). February 1983
Session 1982–83 HC 153

Irritancies in leases. (Scottish Law Commission no. 75). February 1983
Session 1982–83 Cmnd. 8760

Jurisdiction and enforcement. Report of the Scottish Committee. (Scottish Courts Administration)
Scottish Office, 1980

MAY, Justice
The United Kingdom prison services. Report of the committee of inquiry. 1979
Session 1979–80 Cmnd. 7673

MAYALL, W. H.
Principles in design
Design Council, 1980

MAYHEW, P.
Crime and public housing, ed. by M. Hough and P. Mayhew. (Research and Planning Unit: paper 6)
Home Office, 1982

Crime prevention publicity; an assessment, by D. Riley and P. Mayhew. (Research study no. 63)
Home Office, 1980

MAYNARD, Brian A.
Advisory committee on local government audit. 1st report
DoE, 1980

MAYNES, E. S.
Prestel in use: a consumer view
National Consumer Council, 1982

MEADOWS, R.
Spearhead France. Report of the export sub-group of the Knitting S W P
NEDO, 1982

MECHAM, M.
Volunteer care. Report of a seminar, Sunningdale Park, March 1982. (Civil Service College Working Paper no. 33)
Civil Service College, 1982

MEDLIK, S.
Trends in tourism, world experience and England's prospects. Report of a study
English Tourist Board, 1982

MEE, J.
Using role play; an introductory guide, by R. Lewis and J. Mee
MSC, 1981

MEEK, B.
Programming languages. (Guides to Computing Standards no. 15)
National Computing Centre, 1981

MEGAW, Sir John
Civil service pay
Treasury, 1982

Civil service pay. Factual background memorandum on the non-industrial civil service
Civil Service Dept., 1981

Civil service pay. Report of an inquiry; vol. 1: Inquiry's findings vol. 2: Research studies
Session 1981–82 Cmnd. 8590, 8590–I

Civil service pay. Government evidence submitted to the inquiry into non-industrial home civil service pay
Treasury, 1982

MERCER, Eric
English vernacular houses: a study of traditional farmhouses and cottages
Royal Commission on Historical Monuments, 1979

MERCER, R. J.
Grimes Graves, Norfolk, excavations 1971–72: volume I. (Archaeological Reports no. 11)
DoE, 1981

MERRIMAN, J. H. H.
Independent review of the radio spectrum (30–960 MHz) interim report: future use of television bands II and III.
Home Office, 1982
Session 1981–82 Cmnd. 8666

Office machinery SWP progress report 1980
NEDO, 1980

Policy for the U.K. information technology industry, Information Technology S W P
NEDO, 1982

MERRISON, Sir Alec
Royal Commission on the National Health Service. Report. July 1979
Session 1979–80 Cmnd. 7615

A service for patients: conclusions and recommendations of the Royal Commission on the National Health Service: report. (Cmnd. 6502)
Royal Commission on the National Health Service, 1979

Support of university scientific research. Report of the joint working party
Session 1981–82 Cmnd. 8567

MERRY, R.
I started work
MSC, 1981

MESSURIER, Brian Le
South Devon coast path. (Long Distance Footpath Guide no. 9)
Countryside Commission, 1980

MIALL, R. H. C.
The effects of regional policy on manufacturing investment and capital stock within the UK, by R. D. Rees and R. H. C. Miall. (Government Economic Service Working Paper no. 26)
Industry Dept., 1979

MILES, C.
The textile machinery industry. Textile Machinery SWP
NEDO, 1980

MILES, C. (*continued*)
Textile Machinery SWP. Progress report 1980
NEDO, 1980

Textile Machinery SWP. Progress report
NEDO, 1981

MILES, Dillwyn
Castles of Pembrokeshire. (Subject Guide no. 4)
Pembrokeshire Coast National Park, 1979

MILLAR, Ann R.
Debt counselling: an assessment of the services and facilities available to consumer debtors in Scotland. (Research Report for the Scottish Law Commission no. 7)
Scottish Office, 1980

MILLAR, J.
Take up of means-tested benefits in work (DHSS Cohort Study of Unemployed Men Working Paper no. 3)
DHSS, 1982

MILLAR, R. M.
Aspects of bulb flower production. Report of a study tour undertaken in Holland and West Germany, 1979 series
ADAS, 1979

MILLER, Betty
Energy Bill (Bill 11, 1982–83). (Reference Sheet no. 82/13)
House of Commons Library, 1982

Water Bill (Bill 6, 1982–83). (Reference Sheet no. 82/10)
House of Commons Library, 1982

MILLER, Billie A.
Combined medical-legal workshop, Barbados, June 1979. Report
Commonwealth Secretariat, 1980

MILLER, J. C.
Tutoring: the guidance and counselling role of the tutor in vocational preparation. (Further Education Curriculum Review and Development Unit)
DES, 1982

MILLER, K. G.
Domestic electrical appliances sector working party. Progress report
NEDO, 1979

MILLER, Pat
Longitudinal study of children in care
Scottish Education Dept., 1981

MILLER, R.
Occupational mobility of protestants and Roman Catholics in Northern Ireland. (Research Paper no. 4)
Belfast, Fair Employment Agency, 1979

MILLER, W. H.
Building a skilled workforce: a case study of employment and training practices in an oil platform construction yard, by W. H. Miller. (MSC Office for Scotland. Manpower Intelligence and Planning)
MSC, 1981

MILLER, William L.
Oil and the Scottish voter 1974–79, by W. L. Miller, J. Brand and M. Jordan. (North Sea Oil Panel Occasional Paper no. 2)
SSRC, 1981

MILLETT, Peter Julian
Bandara Investments Ltd., Bandara Ceylon Co. Ltd. Investigation under the Companies Act. Report by P. J. Millett and I. M. Bowie
Trade Dept., 1980

The Central Provinces Manganese Ore Co. Ltd., Data Investments Ltd., Vivella Ltd. Investigation under the Companies Act. Report by P. J. Millett and I. M. Bowie
Trade Dept., 1980

Darjeeling Holdings Ltd. Report of investigation under the Companies Act by P. J. Millett and I. M. Bowie
Trade Dept., 1980

MILLINGTON, P. R.
Agriculture conservation and drainage of areas in Holland. Report of a study tour undertaken in Holland, June 1979, by P. R. Millington and others
ADAS, 1979

MILLS, Liz
Public policy research; a review of qualitative methods, by K. Young and L. Mills
SSRC, 1980

MILLS, T. C.
Unobserved components, signal extraction and relationships between macroeconomic time series. (Discussion Paper no. 19)
Bank of England, 1981

MILLWARD, Neil
Company take-overs, management organization and industrial relations, by N. Millward and J. McQueeney. (Manpower Papers no. 16)
Employment Dept., 1981

MILES, C.
Textile Machinery SWP. Progress report 1980
NEDO, 1980

MILNE, Anne
Response to a postal sift of addresses. (New Methodology Series no. NM5)
OPCS, 1980

MINDEL, Richard
Experiment to examine the use of trainability tests in skill centres. Final report by R. Mindel. (Training Services Agency Report no. DTP13)
MSC, 1979

MITCHELL, P.
The labour market for school leavers in Warrington, by G. J. Evans and P. Mitchell. (Manpower Intelligence and Planning)
MSC, 1981

MITCHELL, R.
Nature conservation implications of siting wave energy converters off the Moray Firth, by P. K. Probert and R. Mitchell
Nature Conservancy Council, 1980

Severn tidal power: the natural environment, by R. Mitchell and P. K. Probert
Nature Conservancy Council, 1981

MNOOKIN, Robert H.
Bargaining in the shadow of the law: the case of divorce. (Centre for Socio-legal Studies: Working Paper no. 3)
SSRC, 1979

MOIR, Anne C.
North Sea oil and the Aberdeen economy, by G. A. Mackay and Anne C. Moir. (North Sea Oil Panel Occasional Paper no. 3)
SSRC, 1981

Rural Scotland price survey: spring 1981
Scottish Consumer Council, 1981

MOIR, C. B.
A guide to sources of local labour market information, by T. Fidgett and C. B. Moir. (Reference Paper RP/5/79)
Engineering Industry Training Board, 1979

MONK, Janet
Survey of defenders in debt actions in Scotland. (Research Report for the Scottish Law Commission no. 6; SS1124)
OPCS, 1981

MONTAGU OF BEAULIEU, Lord Edward John Barrington, 3rd Baron
Britain's historic buildings; a policy for their future use
British Tourist Authority, 1980

MONTGOMERY, W.
Energy requirements for pollution control in the British steel industry. Report of a working party. Parts A and B
British Steel, 1979

MOODIE, Margaret
The pattern of maternity services in the Netherlands
DHSS, 1979

MOODY, Mary
Environmental information services in the UK. (Occasional Paper 8)
DoE, 1980

MOODY, Susan
Drunken offenders in Scotland; a review of relevant literature
Scottish Office, 1979

MOORE, B. M.
Inland revenue: experimental tests of numeracy. An interim report. (Recruitment Research Unit Report no. 2)
Civil Service Dept., 1979

Inland revenue: experimental tests of numeracy. Second report. (Recruitment Research Unit Report no. 12)
Civil Service Commission, 1980

Qualifying tests for appointments in administration (1980–81 review). (Recruitment Research Unit Report no. 15)
Civil Service Commission, 1981

The selection and performance of tax inspectors. A follow up study. (Recruitment Research Unit Report no. 8)
Civil Service Commission, 1979

Validation of the language test battery (LTB). (Recruitment Research Unit Report no. 11)
Civil Service Commission, 1980

MOORE, D. J.
A simple method of collecting and drying papaya (pawpaw) latex to produce crude papain. (Rural Technology Guide 8)
Tropical Products Institute, 1980

MOORE, G.
Development work in music. Committee on Primary Education. (Curriculum Paper 16)
Consultative Committee on the Curriculum, 1981

MOORE, Robert
Labour migration and oil. (North Sea Oil Panel Occasional Paper no. 7)
SSRC, 1981

MOORE, W. C.
Diseases of bulbs, 2nd ed. (Reference Book HPD1)
ADAS, 1979

MORCOM, R. Hugh
Orbit Holdings Ltd. Investigation under section 165(b) of the Companies Act, 1948. Report, by A. H. M. Evans and R. H. Morcom
Trade Dept., 1981

MORFETT, J.
Rig with simulated suction lift for measurements of fire pump performance (Scientific Advisory Branch Report 24/81)
Home Office, 1981

MORGAN, B. J. W.
Bord na Mona Irish peat development authority: report of a visit to the Republic of Ireland, 9–10 March 1981
ADAS, 1982

MORGAN, D. E.
The nutritional value of fodder. Report of a visit to France, April 1979
ADAS, 1979

MORGAN, G.
Recording system for bovine foetal data, by C. Richardson and G. Morgan. Report of a visit to Veterinary Research Laboratory, Abbotstown Castleknock, Eire, 25–26 March 1982
ADAS, 1982

MORGAN, H. Gethin
Services for mentally ill people: collaboration between health and social services in community care. Regional study day. Report of the day's proceedings, Bristol, June 1979
DHSS, 1979

MORGAN, J. H.
Meeting of European leptospira workers, 2nd. Report of a visit to France, September 1979, by T. W. A. Little and J. H. Morgan
ADAS, 1979

European leptospirosis workers, France 15–16 October 1981, 3rd meeting, by J. H. Morgan, T. W. A. Little and S. C. Hathaway
ADAS, 1982

MORGAN, John
British Telecom's proposals for increased tariffs
Post Office Users' National Council, 1980

The delivery performance and potential of the Post Offices' mail services. (Report 17)
Post Office Users' National Council, 1979

Post Office proposals for increased inland postal, overseas postal, national girobank and remittance service charges. (Report no. 18)
Post Office User's National Council, 1979

Increased telecommunications charges. Report on Post Office proposals. (Report 19)
Post Office Users' National Council, 1979

Letter post services in the inner London postal area. Report to the Monopolies and Mergers Commission. (Report no. 20)
Post Office Users' National Council, 1979

Increased inland and overseas postal charges. Report on Post Office proposals. (Report 21)
Post Office Users' National Council, 1979

MORGAN, Phillip L.
Employment functions in manufacturing industry. (Government economic service working paper no. 24) (Dept. of Employment Working Paper no. 2)
Dept. of Employment, 1979

Evaluation of the job release scheme, by P. Makeham and P. Morgan. (Research Paper no. 13)
Employment Dept., 1980

MORGAN, S.
Study of housing action areas, the case study reports, 1976–78, by S. Morgan and B. Cullen
Scottish Development Dept., 1981

MORGAN, W. M.
Pest disease control in glasshouse crops, by W. M. Morgan and others
British Crop Protection Council, 1979

MORGAN-GILES, R. F.
Arrest, charge and summons; current practice and resource implications, by R. Gemmill and R. F. Morgan-Giles. (Research Study no. 9)
Royal Commission on Criminal Procedure, 1980

MORLAND, M.
Case of Paul Steven Brown. Report of the committee of inquiry. DHSS. December 1980
Session 1980–81 Cmnd. 8107

MORLEY, Beric M.
Hylton Castle, Tyne and Wear
DoE, 1979

MORRIS, Brian
Countryside consultative committees for museums. Report of a working party
Museums and Galleries Commission, 1982

Museums in Wales. Report
Standing Commission on Museums and Galleries, 1981

MORRIS, H. T.
International symposium on residues in food of animal origin, France, 20–23 May 1981
ADAS, 1982

MORRIS, J. E.
Changing maintenance requirements in the iron and steel industry. A report of a research study
Iron and Steel Industry Training Board, 1979

MORRIS, J. G.
Application of physical techniques in biology. Report of the biological sciences committee
Science Research Council, 1979

MORRIS, J. N.
Two reports on research into services for children and adolescents (1): improving the quality of child health care. Report of the working group
DHSS, 1980

MORRIS, John
Electricity in the home. (Open Science)
Schools Council, 1979

Science at home. (Open Science)
Schools Council, 1979

MORRIS, Pauline
Crime control and the police: a review of research, by P. Morris and K. Heal. (Research Study no. 67)
Home Office, 1981

Police interrogation: review of literature. (Research Study no. 3)
Royal Commission on Criminal Procedure, 1980

MORRIS, R. M.
Review of Home Office statistical services. (Crime Policy Planning Unit)
Home Office, 1980

MORRISON, A.
Inquiry into the teaching of modern studies in SI and SII. Report of a study group of the Scottish Central Committee on Social Subjects
Consultative Committee on the Curriculum, 1980

MORRISON, C. A.
Science budget; a forward look, 1982. Report by the Advisory Board for the Research Councils
DES, 1982

MORRITT, R. A.
Gilgate Holdings Limited, Raybourne Group Limited, Calomefern Limited, Desadean Properties Limited. Investigation under the Companies Act 1948
Trade Dept., 1981

MORTIMER, J. E.
Fur wages council (Great Britain). Report of an inquiry. (Report no. 17)
Advisory, Concilliation and Arbitration Service, 1979

Licensed Residential Establishments and Licensed Restaurant Wages Council. (Report no. 18)
Advisory, Concilliation and Arbitration Service, 1980

The Laundry Wages Council. (Report no. 19)
Advisory, Concilliation and Arbitration Service, 1980

MOSDELL, K. B.
Transplanting techniques in connection with the sugar beet crop. Report of a study tour undertaken in Japan, October 1980
ADAS, 1980

MOSELEY, H. S.
Selective detection assessment – South Kensington, London, by R. P. Jenkins and H. S. Moseley. (Traffic Advisory Unit)
DTp, 1981

MOSELEY, M. J.
Rural development and its relevance to the inner city debate. (The Inner City in Context 9)
SSRC, 1980

MOWL, Colin
Simulations on the Treasury economic model. (Government Economic Service Working Paper no. 34; Treasury Working Paper no. 15)
Treasury, 1980

MOXON, David
Fine enforcement; an evaluation of the practices of individual courts, by P. Softley and D. Moxon. (Research and Planning Unit Paper 12)
Home Office, 1982

MOY, A.
Assessment of furniture designed for handicapped children. Summary report. Part 1. (DHSS Aids Assessment Programme)
DHSS, 1982

MULHOLLAND, J. R.
Jersey cows in Denmark – their breeding, feeding and milk quality. Report of a study tour by J. R. Mulholland and P. E. Farmer
ADAS, 1982

MÜLLER-CHRISTENSEN, Sigrid
Ecclesiastical and imperial vestments in Bamberg. (Conservation Paper 4)
Crafts Advisory Committee, 1979

MUNRO, H. D. R.
The Livingstone scheme; a ten year review (Scottish Health Service Studies, 43)
SHHD, 1982

MURIE, A.
Housing market processes and the inner city, by A. Murie and R. Forrest. (The Inner City in Context 10)
SSRC, 1980

MURRAY, A. J.
Metals, organochlorine pesticides and PCB residue levels in fish and shellfish landed in England and Wales during 1974. (Aquatic Environment Monitoring Report no. 2)
MAFF, 1979

Metals, organochlorine pesticides and PCB residue levels in fish and shellfish landed in England and Wales during 1975, by A. J. Murray. (Aquatic Environment Monitoring Report no. 5)
MAFF, 1981

MURRAY, Dominic
The vocational aspirations and expectations of school leavers in Londonderry and Strabane, by D. Murray and J. Darby. (Research Paper 6)
Fair Employment Agency (Belfast), 1980

MYERS, W.
Access to the countryside for sport and recreation. (Regional Strategy: Subject Report 2) (SCSR(81)68)
Southern Council for Sport and Recreation, 1981

NADIAN, A. K.
European (8th) workshop on drug metabolism, Belgium, September, 1982. Report
ADAS, 1982

NEAL, Ernest
Badgers in woodlands. (Forest Record 103)
Forestry Commission, 1982

NEALE, Sir Alan
Great Universal Stores Plc. and Empire Stores (Bradford) Plc. Report by the Monopolies and Mergers Commission on the existing and proposed mergers. January 1983
Session 1982–83 Cmnd. 8777

Imperial Chemical Industries Plc. and Arthur Holden and Sons Plc. Report on the proposed merger by the Monopolies and Mergers Commission. September 1982
Session 1981–82 Cmnd. 8660

NEEDHAM, P.
International congress (12th) of soil science, New Delhi, February 1982. Report by W. Dermott and P. Needham
ADAS, 1982

Report on 16th colloquium of the International Potash Institute: 'Agricultural yield potentials in agricultural climates', Poland, 22–27 June 1981
ADAS, 1982

NEILL, J. H.
Sheffield and Rotherham labour market study
MSC, 1980

NEWALL, R. S.
Stonehenge, Wiltshire
DoE, 1981

NEWBY, H.
The state of research into social stratification
SSRC, 1982

NEWEY, John
Second terminal, Gatwick and other works. Report of the public inquiry, 29 January – 11 July 1980. Inspector: His Honour John Newey
DoE, 1981

NEWTON, R. G.
Current problems in the conservation of stained glass. (Conservation Paper 7)
Crafts Advisory Committee, 1979

NICOD, Michael
Women on MSC craft courses
MSC, 1982

NICOLL, J.
Patterns of project dissemination. Schools Council Research Team
Schools Council, 1982

NICHOLLS, Donald James
Larkfold Holdings Ltd. Report of investigation under the Companies Act, 1948, by D. J. Nicholls and E. K. Wright
Trade Dept., 1979

NIELSEN, V. C.
Agricultural odours. FAO European network on farm waste utilisation. Report of a visit to Holland, October 1979
ADAS. 1979

Construction and management of livestock slurry stores constructed by the use of concrete pipes: report of a visit to Eire, 3–5 December 1980
ADAS, 1981

FAO consultation on the European co-operative network on animal waste utilization. Report of a visit to Holland, October 1980
ADAS, 1980

Fourth international symposium on livestock wastes, Amarillo, Texas, USA, 15–19 April 1980. Report
ADAS, 1980

International (2nd) symposium on anaerobic digestion, Travemunde, Germany, September 1981; including reports on a study tour of Danish biogas plants, and a visit to F. A. L. Technological Institute, Braunschweig, Germany. September 1981. Report
ADAS, 1982

NIVEN. A.
A critical view on Elechi Amadi's 'The Concubine'. (Nexus Books 01)
Rex Collings for the British Council, 1981

NIXON, J.
Fatherless families on family income supplement (FIS). (Research Report no. 14)
DHSS, 1979

NIXON, Jaqi
Policies for the 16–19 year olds: an overview. (CSC Working Paper no. 18)
Civil Service College, 1980

Review of the supplementary benefits scheme; a case study. (CSC Working Paper no. 25)
Civil Service College, 1980

NIXON, Jon
Teachers in research. A report on the role of the teacher in research. Conference, Birmingham, November 1979
Schools Council, 1980

NOBEL, K. C.
Water control projects. Report of a visit to West Germany, Ocotber 1979, by K. C. Nobel and J. C. Waddington
ADAS, 1979

NOBLE, J. R.
Suckler cow workers meeting, Grange, Dunsany, Republic of Ireland, 9–12 June 1981. Report by J. R. Noble and J. MacLeod
ADAS, 1981

NODDER, T. E.
Organisational and management problems of mental illness hospitals. Report of a working group
DHSS, 1980

NORTHFIELD, Lord W. Donald Chapman
Acquisition and occupancy of agricultural land. Report of the committee of inquiry. July 1979
Session 1979–80 Cmnd. 7599

NORTON, A.
Cocoa, chocolate and sugar confectionery. Report of the sector working group of the Food and Drink Manufacturing EDC
NEDO, 1979

NORTON, Michael
Fund raising, a handbook for minority groups. ed. by M. Morton and H. Blume
Commission for Racial Equality, 1979

NTUK-IDEM, Moses J.
Poly Theatre. Commonwealth Institute Theatre Workshop
Commonwealth Institute, 1980

NUNN, Stuart
The opening and closure of manufacturing units in the United Kingdom, 1966–75. (Government Economic Service Working Paper no. 36)
Industry Dept., 1980

NUSSEY, Clive
A study of routinely available information relating to minor accidents in N.C.B. Derbyshire area, by Clive Nussey and H. Thompson. (Research Paper 19)
Health and Safety Executive, 1982

A survey of minor injuries associated with transport and handling accidents at six collieries in N.C.B. North Derbyshire area, by Clive Nussey and H. Thompson (including Errata). (Research Paper 21)
Health and Safety Executive, 1982

NUTLEY, P.
The learning resources centre at the Civil Service College, Sunningdale. (CSC Working Paper no. 7)
Civil Service College, 1979

NUTLEY, S. D.
Evaluation of accessibility levels in rural areas; an example from rural Wales
Welsh Office, 1981

NUTTALL, B. R.
Out of season lamb production: report of a study tour undertaken in France, 3–11 October 1981
ADAS, 1982

NUTTALL, D. I.
School self-evaluation: accountability with a human face? (SC Programme 1: Purpose and Planning in Schools)
Schools Council, 1981

OATES, N.
'Can-do' cards and profiles; tools for self-assessment, by M. R. Freshwater and N. Oates
MSC, 1982

O'BRIEN, Maureen
A study of an East End night shelter, by M. Drake and M. O'Brien. (Single and Homeless Working Paper 2)
DoE, 1982

O'BRIEN, Sir Richard
Outlook on training. Review of the Employment and Training Act, 1973
MSC, 1980

O'CONNOR, D.
Probabilities of employment on leaving work experience schemes (Government Economic Service Working Paper no. 53)
MSC, 1982

O'CONNOR, Michael
Management and design in the British small boat industry
Design Council, 1980

O'CONNOR, R. M.
The making of standards. (Guides to Computing Standards no. 1)
National Computing Centre, 1981

OGDEN, T. L.
The reproducibility of asbestos counts. (Research Paper 18)
Health and Safety Executive, 1982

OGILVY, Audrey
Inter-regional migration since 1971: an appraisal of data from the national health service central register and labour force surveys. (Occasional Paper 10)
OPCS, 1980

OGLESBY, R. H.
Condensed report on the evaluation of self-recuperative burners for use in small drop forging slot furnaces: main report prepared for the Dept. of Energy, November 1980
Energy Dept., 1981

OLDFIELD, D. G.
Appraisal of marine fouling on offshore structures. (Offshore Technology Paper 6)
Energy Dept., 1980

OLDHAM, S. W.
Design and design management in the UK footwear industry
Design Council, 1982

OLIVER, Peter
Chancery Division of the High Court. Report of the review body
Session 1980–81 Cmnd. 8205

OLIVER, Peter James
AEG-Telefunken (UK) Ltd., Chasgift Ltd. Investigations under the Companies Act, 1948. Report by D. J. Freeman and P. J. Oliver
Trade Dept., 1979

O'NEIL, B. H. St. J.
Caerlaverock Castle, by B. H. St. J. O'Neil, revised by C. J. Tabraham
Scottish Development Dept., 1982

Cliffords Tower, York Castle, 2nd ed., 2nd impr.
DoE, 1982

ONSLOW, Cranley
Report of the Saint Christopher and Nevis constitutional conference, London, December 1982, January 1983
Session 1982–83 Cmnd. 8796

OPIE, R. G.
West Somerset Free Press and Bristol United Press Ltd. A report on the proposed transfer of the West Somerset Free Press, a newspaper of which Farnham Castle Newspapers Ltd. is a proprietor, to British United Press Ltd., April 1980. (The Monopolies and Mergers Commission)
Session 1979–80 HC 546

OPPE, T. E.
Artificial feeds for the young infant. Report of the working party on the composition of foods for infants and young children, committee on medical aspects of food policy. (Reports on Health and Social Subjects 18)
DHSS, 1980

Present day practice in infant feeding, 1980. Report of a working party of the panel on child nutrition; committee on medical aspects of food policy. (Report on Health and Social Subjects 20)
DHSS, 1980

OPPENHEIMER, P. M.
International monetary arrangements; the limits to planning. (Papers Presented to the Panel of Academic Consultants no. 8)
Bank of England, 1979

ORCHARD, D.
Handcuffs: state of art review. (SOAR 006) (Police Scientific Development Branch)
Home Office, 1981

ORDE, M. H.
Report of the working party to examine qualifications for entry to teacher training courses in music
SED, 1982

ORNA, Elizabeth
EITB research 1968–1978. A summary of results and bibliography. (EITB Reference Paper RP/1/79)
Engineering Industry Training Board, 1979

ORR, Alan
Making and revocation of wills. 22nd report of the Law Reform Committee. May 1980
Session 1979–80 Cmnd. 7902

ORSINI, Bruno
Sevesco. The escape of toxic substances at the ICMESA establishment on 10 July 1976 and the consequent potential dangers to health and the environment due to industrial activity
Health and Safety Executive, 1980

OSBORN, H. E.
Civil aviation: energy considerations. Advisory Council on Energy Conservation, Paper 9; Transport Working Group. (Energy paper no. 36)
Energy Dept., 1979

OSBORNE, Michael Charles Anthony
Consolidated Gold Fields Ltd. Report of investigation under the Companies Act, 1948, by B. J. Welsh and M. C. A. Osborne
Trade Dept., 1980

OTTLEY, P.
Computer benefits?: guidelines for local information and advice centres, by P. Ottley and E. Kempson
National Consumer Council, 1982

OWENS, Susan E.
Energy: a register of research, development and demonstration in the UK, part 2: Social sciences
SSRC, 1980

PADDON, A. R.
The production of charcoal in a portable metal kiln, by A. R. Paddon and A. P. Harker. (G119)
Tropical Products Institute, 1979

PAIWALA, A.
Appeals by the prosecution against sentences and acquitals; a survey of the situation in some Commonwealth countries, by A. Paiwala and J. Cottrell
Commonwealth Secretariat, 1982

PALMER, E. R.
Pulping characteristics of *Pinus caribaea* grown in Sri Lanka, by E. R. Palmer and S. Ganguli. (L57)
Tropical Products Institute, 1982

Pulping trials of wood species growing in plantations in Kenya, by E. R. Palmer, J. A. Gibbs and A. P. Dutta. (Report L61)
Tropical Products Institute, 1982

PALMER, Ernest J.
Pollution. (Open Science)
Schools Council, 1979

PALMER, Margaret
Nature conservation and agriculture – can we have both? (Nature Conservation and Agriculture: a Series of Projects for Secondary Schools no. 1)
Nature Conservancy Council, 1980

PANES, J. J.
A survey of the quality of farm milk in England and Wales in relation to European Economic Community proposals
ADAS, 1979

PARK, J. R.
Survey of vinylidene chloride levels in food contact materials and in foods. 3rd report of the steering group on food surveillance, working party on vinylidene chloride. (Food Surveillance Paper 3)
MAFF, 1980

PARKER, S. R.
Work and leisure: trends and prospects
SSRC, 1979

PARKER, Stanley
Older workers and retirement. An enquiry carried out on behalf of the Department of Employment and the Department of Health and Social Security. (Social Survey Division)
OPCS, 1980

PARRY, D. R.
Alfa-Laval symposium on cleaning milking equipment, Sweden, 2–5 September 1980. Report
ADAS, 1981

Annual sessions of the International Dairy Federation, 63rd. Report of a visit to Switzerland
ADAS, 1979

International Dairy Federation. Report on 64th annual session, Bristol, 7–12 September 1980, by D. R. Parry, J. H. Marshall and G. Sinclair
ADAS, 1981

International Dairy Federation, report on 65th annual session, Torremolinos, Spain, 5–9 October 1981
ADAS, 1982

PARSLOE, Eric
Thomson Travel Limited communications study report. (Research Report 80/1)
Air Transport and Travel Industry Training Board, 1980

PARSONS, P. L.
A door-opening tool for fire service use (Joint Committee on Fire Research Report 21)
Home Office, 1982

General fireground lighting equipment for first attendance fire appliances, prepared by J. A. Foster and P. L. Parsons. (Central Fire Brigades Advisory Councils for England and Wales and for Scotland Joint Committee on Fire Research, Research Report no. 13)
Home Office, 1979

Trials of medium and high expansion foams on petrol fires (Scientific Advisory Branch Report 12/81)
Home Office, 1981

PART, Sir Anthony
Direct broadcasting by satellite. Report of the advisory panel on technical transmission standards. November 1982.
Home Office
Session 1982–83 Cmnd. 8751

PARTIS, J.
Intensive apple growing in south west Holland. Report of a visit to Holland, April 1979, by R. R. Stapleton and J. Partis
ADAS, 1979

PASSMORE, S.
Sugar beet. Arable group's report
NEDO, 1982

PATCHETT, K.
International conventions in the field of succession; explanatory documentation prepared for Commonwealth jurisdictions
Commonwealth Secretariat, 1980

PATERSON, Betty F. R.
Nursing appointment procedures: a guide to good practice
National Staff Committee for Nurses and Midwives, 1981

PATERSON, J. B.
Flexible magnetic disk cartridges, by C. R. Claber and J. B. Paterson. (Guides to computing standards no. 4)
National Computing Centre, 1981

PATES, A.
Plumbing's a good job
MSC, 1982

PATON, G.
Scottish English; the language children bring to school. Scottish Committee on Language Arts in the Primary School
Consultative Council on the Curriculum, 1980

PATTERSON, D. S. P.
Danish Mycopathological Society. Report on annual meeting, Denmark, October 1981
ADAS, 1982

International symposium on animal, plant and microbial toxins, 6th. Mycotoxin symposium. Report of a visit to Sweden, August 1979
ADAS, 1979

PATTERSON, K. D.
Deriving and testing rate of growth and higher order growth effects in dynamic economic models, by K. D. Patterson and J. Ryding. (Discussion Paper 21)
Bank of England, 1982

PATTERSON, R. D.
Guidelines for auditory warning systems on civil aircraft (CAA Paper 82017)
Civil Aviation Authority, 1982

PATTIE, G.
Steering group on quality assurance manpower; consultative document
Defence Min., 1980

PAUL, A. A.
McCance and Widdowson's 'The composition of foods' first supplement: amino acids, mg per 100g food, fatty acids, g per 100g food, by A. A. Paul and others
MAFF, 1980

PAUL, Richard K. G.
Development of a fishery for portunid crabs of the genus *Callinectes* in Sinaloa, Mexico
Overseas Development Administration, 1981

PAUL, S.
A study of the CSSB performance of candidates for the Government Economic Service 1974–1978. (Recruitment Research Unit: Report no. 14)
Civil Service Commission, 1981

PAUL, S. E.
Follow up study of H. M. Factory Inspectors, class II. (Recruitment Research Unit Report no. 1)
Civil Service Commission, 1979

PAXMAN, John M.
The use of paramedicals for primary health care in the Commonwealth; a survey of medical-legal issues and alternatives, by J. M. Paxman and others
Commonwealth Secretariat, 1979

PEACOCK, S.
The technician in engineering, part 2: Qualifications and training backgrounds of technicians (Research Report RR/9/2)
Engineering Industry Training Board, 1982

PEARCE, Barbara
Trainee centred reviewing (TCR). (Special Programmes Research and Development Series no. 2)
MSC, 1981

PEARCE, David
The social incidence of environmental costs and benefits: a report to the Panel on Pollution Research of the Research Initiatives Board, by D. Pearce, R. Edwards and T. Harris
SSRC, 1981

The social incidence of environmental costs and benefits, by David Pearce and others
SSRC, 1979

PEARSON, W.
Towards greater independence for the elderly; implications for management. Reports of working parties. Social Work Service Development Group, Northern Region
DHSS, 1982

PEERS, Sir Charles
Carisbrooke Castle, Isle of Wight, 3rd ed.
DoE, 1982

Middleham Castle. repr.
DoE, 1981

Richmond Castle, Yorkshire
DoE, 1981

PENGELLY, R. A.
The health capital programme in Wales. Report of a working party
Welsh Office, 1980

Services for mentally handicapped people. Report of the all-Wales working party
Welsh Office, 1982

PEPIN, G. A.
Mycotoxins in animal disease. Proceedings of a third meeting held at the National College of Food Technology, Weybridge, April 1978. (RGV10)
ADAS, 1979

Mycotoxins in animal disease. Proceedings of a fourth meeting, National College of Food Technology, Weybridge, April 1981. (Reference Book 360)
ADAS, 1982

PERCIVAL, A. J.
Darlington quiet town experiment, September 1976 to September 1978. Report by the working group
Noise Advisory Council, 1981

PERKINS, Elizabeth
What is health education in nursing practice? Report of a development workshop, December 1979. (Training Occasional Paper no. 2)
Health Education Council, 1980

PERRETT, K.
TRAMS (Transport Referencing and Mapping System), by K. Perrett and B. A. Sperring. (HECB/M/4) (Highway Engineering Computer Branch)
DTp, 1980

PERRIMAN, V.
Stationery and printing of forms. (Guides to Computing Standards no. 18)
National Computing Centre, 1981

PERRY, B.
Corrosion principles for engineering technicians. Corrosion Education and Training Working Party
Industry Dept, 1982

PERRY, G.
Glass industry: energy conservation and utilisation in the glass industry. A report by G. Perry and P. J. Doyle. (Energy Audit Service no. 5)
Energy Dept., 1979

PERRY, M. W.
The organisation of the remedial professions in the National Health Service. Report of the sub-group
DHSS, 1979

PERRY, N. H.
Review of statistical services, by Sir Derek Rayner. Report of the study officer for the Departments of Environment and Transport
Central Statistical Office, 1981

PETERS, D. A.
A better life. Report on services for the mentally handicapped in Scotland by the Sub-committee of the Mental Disorder Planning Group
SHHD, 1979

PETERSEN, K. H.
A critical view on John Pepper Clark's 'Selected Poems'.
(Nexus Books 03)
Rex Collings for British Council, 1981

PETTITT, Raymond
Computer aids to housing maintenance management
DoE, 1981

PETTS, K. W.
Air segmented continuous flow automatic analysis in the laboratory, 1979. An essay review. Methods for the Examination of Waters and Associated Materials
DoE, 1980

PEXTON, A. F.
A fuels policy for the UK into the 21st century
South of Scotland Electricity Board, 1980

PHILIPS, Sir Cyril
Royal Commission on Criminal Procedure. Report
Session 1980–81 Cmnd. 8092, 8092–I

PHILLIPS, D. H.
International plant health controls conflicts, problems and co-operation: a European experience. Prepared for the eleventh Commonwealth Forestry Conference, Trinidad, September 1980. (R & D Paper 125)
Forestry Commission, 1980

PHILLIPS, H.
Decay of spherical detonations and shocks. (Technical Paper 7)
Health and Safety Executive, 1980

PHILLIPS, J. C.
Research on the urban fringe, compiled by J. C. Phillips and A. J. Veal. (CURS Conference and Seminar Papers no. 6)
Countryside Commission, 1979

PHILLPOTTS, G. J. O.
Previous convictions, sentence and reconviction; a statistical study. (Research Study no. 53)
Home Office, 1979

PIEARCE, G. D.
Verticillium wilt. (Arboricultural Leaflet 9)
Forestry Commission, 1981

PINCHERLE, G.
Kidney transplants and dialysis. (Topics of Our Time 2)
DHSS, 1979

PINCOTT, Leslie R.
Charges, costs and margins of estate agents. Price Commission Report, August 1979
Session 1979–80 Cmnd. 7647

The future of the printing industries. Report to the National Economic Development Council
NEDO, 1982

Prices, costs and margins in the manufacture and distribution of children's toys and games. Price Commission Report, August 1979
Session 1979–80 Cmnd. 7651

PITTS, Cyril
British process plant industry; achievements
NEDO, 1981

PITZZ, K.
Low-cost science teaching equipment, 3: report of a Commonwealth regional seminar-workshop, Law, Papua, New Guinea, March 1979
Commonwealth Secretariat, 1979

PIXTON, S. W.
Final symposium of the Cost 90 Project (physical properties of foodstuffs). Report of a visit to Belgium, 9–11 September 1981
ADAS, 1982

International symposium on controlled atmosphere storage of grains. Report of a visit to Italy, May 1980, by N. J. Burrell and S. W. Pixton
ADAS, 1980

PLIATSKY, Sir Leo
Non-departmental public bodies. Report. February 1980
Session 1979–80 Cmnd. 7797

PLOWDEN, E. N., Lord
Establishment of an independent element in the investigation of complaints against the police. Report of a working party. Home Office, 1981
Session 1980–81 Cmnd. 8193

Fifth report on top salaries. (Report of the Review Body on Top Salaries no. 18)
Session 1981–82 Cmnd. 8552

POLANI, P. E.
Guidelines for the testing of chemicals for mutagenicity. Report of the committee on mutagenicity of chemicals in food, consumer products and the environment. (Report on Health and Social Subjects 24)
DHSS, 1981

MRC/DHSS joint working group on genetic counselling and service implications of chemical genetics research. Report
MRC, 1979

POLLOCK, M. R.
Winter cauliflower production. Report of a study tour undertaken in France, April 1979
ADAS, 1979

POND, C. C.
Access to Parliamentary resources and information in London libraries
House of Commons, 1982

Procedural changes of 19 July 1982 and supply procedure of the House. (Public Information Office Fact Sheet no. 18)
House of Commons Library, 1982

POOLE, J. B.
Falklands campaign; military accounts and consequences. (Reference Sheet 82/18)
House of Commons Library, 1982

POPE, J. A.
A developing strategy for the West Midlands. Updating and rolling forward of the regional strategy to 1991. The regional economy: problems and proposals. Report of the West Midlands Economic Planning Council and the West Midlands Planning Authorities Conference, July 1979. (J. A. Pope and E. C. J. Whittingham, ch.)
West Midlands Planning Authorities Conference, 1979

PORTMANN, J. E.
Chemical monitoring of residue levels in fish and shellfish landed in England and Wales during 1970–73. (Aquatic Environment Monitoring Report no. 1)
MAFF, 1979

POSNER, M. V.
Institutions in the financial markets; questions and some tentative answers. (Papers Presented to the Panel of Academic Consultants no. 9)
Bank of England, 1979

POSNER, Michael
'Public enterprise in the market place'. (NICG Occasional Paper no. 1)
Nationalised Industries' Chairmen's Group, 1979

POSTLES, J. E.
Working party on the staffing requirements for control stores. Report. First revision
DHSS, 1979

POTTER, J.
Public transport. (Special Paper no. 6)
National Consumer Council, 1982

POTTER, R. F.
Salad discussion group visit to Holland. Report of a visit, March 1980
ADAS, 1980

POUNCE, R. J.
Industrial movement in the United Kingdom 1966–75
Industry Dept., 1981

POWER, Anne
Priority estates project; upgrading problem council estates
DoE, 1980

POWER, M. G.
Retirement between 60 and 65; an examination of civil service policy and practice. Report of the Joint Committee on Retirement
Civil Service Dept., 1979

PRATT, M. J.
Building societies: an econometric model. (Discussion Paper no. 11)
Bank of England, 1980

PRESCOTT-CLARKE, P.
Organising house adaptations for disabled people. A research study
DoE, 1982

PRICE, B. T.
Lifts report. Progress reports of the Mechanical Handling Sector Working Party
NEDO, 1979

Lifting and winding equipment industry. Progress of the Mechanical Handling Sector Working Party
NEDO, 1979

PRICE, F.
Tourism growth and London accommodation. Report on a conference, 5 December 1978
British Tourist Authority, 1979

PRICE, Robert
Profiles of union growth; a comparative statistical portrait of eight countries, by G. S. Bain and R. Price. (Warwick Studies in Industrial Relations) (Industrial Relations Research Unit)
SSRC, 1980

PRICE, S. G.
Introducing the electronic office
National Computing Centre, 1979

PRINCE, W.
Dressing, cleaning and finishing operator training guide book
Foundry Industry Training Committee, 1979

PRITCHARD, D. G.
Epidemiology of respiratory disease in cattle and pigs and haemophilus infections of domestic animals: report of a study tour undertaken in Canada, 20 August – 7 September 1981
ADAS, 1982

PRITCHARD, J. A. T.
Security in communications systems
National Computing Centre, 1982

PRITCHARD, T.
Nature conservation in the marine environment. Report of the NCC/NERC Joint Working Party on Marine Wildlife Conservation
Nature Conservancy Council, 1979

PROBERT, P. K.
Nature conservation implications of siting wave energy converters off the Moray Firth, by P. K. Probert and R. Mitchell
Nature Conservancy Council, 1980

Severn tidal power: the natural environment, by R. Mitchell and P. K. Probert
Nature Conservancy Council, 1981

Severn tidal power: potential effects of altered drainage patterns on freshwater wetlands
Nature Conservancy Council, 1981

PUGH, L.
The development of intermediate treatment in Wales; working together in intermediate treatment. Report of the residential workshop, Abergavenny, November 1979. (Social Work Service)
Welsh Office, 1979

PULLING, F. H.
Dunlop Holdings Ltd. Interim report of investigation under the Companies Act, 1948, by C. W. M. Ingram and F. H. Pulling
Trade Dept., 1981

PURDOM, D.
Enforcement of Trade Descriptions Act in Scotland, by D. Purdom and E. Walker
Scottish Consumer Council, 1980

PURDY, I.
A regional strategy for sport and recreation. Issues report (with) summary
Eastern Council for Sport and Recreation, 1980

PYPER, R.
Study of certification procedure and field inspection techniques relating to seed potatoes: report of a study tour undertaken in Holland, June 1980
ADAS, 1981

QUENNELL, A. M.
Stratigraphic correlation of Turkey, Iran and Pakistan, by S. M. I. Shah and A. M. Quennell. 2 vols
Overseas Development Administration, 1980

QUESNE, G. Le
see: **LE QUESNE, G.**

QUEST, M.
The Way to Work: new schemes to prepare young people for jobs in the hotel and catering industry
Hotel and Catering Industry Training Board, 1982

QUICK, A. J.
The rotoradial milking parlour. Report of a visit to Holland September 1979
ADAS, 1979

QUICKE, J. G.
Milk production in the European Community: a report by the Agriculture EDC's Livestock Group
NEDO, 1981

RABY, F. J. E.
Framlingham Castle, Suffolk, by F. J. E. Raby and P. K. Baillie Reynolds
DoE, 1980

Thetford Priory, Norfolk
DoE, 1979

RABY, L.
Supervision – now and then. A report of a research study into the role and training of supervisors in the iron and steel industry carried out by the Industrial Training Service. (Research Steering Group)
Iron and Steel Industry Training Board, 1980

RACE, D. G.
The Cherries Group Home: a beginning, by D. G. and D. M. Race
DHSS, 1979

RACE, D. M.
The Cherries Group Home: a beginning, by D. G. and D. M. Race
DHSS, 1979

RADFORD, C. A. Ralegh
Dolbadarn Castle, Gwynedd
Welsh Office, 1980

Grosmont Castle, Gwent
Welsh Office, 1980

Llawhaden Castle, Dyfed
Welsh Office, 1980

Ogmore Castle, Mid Glamorgan
Welsh Office, 1980

The Pillar of Eliseg, Clwyd
Welsh Office, 1980

Restormel Castle
DoE, 1980

Strat Florida Abbey, Dyfed
Welsh Office, 1980

White Castle, Gwent (Official Handbook)
Welsh Office, 1982

RADNOR, Alan
Living in the future
Independent Television Authority, 1981

RAE, D.
Experimental coal-dust explosions in the Buxton full-scale surface gallery, IX - asymmetry in water and coal dust explosions. (Technical Report 6)
Health and Safety Executive, 1980

Experimental coal-dust explosions in the Buxton full-scale surface gallery XII, by D. Rae and L. C. W. West. (Research Paper no. 16)
Health and Safety Executive, 1982

RAINE, Neale
Manufacturing efficiency checklists. (Manufacturing Efficiency Action Team, Printing Machinery SWP). J. Hinde and N. Raine, ch.
NEDO, 1980

RAMPHAL, Shridath
Address to the eighth public relations world congress, London, May 1979. (Commonwealth information)
Commonwealth Secretariat, 1979

Luncheon address to the diplomatic and commonwealth writers' association and the foreign press association, London, 17 July 1979. (Commonwealth Information)
Commonwealth Secretariat, 1979

Reflections on Lusaka. Address, London, September 1979. (Commonwealth Information)
Commonwealth Secretariat, 1979

Speech by the commonwealth secretary-general at the opening session of the commonwealth finance ministers' meeting, Valletta, Malta, September 1979. (Commonwealth Information)
Commonwealth Secretariat, 1979

RAMPTON, Anthony
West Indian children in our schools. Interim report of the committee of inquiry into the education of children from ethnic minority groups. Dept. of Education and Science, 1981
Session 1980–81 Cmnd. 8273

RAMSAY,¾ Malcolm
City-centre crime; the scope for situational prevention. (Research and Planning Unit Paper 10)
Home Office, 1982

RANDELL, J.
Health education in the workplace: a report of a workshop organised and sponsored by the Health Education Council, February 1980, by J. Randell and J. McEwen
Health Education Council, 1980

RANDS, J. G.
Regional European conference (13th) of the international commission on irrigation and drainage. Report
ADAS, 1982

RATCLIFFE, John
Land acquisition and disposal. (SSRC Planning Reviews no. 3)
SSRC, 1982

RAUTA, I.
Extending the electoral register – 2: two surveys of public acceptability, by A. J. Manners and I. Rauta. (Occasional Paper 21)
OPCS, 1981

RAWLING, E.
Local issues and enquiry-based learning. (Curriculum Development: Geography 16–19, Occasional Paper no. 2)
Schools Council, 1981

RAY, C.
Handbook for teacher-librarians. (Commonwealth Education Handbooks)
Commonwealth Secretariat, 1981

RAY, J. W.
Change for the better. How eight companies in the electrical engineering industry took steps to increase their productivity. Productivity Sub-group of the Electrical Engineering EDC.
NEDO, 1980

RAYNER, B. W.
Southern region unusual train services 1979, by B. W. Rayner and J. F. Chapter
Southern Electric Group, 1979

RAYNER, Derek.
Review of adminstrative forms. Report to the Prime Minister
Cabinet Office, 1982

Review of Government statistical services: report to the Prime Minister
Cabinet Office, 1980

Review of statistical services, by Sir Derek Rayner. Report of the study officer (NH Perry) for the Departments of Environment and Transport
Central Statistical Office, 1981

Review of support services in research and development and allied scientific establishments. Report to the Prime Minister
Management and Personnel Office, 1982

A study of road construction units in consultation with Sir D. Rayner. Report to the Minister
DTp, 1980

RAYSON, D. W.
Individual assessment and performance evaluation of UK civil servants. Paper presented to the International Personnel Management Association's 7th international symposium, 1979
Civil Service Dept., 1979

RAZZELL, E. J.
Improving policy analysis in DHSS. (CSC Working Paper no. 19)
Civil Service College, 1980

Open government: an analytical framework. (CSC Working Paper 8)
Civil Service College, 1979

READ, C. N.
Cable systems. A report by the information technology advisory panel working group
Cabinet Office, 1982

READ, W. C. S.
Brucella ovis complement fixation test methods and standardisation procedures: report of a visit to France, 9–12 June 1981, by C. J. Archer and W. C. S. Read
ADAS, 1981

READER, K. M.
The civil service commission 1855–1975, by K. M. Reader. (Civil Service Studies 5)
Civil Service Dept., 1981

REAY, I. M.
Runway capacity and aircraft delays at Gatwick Airport, by I. M. Reay and H. K. Logan. (CAA Paper 81002)
Civil Aviation Authority, 1981

REDMAN, P. L.
Hay drying and Handlingsy's terms. Report on a visit to Sweden, January 1982
ADAS, 1982

Mechanisation for the feeding and treatment of forages. Report of a study tour undertaken in Denmark and Sweden, March 1979
ADAS, 1979

REDWOOD, John
National Enterprise Board; a case for euthanasia, by M. Grylls and J. Redwood
National Enterprise Board, 1980

REED, E. C.
Manual of sewer condition classification. Standing technical committee on sewers and water mains. (Standing Technical Committee Reports no. 24)
National Water Council, 1980

Sewer and water main records. Standing technical committee on sewers and water mains. (Standing Technical Committee Reports no. 25)
National Water Council, 1980

REES, J.
Geographical agenda for a changing world, by B. T. Robson and J. Rees
SSRC, 1982

REES, R. D.
The effects of regional policy on manufacturing investment and capital stock within the UK, by R. D. Rees and R. H. C. Miall. (Government Economic Service Working Paper no. 26)
Industry Dept., 1979

REES, W. A.
International (3rd) theriological congress. Report by W. A. Rees and J. H. Greaves
ADAS, 1982

REEVES, F.
The concept of prejudice: an evaluative review. (Research Unit on Ethnic Relations, Working Papers on Ethnic Relations no. 17)
SSRC, 1982

REID, Margaret I.
Balancing the equation: a study of women and science and technology within F. E., by Shelia M. Stoney and Margaret I. Reid. (Project Report PR10) (Further Education Curriculum Review and Development Unit)
Dept. Education and Science, 1981

Further opportunities in focus; a study of bridging courses for women, by S. M. Stoney and M. I. Reid. Further Education Curriculum Review and Development Unit
Dept. Education and Science, 1980

RENDALL, N. A.
Report of the Marine Fouling Working Party for the director of Petroleum Engineering Division. (OTP4)
DoE, 1980

REX, J.
Unemployment and racial conflict in the inner city, by J. Rex and M. Cross. (Research Unit on Ethnic Relations, Working Papers on Ethnic Relations no. 16)
SSRC, 1982

REYNOLDS, P. K. Baillie
Framlingham Castle, Suffolk, by F. J. E. Raby and P. K. Baillie Reynolds
DoE, 1980

Thornton Abbey, Humberside, by A. Clapham and P. K. B. Reynolds. 2nd ed., 8th pr.
DoE, 1982

RHODES, J. R.
Adult dental health survey Northern Ireland 1979, by J. R. Rhodes and T. H. Haire
DHSS for N.I., 1981

RICH, L. A.
Elements of bookkeeping by L. A. Rich and T. J. Terry. (Small Firms Service)
Industry Dept., 1980

Elements of bookkeeping, by L. A. Rich and T. J. Terry. (Small Firms Service)
Industry Dept., 1981 (reprinted 1982)

RICHARDS, E. G.
Developments towards whole area utilization of softwoods, by E. G. Richards. Prepared for the eleventh Commonwealth Forestry Conference, Trinidad, September 1980. (Forestry Commission, R & D Paper 128)
Forestry Commission, 1980

RICHARDS, E. L.
FMC Corporation, Merek and Co. Inc., and Alginate Industries Ltd. A report on the proposed mergers by the Monopolies and Mergers Commission. July 1979
Session 1979–80 HC 175

Ice cream and water ices. A report on the supply in the UK. Monopolies and Mergers Commission. August 1979
Session 1979–80 Cmnd. 7632

RICHARDSON, C.
Recording system for bovine foetal data, by C. Richardson and G. Morgan. Report of a visit to Veterinary Research Laboratory, Abbotstown Castleknock, Eire, 25–26 March 1982
ADAS, 1982

RICHARDSON, J. J.
Swedish pollution control agencies
SSRC, 1980

RICHARDSON, J. S.
Balvenie Castle, by J. S. Richardson and M. E. Root
Scottish Development Dept., 1980

Dirleton Castle, by J. S. Richardson, amended by C. J. Tabraham
Scottish Development Dept., 1982

Dundrennan Abbey by the late J. S. Richardson, revised by C. J. Tabraham
Scottish Development Dept., 1981

RICHARDSON, J. S. *(continued)*
Elgin cathedral; the cathedral kirk of Moray. History by H. B. Mackintosh, description by J. S. Richardson
Scottish Development Dept., 1980

Huntingtower Castle
Scottish Development Dept., 1982

Tantallon Castle, 3rd ed.
DoE, 1980

RICHARDSON, P.
Money and prices; a simulation study using the Treasury macroeconomic model. (Government Economic Service Working Paper 41)
Treasury, 1981

RICKARD, D. F.
Aspects of agricultural structure, marketing, co-operative systems and fixed equipment. Report of a visit to West Germany, October 1979
ADAS, 1979

RICKARD, P. C.
Early carrot production in the Nantes area of Loir Atlantique, France: report of a study tour undertaken in France, May 1981
ADAS, 1982

RICKWOOD, Pat
The story of access in the Peak District
Peak Park Joint Planning Board, 1982

RIDLEY, W. F.
Leakage control policy and practice. (Standing Technical Committee Reports no. 26). Technical Working Group on Waste of Water
National Water Council, 1980

RIGBY, M.
Friesan heifer rearing. A review of management practice, 1979
ADAS, 1979

RIGGE, Marianne
Building societies and the consumer. A report by M. Rigge and M. Young
National Consumer Council, 1981

RIGOLD, S. E.
Baconsthorpe Castle, Norfolk
DoE, 1981

RILEY, D.
Crime prevention publicity; an assessment, by D. Riley and P. Mayhew. (Research Study no. 63)
Home Office, 1980

RILEY, J. E.
Effects of new animal welfare laws in Switzerland. Report by G. H. Stewart and J. E. Riley
ADAS, 1982

RITCHIE, A.
Competitiveness and manufactured exports; some tests of the Treasury model specification by A. Ritchie and J. Hicklin. (Government Economic Service Working Paper 51)
Treasury, 1981

RITCHIE, Jane
Access to primary health care: an enquiry carried out on behalf of the United Kingdom Health Departments, by J. Ritchie, A. Jacoby, M. Bone. (Social Survey Division SS1102)
OPCS, 1981

RIVETT, B. H. P.
Industrial review: petrochemicals. (Chemicals EDC: Petrochemicals SWP)
NEDO, 1981

Petrochemicals SWP progress report 1980
NEDO, 1980

RIXON, Shelagh
Communication games, by D. Byrne and S. Rixon. (ELT Guide 1)
British Council, 1979

ROBBINS, D.
Loading the law: a study of transmitted deprivation, ethnic minorities and affirmative action, by A. Little and D. Robbins. (Summary)
Commission for Racial Equality, 1982

ROBBINS, S. R. J.
The markets for selected herbaceous essential oils, by S. R. J. Robbins and P. Greenhalgh. (G120)
Tropical Products Institute, 1979

Selected markets for the essential oils of patchouli and vetiver. (Report G167)
Tropical Products Institute, 1982

ROBERTS, D. H.
Proposed new initiatives in computing and computer applications. Report of a SRC panel
Science Re!;search Council, 1979

ROBERTS, F.
A preliminary energy audit of combined heat and power; district heating for a large UK city together with some alternative systems. (ETSU Report no. CR/18)
Energy Technology Support Unit, 1979

ROBERTS, J. E.
Making progress? A special needs document. Further Education Unit
DES, 1982

ROBERTS, John
The commercial sector in leisure. (A Review for the SC/SSRC Joint Panel on Leisure and Recreation Research)
Sports Council, 1979

ROBERTS, K.
Unregistered youth unemployment and outreach careers work: final report, part one: non-registration, by K. Roberts, J. Duggan and M. Noble. (Research Paper no. 31)
Employment Dept., 1981

ROBERTSON, J. S.
Agricultural Engineers Association mission to China, December 1980. Report
ADAS, 1981

Agricultural export mission to Finland, Sweden and Norway, September/October 1980. Report
ADAS, 1980

British narcissus exhibit and technical symposium. Report of a visit to Holland, February 1979, by J. S. Robertson and others
ADAS, 1979

Exhibition of narcissus from Britain, 2nd biennial, at Treslong Centre, Hillegom, Holland, February 1981
ADAS, 1981

The market for British agricultural products in Finland, Sweden and Norway: report of a trade mission organised by the Agricultural Engineers Association
ADAS, 1981

ROBINS, J.
Motor cycle rider training. Report of the advisory committee
DTp, 1979

ROBINS, W. E. C.
Treatment and rehabilitation. Report of the advisory council on the misuse of drugs
DHSS, 1982

ROBINSON, R. E. S.
Solvent abuse and children's hearings: consultative memorandum. (Special Work Services Group)
Scottish Education Department, 1981

ROBINSON, T. W.
Exmoor national park; interpretative plan study. A research report. (CCP 123)
Countryside Commission, 1979

ROBSON, B. T.
Geographical agenda for a changing world, by B. T. Robson and J. Rees
SSRC, 1982

ROE, Alan
Childrens' and adults' units at the Gloucester Centre. A. Roe in association with George Grey and partners. (Mental Health Buildings Evaluation. Report P1)
DHSS, 1980

ROE, S. A.
Health service residential accommodation for severely mentally handicapped people. Architectural and planning consultant: S. A. Roe. (Mental Health Buildings Evaluation Pamphlet 2, 2nd ed.)
DHSS, 1982

ROEBUCK, J. F.
Latest developments at Limburgerhof, BASF station and farm trials in the surrounding area. Report of a visit to West Germany, July-August 1979, by J. F. Roebuck and D. C. Gwynne
ADAS, 1979

ROLL OF IPSDEN, Lord Eric
The tripartite approach to industrial recovery. A guide for financial institutions. Committee for finance for industry
NEDO, 1980

ROLLO, J. M. C.
The CAP and resource flows among EEC member states, by J. M. C. Rollo and K. S. Warwick. (Government Economic Service Working Paper no. 27)
Treasury, 1979

ROOT, Margaret E.
Balvenie Castle, by J. S. Richardson and M. E. Root
Scottish Development Dept., 1980

ROSE, G.
Plascon greenhouse. Report of a visit to Switzerland, by M. Goltz and G. Rose
ADAS, 1980

ROSE, K. S. B.
The coke making industry; energy consumption and conservation in the coke making industry, by P. B. Taylor and K. S. B. Rose. (Energy Audit Series no. 9)
Dept. Energy, 1979

ROSENBROCK, H. H.
Engineers and the work that people do. (Work Research Unit Occasional Paper 21)
Employment Dept., 1981

ROSENBURG, L.
Housing investment strategies for difficult-to-let public sector housing estates, by J. Gilbert and L. Rosenburg
Scottish Office, 1981

ROSS, H. McG.
Character sets and coding. (Guides to Computing Standards no. 9)
National Computing Centre, 1981

Fundamental aspects. (Guides to Computing Standards no. 22.1)
National Computing Centre, 1981

ROSS, J.
Rabbit control methods. Report of a visit to Australia, March-June 1979
ADAS, 1979

ROSTON, B.
Safety. (Guides to Computing Standards no. 12)
National Computing Centre, 1981

ROTHMAN, James
Further development of an income surrogate. Report of a research contract
DoE, 1979

ROTHSCHILD, Nathaniel M. V., 3rd Baron
Enquiry into the Social Science Research Council. May 1982. DES
Session 1981-82 Cmnd. 8554

ROUND, K. M.
Apple juice production. Report of a visit to West Germany and Switzerland, October 1979
ADAS, 1979

ROUTH, D. T.
A developing strategy for the West Midlands. Updating and rolling forward of the regional strategy to 1991. Report of the Joint Monitoring Steering Group. 2 vols.
West Midlands Planning Authorities Conference, 1979

ROWE, D. C. F.
Seed manual for ornamental trees and shrubs, by A. G. Gordon and D. C. F. Rowe. (Bulletin 59)
Forestry Commission, 1982

ROWELL, D. J.
Nursery stock production in the Loire valley: report of a study tour undertaken in France, 6–11 September 1981
ADAS, 1982

ROWELL, W. H. M.
Initiating action learning programmes
MSC, 1980

ROWLAND, R. T.
Northern Ireland Housing Executive contracts. Report of the investigatory commission. July 1979
Session 1979–80 Cmnd. 7586

ROWLANDS, A.
Pasture improvement including the use of herbicides. (Grassland practice no. 9; Booklet 2049)
ADAS, 1980

ROYCE, D. N.
The Queen's awards for export and technology. Report of the 1979 Working Group on Invisible Exports
Industry Dept., 1980

RUDD, G. T.
Fire policy reviewed. Fire Service Research and Training Trust lecture, 1980
Home Office, 1980

Fire caused by vandalism. Report of a Home Office working party
Home Office, 1980

RUNCIE, R., Archbp. of Canterbury
Pastoral (Amendment) Measure. Report of the Ecclesiastical Committee. 1982
Session 1981–82 HC 293, HL 110

RUSSELL, R. D.
Research on grass/clover. Report of a study visit to Eire, October 1980
ADAS, 1980

RYDING, J.
Deriving and testing rate of growth and higher order growth effects in dynamic economic models, by K. D. Patterson and J. Ryding. (Discussion Paper 21)
Bank of England, 1982

SADLER, Peter
The Welsh social accounts, 1968: a labour dimension, by P. Sadler and R. Jarvis
Welsh Council, 1979

ST. JOHN, H. D.
A review of current practice in the design and installation of piles for offshore structures. (Offshore Technology Paper 5)
Energy Dept., 1980

SAINTY, J. C.
Parliamentary functions of the sovereign since 1509. (Memo no. 64)
House of Lords Record Office, 1980

SALMON, Goeffrey
The working office
Design Council, 1979

SALTER, L. S.
Bulk pasteurisation and spawning system for mushroom production. Report of a visit to Holland, February 1979, by J. B. Finney and L. S. Salter
ADAS, 1979

SAMES, T.
Wildlife in towns; a teachers' guide
Nature Conservancy Council, 1982

SAMUEL, M. P.
Planning control to protect agricultural land. Report of a study tour in the Netherlands by E. H. B. Martyn and M. P. Samuel
ADAS, 1982

SAMWELL, Stanley David
Peachey Property Corporation Ltd. Report of investigation under the Companies Act, 1948, by R. I. Kidwell and S. D. Samwell
Trade Dept., 1979

SANDEMAN, Roland Stewart
Marketing farm produce; the challenge for the 80's. Papers presented at a conference at Shepton Mallet, November 1978
Central Council for Agricultural and Horticultural Co-operation, 1980

SANDERS, P. F.
An investigation into the growth of 'sewage fungus' in the lower River Don, Aberdeenshire, 1979–81
Scottish Development Agency, 1982

SANDS, Margaret
Handling classroom groups, by T. Kerry and M. Sands. (DES Teacher Education Project)
Macmillan for DES, 1982

Mixed ability teaching in the early years of the secondary school, by T. Kerry and M. Sands. (DES Teacher Education Project)
Macmillan for DES, 1982

SANGSTER, G. I.
A study of the fish capture process in a bottom trawl by direct observations from a towed underwater vehicle, by J. Main and G. I. Sangster. (Scottish Fisheries Research Report no. 23)
Agriculture and Fisheries for Scotland Dept., 1981

SAUNDERS, A. D.
Bernard Castle, 3rd ed.
DoE, 1982

Lydford Saxon town and castle, 2nd ed.
DoE, 1982

SAUNDERS, Christopher
A six-country comparison of the distribution of industrial earnings in the 1970's, by C. Saunders and D. Marsden. (Background Paper no. 8)
Royal Commission on the Distribution of Income and Wealth, 1979

SAVAGE, M. J.
Report of an exchange year in New Zealand, 1980–1981
ADAS, 1981

SAVILLE, C. H.
Boarding education. Report of a DES/CLEA working group
Dept. Education and Science, 1980

SAVILLE, I. D.
The sterling/dollar rate in the floating rate period: the rate of money, prices and intervention. (Discussion Paper no. 9)
Bank of England, 1980

SAYCE, R. B.
Agriculture and the countryside. Report of a visit to West Germany, March 1979, by R. B. Sayce and M. J. Finnigan
ADAS, 1979

SCARMAN, Leslie George
Brixton disorders, 10–12 April 1981. Report of an inquiry. November 1981
Session 1981–82 Cmnd. 8427

SCHAFFER, H. R.
Children in need of care. The report of an Advisory Panel to the Research Initiatives Board
SSRC, 1980

SCHAFFER, R.
Economies of converting oil to coal
Energy Dept., 1982

SCHOFIELD, W. N.
A review of the literature on methods of assessing the personal and social development of young people. (Assessment of Performance Unit)
DES, 1980

SCOPES, Nigel
Pest and disease control handbook
British Crop Protection Council, 1979

SCOTT, Angus
Social impact of large-scale industrial developments. (North Sea Oil Panel Occasional Paper no. 10)
SSRC, 1982

SCOTT, B. M.
Muscle hypertrophy of genetic origin and its utilization to improve beef production. Report of a visit to France, June 1980, by R. Bradley and B. M. Scott
ADAS, 1980

SCOTT, Sir Bernard
Value of pensions. Report of the inquiry. 1981
Session 1980–81 Cmnd. 8147

SCOTT, Ian
Potential of West Africa and Egypt as direct markets for UK produced fish and fish products. (FERU Occasional Paper no. 3 1980)
White Fish Authority, 1980

Sources of statistics pertaining to the British fishing industry. (FERU Occasional Paper Series no. 3, 1981)
White Fish Authority, 1981

SCOTT, M. A.
Seminar for instructors in horticulture. Report of a visit to Eire, January–February 1979
ADAS, 1979

Symposium on Nutricote: report of a visit to Holland, 21–22 October 1981
ADAS, 1982

SCOTT, M. Fg.
The arguments for and against protectionism. Papers by M. Fg. Scott and W. A. H. Godley. (Papers Presented to the Panel of Academic Consultants no. 10)
Bank of England, 1980

SCOTT, P. R. D.
Introducing data communications standards
National Computing Centre, 1979

Modems in data communications
National Computing Centre, 1980

SCOULLAR, Brian
Farmers' decision-making processes. (Extension Development Unit Report no. 14)
Agricultural Development and Advisory Service, 1979

SCRUTON, C.
Introduction to wind effects on structures. (Engineering Design Guide no. 40)
Design Council, 1981

SCUDAMORE, K. A.
Visit to Agriculture Canada Research Institute, June 1980
ADAS, 1980

SCURFIELD, J. A.
Waste food processing. Report of a study tour undertaken in Denmark, June 1980
ADAS, 1980

SEABRIGHT, Diana
Fire and care; an enquiry into fire precautions in residential homes
Personal Social Services Council, 1979

SEAWARD, Dennis R.
Sea area atlas of the marine molluscs of Britain and Ireland
Nature Conservancy Council, 1982

SEDDON, J. W.
The application of a behavioural regime to disturbed young offenders, by J. E. Cullen and J. W. Seddon. (DPS Report Series I, no. 15)
Home Office, 1980

SEERS, Dudley
The rehabilitation of the economy of Uganda; a report by a Commonwealth team of experts. 2 volumes
Commonwealth Secretariat, 1979

SEMBACH, K. J.
Contemporary furniture, an international review of modern furniture, 1950 to the present
Design Council, 1982

SEMPLE, A. G.
Design costs. Report of the working group
Property Services Agency, 1982

SENKER, P.
Designing the future. The implications of CAD interactive graphics for employment and skills in the British engineering industry, by E. Arnold and P. Senker (Occasional Paper OP/9)
Engineering Industry Training Board, 1982

New technology and employment, by E. Braun and P. Senker
MSC, 1982

SERPELL, David
Ordnance survey review committee report, July 1979
Ordnance Survey, 1979

SERVICE, M. J.
Occupational safety of fishermen. Report of the working group
Trade Dept., 1979

SEXTON, B.
Technical supplement on the analysis of APU monitoring in mathematics, by B. Sexton and M. Cresswell. (APU (Stat) (81) 1)
DES, 1981

SEYMOUR, Paul R.
Invertebrates of economic importance in Britain: common and scientific names. 3rd ed.
ADAS, 1979

SHACKLETON, Lord Edward Arthur Alexander
Falkland Islands economic study, 1982
Session 1981–82 Cmnd. 8653

SHAH, S. H. Ibrahim
Stratigraphic correlation of Turkey, Iran and Pakistan, by S. M. I. Shah and A. M. Quennell. 2 vols.
Overseas Development Administration, 1980

SHANG, A.
Television in a multi-racial society. A research report by M. Anwar and A. Shang
Commission for Racial Equality, 1982

SHANKS, N. J.
Police community involvement
Scottish Office, 1981

SHAPIRO, D. M.
Future development of libraries: the organisational and policy framework. A report by the Library Advisory Council
DES, 1979

SHARP R. J. A.
Rents assessment panel procedures. Report of the working party
DOE, 1981

SHEARD, G. F.
Greenhouse crop production in the USSR with particular reference to the use of reject heat. Report of a visit to the USSR under the ASCAR agreement, March 1978, by G. F. Sheard and others
ADAS, 1978

SHELDON, H. N.
Community councils in the Strathclyde region. 1976–79, by D. F. Cosgrove and H. N. Sheldon. (Central Research Unit)
Scottish Office, 1980

SHEPHERD, Lord Malcolm Newington, *2nd Baron*
Civil service pay research unit board report on the special reference to the board concerning civil service scientists
Civil Service Department, 1980

SHERLOCK, D.
North Leigh Roman villa, Oxfordshire, by D. R. Wilson and D. Sherlock
DoE, 1980

SHIELLS, E.
Rayner scrutiny: DHSS activities in support of health care exports: report by scrutiny team. (C. Graham and E. Shiells)
DHSS, 1980

SHIPWAY, M. R.
Unrefrigerated (high temperature) storage of onions. Report of a visit to Brazil, October 1979
ADAS, 1979

SHOOTER, Philip
Birds: where to watch them in the Peak National Park, rev. ed., by P. Shooter and S. Anthony
Peak National Park, 1979

SHOOTER, R. A.
The 1978 Birmingham smallpox occurrence. Report of the investigation into the cause, July 1980
Session 1979–80 HC 668

SIDAWAY, Janet
The scope for castings exports: a report on the experience of twelve UK foundries. (Foundries EDC)
NEDO, 1980

SIDDONS, Suzy
Britain: four countries, one kingdom, by J. Ellenby and S. Siddons
British Tourist Authority, 1980

SILLARS, Angus
Design education at secondary level in Scotland. A working party report
Design Council, 1981

SILLITOE, K.
Ethnic origins 4: an experiment in the use of a direct question about ethnicity, for the census. (Occasional Paper 24)
OPCS, 1981

SIMMINS, P. H.
Pig production in Côtes du Nord. Report of a visit
ADAS, 1982

SIMONS, G. L.
Computers in engineering and manufacture
National Computing Centre, 1982

Robots in industry
National Computing Centre, 1980

Women in computing
National Computing Centre, 1981

SIMPSON, Anne Turner
Historic Annan: the archaeological implications of development. (Scottish Burgh Survey)
Scottish Development Dept., 1981

Historic Auchtermuchty: the archaeological implications of development, by A. T. Simpson and S. Stevenson. (Scottish Burgh Survey)
Scottish Development Dept., 1981

Historic Crail: the archaeological implications of development, by A. T. Simpson and S. Stevenson. (Scottish Burgh Survey)
Scottish Development Dept., 1981

Historic Cupar: the archaeological implications of development, by A. T. Simpson and S. Stevenson. (Scottish Burgh Survey)
Scottish Development Dept., 1981

Historic Dunbar: the archaeological implications of development, (Scottish Burgh Survey)
Scottish Development Dept., 1981

Historic Duns: the archaeological implications of development, by A. T. Simpson and S. Stevenson. (Scottish Burgh Survey)
Scottish Development Dept., 1981

Historic Forres: the archaeological implications of development, by A. T. Simpson and S. Stevenson. (Scottish Burgh Survey)
Scottish Development Department, 1982

Historic Hawick: the archaeological implications of development, by A. T. Simpson and S. Stevenson. (Scottish Burgh Survey)
Scottish Development Dept., 1980

Historic Irvine: the archaeological implications of development, by A. T. Simpson and S. Stevenson. (Scottish Burgh Survey)
Scottish Development Dept., 1980

Historic Kelso: the archaeological implications of development, by A. T. Simpson and S. Stevenson. (Scottish Burgh Survey)
Scottish Development Dept., 1980

Historic Kilmarnock: the archaeological implications of development, by A. T. Simpson and S. Stevenson. (Scottish Burgh Survey)
Scottish Development Dept., 1981

Historic Kilwinning: the archaeological implications of development, by A. T. Simpson and S. Stevenson. (Scottish Burgh Survey)
Scottish development Dept., 1981

Historic Kinghorn: the archaeological implications of development, by A. T. Simpson and S. Stevenson. (Scottish Burgh Survey)
Scottish Development Dept., 1981

Historic Lanark: the archaeological implications of development, by A. T. Simpson and S. Stevenson. (Scottish Burgh Survey)
Scottish Development Dept., 1981

Historic Lauder: the archaeological implications of development, by A. T. Simpson and S. Stevenson. (Scottish Burgh Survey)
Scottish Development Dept., 1980

Historic Linlithgow: the archaeological implications of development, by A. T. Simpson and S. Stevenson. (Scottish Burgh Survey)
Scottish Development Dept., 1981

Historic Lochmaben: the archaeological implications of development, by A. T. Simpson and S. Stevenson. (Scottish Burgh Survey)
Scottish Development Dept., 1980

Historic North Berwick: the archaeological implications of development. (Scottish Burgh Survey)
Scottish Development Dept., 1981

Historic Perth: the archaeological implications of development, by A. T. Simpson and S. Stevenson. (Scottish Burgh Survey)
Scottish Development Dept., 1982

Historic Pittenweem: the archaeological implications of development, by A. T. Simpson and S. Stevenson. (Scottish Burgh Survey)
Scottish Development Dept., 1981

Historic St Andrews: the archaeological implications of development, by A. T. Simpson and S. Stevenson. (Scottish Burgh Survey)
Scottish Development Dept., 1982

Historic Selkirk: the archaeological implications of development, by A. T. Simpson and S. Stevenson. (Scottish Burgh Survey)
Scottish Development Dept., 1980

Historic Wigtown: the archaeological implications of development. (Scottish Burgh Survey)
Scottish Development Dept., 1981

SIMPSON, Alan
I'll never forget what's his name. A popular guide to the Scarman report
Commission for Racial Equality, 1982

SIMPSON, J. V.
The cost of living in Northern Ireland. A report prepared by C. W. Jefferson and J. V. Simpson
Northern Ireland Consumer Council, 1980

SIMPSON, R.
Tourist information and countryside management. Report of a study
Peak National Park Study Centre, 1979

SIMPSON, Robin
Access to primary care. (Research Paper no. 6)
Royal Commission on the National Health Service, 1979

SIMPSON, W.
Asbestos: final report of the advisory committee. 2 vols.
Health and Safety Commission, 1979

SIMPSON, W. Douglas
Brough Castle, 2nd ed.
DoE, 1982

Craigmillar Castle, 2nd ed.
Scottish Development Office, 1980

Dunstaffnage Castle
Scottish Development Dept., 1981

Edzell Castle
Scottish Development Dept., 1982

Hermitage Castle
Scottish Development Dept., 1982

SIMS, T. V.
Carnation study group visit to Holland, October 1981. Report. (FR6710)
ADAS, 1982

International congress of soil-less culture, 5th. Report of a visit to Holland, May 1980
ADAS, 1980

Protective horticulture. Report of a visit to Japan, March 1979
ADAS, 1979

SINGER, A. E.
Electronic Computers SWP. Progress report, 1979
NEDO, 1979

SINGH, R.
Minorities in the market place; a study of south Asian and west Indian shoppers in Bradford, by R. Singh and S. Green
National Consumer Council, 1982

SISSON, D. G.
Symposium on managerial and economic aspects of large livestock holdings, and technical, economic and sanitary aspects of buildings and equipment. Report of a visit to Spain, October 1981, by W. Watson and D. Sisson
ADAS, 1982

Examination of legislative framework and quarrying techniques affecting the French sand and gravel industry. Report of a study tour undertaken in France, June 1979
ADAS, 1979

SLIMMINGS, W. K. M.
Review Board for Government Contracts report on the third general review of the profit formula for non-competitive government contracts
Treasury, 1980

SLOANE, P. J.
Earnings gap between men and women in Britain. Joint EOC/SSRC Panel on Equal Opportunities Research
SSRC, 1981

SMALL, C. J.
New international economic order. Report on the study course held July 1978
Commonwealth Institute, 1979

SMART, Ian
Multinational arrangements for the nuclear fuel cycle. (Energy Paper no. 43)
Energy Dept., 1980

SMITH OF MARLOW, Lord Rodney
The removal of cadaveric organs for transplantation; a code of practice drawn up by a working party
DHSS, 1979

SMITH. Alan
Selected markets for chillies and paprika. (G155)
Tropical Products Institute, 1982

Selected markets for turmeric, coriander seed, cumin seed, fenugreek seed and curry powder. (Report G165)
Tropical Products Institute, 1982

SMITH, B. R.
ISHS international symposium on 'More profitable use of energy in protected cultivation', Dublin, Eire, September 1980. Report
ADAS, 1981

Utilisation of reject heat in horticulture. Report of a visit to Romania, by B. R. Smith and G. D. Drakes, May 1979
ADAS, 1979

SMITH, Celia
New to Britain: a study of some new developments in tourist attraction
British Tourist Authority, 1980

SMITH, David
Life-sentence prisoners. (Research Study no. 51)
Home Office, 1979

SMITH, David J.
Education, training and careers of professional engineers, by R. Berthoud and D. J. Smith
Industry Dept., 1980

SMITH, Eve
Taxonomy in Britain. Report by the Review Group of the Advisory Board for the Research Councils
Dept. Education and Science, 1979

SMITH, G.
Patterns of representation of the parties in unfair dismissal cases: a review of the evidence, by W. R. Hawes and G. Smith. (Research Paper no. 22)
Employment Dept., 1981

SMITH, I. G. N.
Disease control and welfare of farm animals in markets and in transit. Report of a visit to France
ADAS, 1982

SMITH, J.
Symposium on economic and technological aspects of sugar beet production. Report of a visit to USSR, September 1979, by J. B. Finney and J. Smith
ADAS, 1979

SMITH, J. Beverley
Bronllys Castle, Powys
Welsh Office, 1981

SMITH, J. C. C.
Assessing target allocations within the Thames regions. Report of a joint working group of the Thames regional health authorities
DHSS, 1979

SMITH, J. R.
Protected vegetable cropping. Report of a visit to Holland, May 1979, by C. A. Garside and J. R. Smith
ADAS, 1979

SMITH, N. B.
Wool Textile EDC. Progress report 1980
NEDO, 1980

Wool Textile EDC. Progress report 1981
NEDO, 1981

SMITH, Paul
Pig production: report of a visit to Federal Republic of
Germany, June 1981, by G. Aitken and P. Smith
ADAS, 1981

Production, handling and feeding of fish silage to pigs.
Report of a study tour undertaken in Denmark, September
1980
ADAS, 1980

SMITH, R. L.
Progress towards universal primary education. A
commonwealth survey
Commonwealth Secretariat, 1979

SMITH, R. M.
Tenement rehabilitation to provide sheltered housing; a
case study and general perspective
National Building Agency, 1980

SMITH, R. O.
Forest fire fighting with foam, by M. J. R. Ingoldby and
R. O. Smith. (Leaflet no. 80)
Forestry Commission, 1982

SMITH, Richard
Introducing new technology into the office. (Work
Research Unit Occasional Paper 20)
Employment Dept., 1981

SMITH, Robert
Impacts of telecommunications on planning and transport.
(Research Report no. 24)
DoE, 1979

SMOUT, J. K.
Energy from waste. Report of the Waste as Fuel Working
Party
Energy Dept., 1979

SNELL, M. W.
Equal pay and opportunities: a study of the implement-
ation and effects of the Equal Pay and Sex Discrimination
Acts in 26 organizations, by M. W. Snell, P. Glucklich and
M. Povall. (Research Paper no. 20)
Employment Dept., 1981

SNOW, Ruth
Home and family 8–13: handbook for group leaders.
(Schools Council Project: Home Economics in the Middle
Years)
Schools Council, 1979

SOFTLEY, Paul
Fine enforcement; an evaluation of the practices of indivi-
dual courts, by P. Softley and D. Moxon (Research and
Planning Unit Paper 12)
Home Office, 1982

An observational study in four police stations. (Research
Study no. 4)
Royal Commission on Criminal Procedure, 1980

Police interrogation: an observational study in four police
stations. (Research Study no. 61)
Home Office, 1980

SOJKA, W. J.
Tour of veterinary establishments. Report of a visit to
Mexico, April/May 1979
ADAS, 1979

SOUTHGATE, B. J.
International symposium on the ecology of bruchids (seed
beetles) attacking legume (pulses). Report of a visit to
France, April 1980
ADAS, 1980

Visit to an INRA laboratory to study methods developed
for acoustic detection of insects in grain: report of a visit
to France, 20–23 July 1981
ADAS, 1982

SOUTHGATE, Peter
Ethnic minorities, crime and policing; a survey of the
experiences of West Indians and whites. (Research Study
no. 70)
Home Office, 1981

Police probationer training in race relations. (Research and
Planning Unit Paper 8)
Home Office, 1982

Public disorder; a review of research and a study in one
inner city area. (Research Study no. 72)
Home Office, 1982

SOUTHGATE, Vera
Extending beginning reading, by V. Southgate, H. Arnold
and S. Johnson. (Schools Council Project)
Schools Council, 1981

SPACKMAN, D.
Aspects of poultry production. ADAS, study tour
programme, 1980/81, by B. Hodgetts and D. Spackman
ADAS, 1980

SPARKE, Penny
Ettore Sottsass, Jnr.
Design Council, 1982

SPEAK, M
Male midwives; a report of two studies, by M. Speak and
J. Aitken-Swan
DHSS, 1982

SPEAKE, Barbara
Young persons' work preparation courses – a systematic
evaluation, by Barbara Speake and Edward Whelan
Employment Service Agency, 1979

SPEDDING, A.
Results for cereal beef, calf rearing and maize silage beef
in 1981. (Beef Improvement Services Data Sheet 82/3)
Meat and Livestock Commission, 1982

SPEED, K.
Royal dockyards; a framework for the future. Consultative
document on the dockyard study. 2 vols.
Defence Min., 1980

SPELLERBERG, I. F.
Reptiles and amphibians in woodlands. (Forest Record
123)
Forestry Commission, 1982

SPERRING, B. A.
TRAMS (Transport Referencing and Mapping System),
by K. Perrett and B. A. Sperring. (Highway Engineering
Computer Branch)
DTp, 1980

SPICER, J. S.
Property information systems for government. The report
of the national gazetteer pilot study, by J. S. Spicer and
others. (Research Report 30)
DoE, 1980

SPINKS, A.
Biotechnology. Report of a joint working party
Cabinet Office, 1980

SPOKES, A. H.
Comments on 'a happier old age', by the PSSC's policy group on the elderly
Personal Social Services Council, 1979

SQUIRES, Tony
Computer security; the personnel aspect
National Computing Centre, 1980

STADEN, Frances M.
The impact of the mobility allowance; an evaluative study, by K. R. Cooke and F. M. Staden. (Research Report no. 7)
DHSS, 1981

STAMP, R. A. G.
An assessment of the capacity of the Daventry Sectors at the London air traffic control centre, summer 1978. (CAA Paper 79022)
Civil Aviation Authority, 1979

The magnitude and causes of departure delays at London Heathrow Airport, summer 1978, by R. A. G. Stamp and A. E. Drew. (CAA Paper 80006)
Civil Aviation Authority, 1980

STAMPER, P.
Interim report on the 32nd session of the Wharron Research Project, North Yorkshire, 4–24 July 1981. (Medieval Village Research Group)
DoE, 1981

STANIFORTH, A. R.
Straw utilisation. Report on a visit to Belgium, France and Spain, August 1980
ADAS, 1981

STANSFIELD, G.
Experimental work on 1) trenched v trenchless drainage, 2) evaluation of filters, 3) benefits of drainage: report of a study tour undertaken in Denmark, 8–15 August 1981
ADAS, 1982

STANTON, Chris
Research in noise and vibration. A selection of short articles illustrating how basic research can be used to solve specific industrial problems by applying the latest scientific techniques, prepared by Harry Challis and Chris Stanton
Science Research Council, 1979

Research in tribology and bearings, by C. Stanton and H. Challis
Science Research Council, 1980

STAPLETON, R. R.
Intensive apple growing in south west Holland. Report of a visit to Holland, April 1979, by R. R. Stapleton and J. Partis
ADAS, 1979

STARES, Rodney
Ethnic minorities; their involvement in MSC special programmes. (Special Programmes Research and Development Series no. 6)
MSC, 1982

STARR, J. R.
International biometeorological congress. Report of a visit to Israel, September 1979
ADAS, 1979

STEEL, D. I. A.
Marketing of fish and fishery products in Europe, 4: France. (Fishery Economics Research Unit, Occasional Paper 1980/2)
White Fish Authority, 1980

North Sea oil and British fishing; some lines of approach. (Occasional Paper 1981/1)
White Fish Authority, 1981

STEELE, J. R.
The need for a third London airport. Report of the Advisory Committee on Airports Policy
Trade Dept., 1979

STEER, David
Uncovering crime; the police role. (Research Study no. 7)
Royal Commission on Criminal Procedure, 1980

STEER, P. A. T.
Mechanical harvesting of strawberries. Report of a study tour undertaken in USA, 1979 series
ADAS, 1979

STEPHENS, B.
A new bias. A report on the future of provision for bowls
Sports Council, 1982

STERLING, R. S.
Structure and management of health and personal social services in Northern Ireland. Report of the advisory group
DHSS for N.I., 1981

STEVENS, A. J.
Australian veterinary association conference. Report of a visit to Australia, May 1979
ADAS, 1979

Symposium on veterinary epidemiology and economics. Report of a visit to Australia, May 1979, by A. J. Stevens and G. Davies
ADAS, 1979

STEVENS, C. P.
Watercress growing areas of France. Report of a visit to France, September 1979
ADAS, 1979

STEVENS, D. S.
Open-cast coal restoration: report of a visit to the USA, 12–27 June 1980, by D. S. Stevens and R. J. W. Dight
ADAS, 1981

STEVENS, F. R. W.
Establishment of trees on regraded colliery spoil heaps: a review of problems and practice, by J. Jobling and F. R. W. Stevens. (Occasional Paper no. 7)
Forestry Commission, 1980

STEVENS, Philip
Abstracts of race relations research, ed. by G. Mair and P. Stevens (Research and Planning Unit Paper, 7)
Home Office, 1982

Race, crime and arrests, by P. Stevens and C. F. Willis. (Research Study no. 58)
Home Office, 1979

STEVENSON, Sylvia
Historic Annan: the archaeological implications of development. (Scottish Burgh Survey)
Scottish Development Dept., 1981

Historic Auchtermuchty: the archaeological implications of development by A. T. Simpson and S. Stevenson. (Scottish Burgh Survey)
Scottish Development Department, 1981

Historic Crail: the archaeological implications of development, by A. T. Simpson and S. Stevenson. (Scottish Burgh Survey)
Scottish Development Dept., 1981

Historic Cupar: the archaeological implications of development, by A. T. Simpson and S. Stevenson. (Scottish Burgh Survey)
Scottish Development Dept., 1981

Historic Dunbar: the archaeological implications of development (Scottish Burgh Survey)
Scottish Development Dept., 1981

STEVENSON, Sylvia *(continued)*
Historic Duns: the archaeological implications of development, by A. T. Simpson and S. Stevenson. (Scottish Burgh Survey)
Scottish Development Dept., 1981

Historic Forres: the archaeological implications of development, by A. T. Simpson and S. Stevenson (Scottish Burgh Survey)
Scottish Development Department, 1982

Historic Hawick: the archaeological implications of development, by A. T. Simpson and S. Stevenson. (Scottish Burgh Survey)
Scottish Development Dept., 1980

Historic Irvine: the archaeological implications of development, by A. T. Simpson and S. Stevenson. (Scottish Burgh Survey)
Scottish Development Dept., 1980

Historic Kelso: the archaeological implications of development, by A. T. Simpson and S. Stevenson. (Scottish Burgh Survey)
Scottish Development Dept., 1980

Historic Kilmarnock: the archaeological implications of development, by A. T. Simpson and S. Stevenson. (Scottish Burgh Survey)
Scottish Development Dept., 1981

Historic Kilwinning: the archaeological implications of development, by A. T. Simpson and S. Stevenson. (Scottish Burgh Survey)
Scottish Development Dept., 1981

Historic Kinghorn: the archaeological implications of development, by A. T. Simpson and S. Stevenson. (Scottish Burgh Survey)
Scottish Development Dept., 1981

Historic Lanark: the archaeological implications of development, by A. T. Simpson and S. Stevenson. (Scottish Burgh Survey)
Scottish Development Dept., 1981

Historic Lauder: the archaeological implications of development, by A. T. Simpson and S. Stevenson. (Scottish Burgh Survey)
Scottish Development Dept., 1980

Historic Linlithgow: the archaeological implications of development, by A. T. Simpson and S. Stevenson. (Scottish Burgh Survey)
Scottish Development Dept., 1981

Historic Lochmaben: the archaeological implications of development, by A. T. Simpson and S. Stevenson. (Scottish Burgh Survey)
Scottish Development Dept., 1980

Historic North Berwick: the archaeological implications of development. (Scottish Burgh Survey)
Scottish Development Dept., 1981

Historic Perth: the archaeological implications of development, by A. T. Simpson and S. Stevenson. (Scottish Burgh Survey)
Scottish Development Department, 1982

Historic Pittenweem: the archaeological implications of development, by A. T. Simpson and S. Stevenson. (Scottish Burgh Survey)
Scottish Development Dept., 1981

Historic St Andrews: the archaeological implications of development, by A. T. Simpson and S. Stevenson. (Scottish Burgh Survey)
Scottish Development Dept., 1981

Historic Selkirk: the archaeological implications of development, by A. T. Simpson and S. Stevenson. (Scottish Burgh Survey)
Scottish Development Dept., 1980

Historic Wigtown: the archaeological implications of development. (Scottish Burgh Survey)
Scottish Development Dept., 1981

STEWART, Lord Ewan George Francis
Motorist and fixed penalties. 1st report by the committee on alternatives to prosecution. Scottish Home and Health Dept.
Session 1979/80 Cmnd. 8027

STEWART, Averil M.
Study of occupational therapy teaching resources in the United Kingdom
Occupational Therapists Board, 1979

STEWART, Sir Frederick
Advisory board for the research councils. 3rd report. 1976–78. February 1979
Session 1978–79 Cmnd. 7467

STEWART, G. H.
Effects of new animal welfare laws in Switzerland. Report by G. H. Stewart and J. E. Riley
ADAS, 1982

STOAKLEY, J. T.
Pine Beauty Moth. (Forest Record 120)
Forestry Commission, 1979

STODART, Anthony
Local government in Scotland. Report of the committee of inquiry
Scottish Office, 1981

STOKER, R. B.
Geographical stability of a typical trip generation model, by C. P. Hayfield and R. B. Stoker. (LTR Working Paper 11)
Transport Dept., 1979

STOKES, Edith M.
Providing for movement and dance; activities and facilities in the Bedford area, by E. M. Stokes and S. Glyptis. (Research Working Papers 16)
Sports Council, 1979

STONE, P. J.
An investigation of Romanov and Charollaise sheep. Report of a study tour, June 1979
ADAS, 1979

Sheep veterinary society. Report of a visit to France, May/June 1979, by P. J. Stone and others
ADAS, 1979

STONES, E.
The House of Commons: general information. (Education Sheets 4)
House of Commons, 1982

Parliament and government. (Education Sheets 1)
House of Commons, 1982

STONEY, Sheila M.
Balancing the equation: a study of women and science and technology within FE, by Sheila M. Stoney and Margaret I. Reid. (Further Education Curriculum Review and Development Unit Project Report PR10)
Dept. Education and Science, 1982

Further opportunities in focus: a study of bridging courses for women, by S. M. Stoney and M. I. Reid. Further Education Curriculum Review and Development Unit
Dept. Education and Science, 1980

STOTESBURY, H. W.
Marriage matters. A consultative document by the Working Party on Marriage Guidance
Home Office, 1979

STOUT, H. P.
Hovercraft noise. Report by a Working Group of the Noise Advisory Council
DoE, 1980

STRANGE, E. S.
An introduction to commercial fishing gear and methods used in Scotland. (Scottish Fisheries Information Pamphlet no. 1, 1981; 2nd edn., rev.)
Agriculture and Fisheries for Scotland Dept., 1982

STRATHCONA and MOUNT ROYAL, Lord Donald Euan Palmer Howard, *4th Baron*
Ministry of Defence research and development establishment; consultative document. Report of the steering group
Defence Min., 1980

STREETEN, B. R.
Storm surge barrier in the eastern Scheldt. Report of a visit to Holland, May 1980
ADAS, 1980

STRINGER, Peter
Assessment of mobilising times in fire brigade control rooms, by P. Stringer and J. Warren. (Scientific Advisory Branch Technical Memorandum 4/80)
Home Office, 1980

Tape-slide for public participation in planning, by P. Stringer and D. Uzzell
DoE, 1980

STROUTS, R. G.
Phytophthora diseases of trees and shrubs. (Arboriculture Leaflet 8)
DoE, 1981

STRUTT, Nigel
Water for agriculture: future needs
Advisory Council for Agriculture and Horticulture in E & W, 1980

STUART-SMITH, Murray
Grays Building Society. Report of investigation under the Building Societies Act, 1962, by I. H. Davison and M. Stuart-Smith. May 1979
Session 1979–80 Cmnd. 7557

STUBBS, Alan
The conservation of snails, slugs and freshwater mussels, by M. Kerney and A. Stubbs
Nature Conservancy Council, 1980

STURTRIDGE, Gill
Simulations, by D. Herbert and G. Sturtridge. (ELT Guide 2)
British Council, 1979

SUGDEN, T. M.
Some aspects of safety in pressurised water reactors. Advisory Committee on the Safety of Nuclear Installations
Health and Safety Executive, 1982

SUMMERS, C. F.
The scientific background to seal stock management in Great Britain. (Publications Series C no. 21)
Natural Environment Research Council, 1979

SURTEES. H.
Materials handling: packing for profit. A practical guide to load utilisation. Committee for Materials Handling Industry Dept., 1979

SUTCLIFFE, F.
Guide book for the training of slingers
Foundry Industry Training Committee, 1979

SUTCLIFFE, P. J.
Introduction to fish handling and processing, by I. J. Clucas and P. J. Sutcliffe. (G143)
Tropical Products Institute, 1981

SUTTON, S. W.
'So you want to farm?' M. J. Field and S. W. Sutton. (Socio-economics Paper no. 12; booklet no. 2012)
ADAS, 1979

SWALES, Terry
Record of personal achievement, an independent evaluation of the Swindon RPA scheme. (Pamphlet 16)
Schools Council, 1979

SWAN, A.
The care and conservation of photographic material
Crafts Council, 1981

SWANNACK, K. P.
Acid milk feeding to calves. Report of a visit to Holland, August 1979
ADAS, 1979

Calf transport, veal production and manufacture of calf milk replacer (visit to Normandie veau and union laitiers Normande). Report of a visit to France, October 1980
ADAS, 1980

SWATMAN, Mary
A study of aspects of co-operation in Dutch potato marketing. (James E. Rennie Awards Report no. 8)
Potato Marketing Board, 1980

SWEETMAN, H.
North Atlantic MNPS airspace operations manual, ed. by H. Sweetman and L. Lee
Civil Aviation Authority, 1979

SWINNERTON-DYER, Peter
Post graduate education, report of the working party.
Advisory Board for the Research Councils, 1982
Session 1981–82 Cmnd. 8537

SYLVESTER-BRADLEY, R.
Physiology of legumes and their cultivation in South America: report of a visit to Peru, Colombia and Brazil, 12 April–6 May 1980
ADAS, 1981

Symposium on aspects and prospects of plant growth regulations, Wageningen, Holland, November 1980 and discussion in nitrate reductase activity in wheat crops, Belgium, November 1980
ADAS, 1980

SYLVESTER-EVANS, Alun
Urban renaissance; a better life in towns
DoE, 1980

SYMONS G. D.
Review of geotechnical research programme: part 1 – gravity structures, for the Offshore Energy Technology Board. (OTP 10)
Energy Dept., 1982

TABONY, R. C.
Quintiles of the dates of return to, and loss of, field capacity and of hydrologically effective precipitation over England and Wales. (Hydrological Memorandum 42)
Meterological Office, 1979

TABRAHAM, C. J.
Caerlaverock Castle, by B. H. St. J. O'Neil, revised by C. J. Tabraham
Scottish Development Dept., 1982

Dirleton Castle, by J. S. Richardson, amended by C. J. Tabraham
Scottish Development Dept., 1982

Dundrennan Abbey, by the late J. S. Richardson, revised by C. J. Tabraham
Scottish Development Dept., 1981

TAIT, Geoff
Golden Gatwick: 50 years of aviation, by John King and Geoff Tait
British Airports Authority, 1980

TALBOT, Margaret
Women and leisure, a state of the art review
Sports Council, 1979

TALENT, C. J. W.
Protected vegetable production. Report of a visit to Holland, May 1980 , by V. H. Crindle and C. J. W. Talent
ADAS, 1980

TALMAN, A. J.
Simple flow meters and watertable meters for field experiments. (Field Drainage Experimental Unit Technical Report 79/1)
ADAS, 1980

TANBURN, Jennifer
Food distribution: its impact on marketing in the '80s
Central Council for Agricultural and Horticultural Co-operation, 1981

TANFIELD, J.
By-election results since the general election of May 1979, by J. Tanfield and R. Clements. (Research Note no. 79)
House of Commons, 1982

Statistical digest of by-election results since the general election of May 1979, by J. Tanfield and R. Clements. (Factsheet no. 16)
House of Commons, 1982

TARLING, Roger
Sentencing practice in magistrates' courts. (Research Study no. 56)
Home Office, 1979

Taking offenders out of circulation, by S. Brody and R. Tarling. (Research Study no. 64)
Home Office, 1980

TASKER, M. L.
Seabird movement at coastal sites around Great Britain and Ireland 1978–1980, by P. H. Jones and M. L. Tasker
Nature Conservancy Council, 1982

TATHAM, P. B.
Production and marketing of dry bulb onions. Report of a study tour undertaken in Spain, June 1979
ADAS, 1979

TATTON-BROWN, Charlotte
Impact of employment legislation on small firms, by R. Clifton and C. Tatton-Brown. (Research Paper no. 6)
Employment Dept., 1979

TAYLOR, A. J.
Beaumaris Castle
Welsh Office, 1980

Conway Castle and town walls. 9th impr.
DoE, 1979

Harlech Castle. (Official handbook)
DoE, 1980

Jewel Tower, Westminster, 2nd ed.
DoE, 1982

TAYLOR, C. T.
'Real' national saving and its sectoral composition, by C. T. Taylor and A. R. Threadgold. (Discussion Paper no. 6)
Bank of England, 1979

TAYLOR, D.
Environmental studies in the primary school; the development policy. Committee on Primary Education
Consultative Committee on the Curriculum, 1981

TAYLOR, J. A.
Recreation; weather and climate; state of the art review
Sports Council and SSRC, 1979

TAYLOR, K.
Systems of dairy farming, 1: The specialist grassland farm (Farm Management Service Report no. 32)
Milk Marketing Board, 1982

TAYLOR, K. C.
A seminar on food hygiene. Report of a visit to France, June 1979
ADAS, 1979

TAYLOR, Lynda King
Notes on job enrichment and motivation. (Work Research Unit Paper no. 9)
Employment Dept., 1979

TAYLOR, N. C.
Evaluation of electromagnetic flow guage at Spondon. Report
Water Data Unit, 1980

TAYLOR, P. B.
The coke making industry; energy consumption and conservation in the coke making industry, by P. B. Taylor and K. S. B. Rose. (Energy Audit Series no. 9)
Energy Dept., 1979

The iron and steel industry: energy consumption and conservation in the iron and steel industry: a report prepared for the DE. (Energy Audit Series no. 16)
Energy Dept., 1982

TEMPLEMAN, Margaret
Competition policy and the Scottish air traveller
Scottish Consumer Council, 1979

TERRY, T. J.
Elements of bookkeeping, by L. A. Rich and T. J. Terry. (Small Firms Service)
Industry Dept., 1980

Elements of bookkeeping, by L. A. Rich and T. J. Terry. (Small Firms Service)
Industry Dept., 1981 (repr., 1982)

Management accounting, by T. J. Terry. (Small Firms Service Series)
Industry Dept., 1980

TETTENBORN, R. G.
Welsh Rate Support Grant Joint Working Party. Report of the Sub-group on Education
Welsh Office, 1980

THOMAS, A. I.
Evaluation of the MSC Training Services Divisions' essay in management development through action learning, by A. I. Thomas and R. J. Kitching. (Training Services Division Report no. 15)
MSC, 1979

Research associated with human learning – MSC activities, by A. Thomas. (Training Services Division Report no. DTP 26)
MSC, 1980

THOMAS, A. J.
Audit of computer systems, by A. J. Thomas and I. J. Douglas
National Computing Centre, 1981

THOMAS, B.
Workshop in 'impact of chlorinated dioxins and related compounds in the environment'. Report
ADAS, 1980

THOMAS, F. J.
Complete diet feeding of dairy cows. Second year report; investigation carried out during 1977–78
ADAS, 1980

THOMAS, George
Boundary commission for Northern Ireland. 3rd periodical report on parliamentary constituencies and 1st supplementary report on the number of members to be returned to the Northern Ireland Assembly by each of those constituencies. November 1982
Session 1982–83 Cmnd. 8753

Boundary commission for Scotland. 3rd periodical report. 2 vols.
Session 1982–83 Cmnd. 8794

THOMAS, J. F. A.
Cadmium in the environment and its significance to man; an inter-departmental report. Central Directorate on Environmental Pollution. (Pollution Paper no. 17)
DoE, 1980

Shipham survey committee final report on metal contamination at Shipham
DoE, 1982

THOMAS, T. H.
Plant growth regulator potential and practice
British Crop Protection Council, 1982

THOMPSON, A. Hamilton
Lindisfarne Priory, Northumberland. (DoE Official Handbook)
DoE, 1980

THOMPSON, Alan
Experience and participation. Report of the review group on the youth service in England. October 1982. Education and Science Dept
Session 1981–82 Cmnd. 8686

THOMPSON, A. K.
The storage and handling of kiwifruit. (G159)
Tropical Products Institute, 1982

The storage and handling of onions. (G160)
Tropical Products Institute, 1982

THOMPSON, D. M.
Notes of the budgetary structure of developing countries
Treasury, 1979

THOMPSON, George
Resources available for continuing education in Northern Ireland. The report of the resources panel of the council for continuing education
Dept. of Education for N.I., 1979

THOMPSON, H.
A study of routinely available information relating to minor accidents in NCB North Derbyshire area, by Clive Nussey and H. Thompson. (Research Paper 19)
Health and Safety Executive, 1982

A survey of minor injuries associated with transport and handling accidents at six collieries in NCB North Derbyshire area, by Clive Nussey and H. Thompson (including Errata). (Research Paper 21)
Health and Safety Executive, 1982

THOMPSON, H. V.
First Worldwide Furbearer Conference, Frostburg, Maryland, USA, 3–11 August 1980. Report
ADAS, 1981

THOMPSON, J. K.
Policies and programmes for disabled people in the Commonwealth. Report of a survey
Commonwealth Secretariat, 1982

THOMPSON, K. C.
Atomic absorption spectrophotometry, 1979 version. An essay review. (Methods for the Examination of Waters and Associated Materials)
DoE, 1979

THOMPSON, L. H.
Survey of sewage sludge composition (1977 data). Standing Committee on the Disposal of Sewage Sludge. Sub-committee on Disposal of Sewage Sludge to Land, working group I
DOE, 1981

THOMPSON, Linda A. S.
'Young people starting work'. Introduction and interim progress report. (Training Services Division Report no. DTP 24)
MSC, 1980

THOMPSON, M. W.
Kenilworth Castle. 3rd pr
DoE, 1982

Pickering Castle, North Yorkshire
DoE, 1981

THOMPSON, N. B. W.
Legal basis of further education. A review
DES, 1981

THOMPSON, R. H.
24th annual meeting of the collaborative international pesticides analytical council and the FAO panel of experts on specifications – Spain 21–30 May 1980. Report, by R. H. Thompson and J. F. Lovett
ADAS, 1981

Annual meeting of CIPAC and meeting of the FAO panel of experts on pesticide specifications. Report of a visit to USA, May–June 1979, by R. H. Thompson and J. F. Lovett
ADAS, 1979

THOMPSON, R. R.
National conference on terotechnology in higher education, April 1979
Industry Dept., 1979

THOMSON, A. M.
Nutritional surveillance: second report of the sub-committee. (Report on Health and Special Subjects 21)
DHSS, 1981

THOMSON, Kenneth J.
Farming in the fringe. (CCP 142)
Countryside Commission, 1981

THOMSON, L. H.
Recent trends in the Scottish energy market, by S. F. Hampson and L. H. Thomson. (ESU Discussion Paper no. 1)
Scottish Economic Planning Dept., 1979

THORPE, J.
Analysis of bird strikes to UK registered aircraft 1977. (CAA Paper 79001)
Civil Aviation Authority, 1979

Analysis of bird strikes to UK registered aircraft 1978; civil aircraft over 5700 kg maximum weight. (CAA Paper 80016)
Civil Aviation Authority, 1980

Analysis of bird strikes to UK registered aircraft 1979; civil aircraft over 5700 kg maximum weight. (CAA Paper 81004)
Civil Aviation Authority, 1981

Analysis of bird strikes to UK registered aircraft 1980; civil aircraft over 5700 kg maximum weight. (CAA Paper 81013)
Civil Aviation Authority, 1981

THORPE, Jennifer
Social inquiry reports: a survey. (Research Study no. 48)
Home Office, 1979

THORPE, R. D.
Guidelines for short courses for the training of sports leaders
Sports Council East Midland Region, 1982

THREADGOLD, A. R.
'Real' national saving and its sectoral composition, by C. T. Taylor and A. R. Threadgold. (Discussion Paper no. 6)
Bank of England, 1979

THWAITES, A. T.
Technological change and the inner city, by J. B. Goddard and A. T. Thwaites. (The Inner City in Context 4)
SSRC, 1980

TIBBITT, J. E.
Day services for the elderly and elderly with mental disability in Scotland, by J. E. Tibbitt and J. Tombs. (Scottish Day Services Study. Central Research Unit Papers)
Scottish Office, 1981

TIETZ, S. B.
Building products – competing at home and abroad. Action Group on Building Materials. Summary by Industrial Market Research Ltd for the Building E D C
NEDO, 1982

Building products – competing at home and abroad. A follow-up study of exports and imports of selected building products. Summary report
NEDO, 1982

TIMBURG, G. C.
Services for the elderly with mental disability in Scotland. A report by a programme planning group
SHHD, 1979

TIMMINS, W. H.
A stirrup-operated coconut grater, by J. E. Cecil and W. H. Timmins. (Rural Technology Guide, 6)
Tropical Products Institute, 1980

TINDALE, P. R.
Infill development. Report by a working party
DoE, 1979

TINKER, Anthea
Families in flats by J. Littlewood and A. Tinker
DoE, 1981

Housing the elderly near relatives: moving and other options. (HDD Occasional Paper 1/80)
DoE, 1980

TINLEY, G. H.
Cucumber and sweet pepper production. Report of a study tour undertaken in Holland, May 1979
ADAS, 1979

ISHS working party on greenhouse cucumbers. Report of a visit to Holland, May 1980
ADAS, 1980

Minor vegetable crops under protection. Report of a visit to Holland
ADAS, 1982

TITE, R. L.
Mushroom production, by P. G. Allen and R. L. Tite. Report of a study tour in Holland, March 1980
ADAS, 1980

TITTENSOR, A. M.
Mammals research institute of the Polish academy of sciences. (Comments on land use in Czechoslovakia and Poland). Report of a visit to Poland, June 1979
ADAS, 1979

TIVY, Joy
The effect of recreation on freshwater lochs and reservoirs in Scotland
Countryside Commission for Scotland, 1980

TODD, D.
Impact of indirect taxes on households, by D. Todd and V. Hamilton (Government Economic Service Working Paper 44)
Treasury, 1981

TODD, J. E.
Adult dental health; England and Wales, 1968–78, by J. E. Todd and A. M. Walker
OPCS, 1980

Electoral registration in 1981, by J. E. Todd and B. Butcher
OPCS, 1982

Electoral registration process in the United Kingdom, by J. E. Todd and P. A. Dodd. (Social Survey Division SS1171)
OPCS, 1982

People as pedestrians, by J. E. Todd and A. M. Walker. (Social Survey Div.)
OPCS, 1980

TOLLEY, George
A basis for choice. Report of a study group on post–16 pre-employment courses, by the Further Education Curriculum Review and Development Unit
DES, 1979

TOMASIN, K.
Safety in steel erection. Report of a sub-committee of the joint advisory committee on safety and health in the construction industries
Health and Safety Executive, 1979

TOMBS, Francis
British nuclear achievements
Electricity Council, 1979

Nuclear energy past, present and future. (Anniversary lecture, November 1980)
Electricity Council, 1980

A review of nuclear power in the United Kingdom
Electricity Council, 1980

The role of nationalised industries. Based on a lecture to the Bristol Centre of the Institute of Bankers on November 11, 1980
Electricity Council, 1980

TOMBS, J.
Day services for the elderly and elderly with mental disability in Scotland, by J. E. Tibbitt and J. Tombs. (Scottish Day Services Study. Central Research Unit Papers)
Scottish Office, 1981

TOMLINSON, Alan
Leisure and the role of club and voluntary groups. (A review for the SC/SSCR Joint Panel on Leisure and Recreation Research)
Sports Council, 1979

TORRANCE, L.
International congress on virology, report on the 5th, Strasbourg, France, 1–12 August 1981
ADAS, 1982

TOUGH, Jean
Talk for teaching and learning. (Schools Council Communication Skills Project: 7–13)
Schools Council, 1979

TOWNSEND, Peter
Study tour of European nature parks. A report
Peak National Park, 1979

European 'Natur' parks, a study tour report
Peak National Park, 1979

TRAINOR, M.
Recent changes in the female labour market in Northern Ireland, by J. M. Trewsdale and M. Trainor. (Womanpower no. 2)
Equal Opportunities Commission for Northern Ireland, 1981

TRAVIS, A. S.
The state and leisure provision. (A Review for the SC/SSRC Joint Panel on Leisure and Recreation Research)
Sports Council, 1979

TREASURE, J. A. P.
Domestic Electrical Appliances SWP. Progress report 1980
NEDO, 1980

TREWSDALE, J. M.
Recent changes in the female labour market in Northern Ireland, by J. M. Trewsdale and M. Trainor. (Womanpower no. 2)
Equal Opportunities Commission for Northern Ireland, 1981

TRIANCE, J. M.
COBOL programming
National Computing Centre, 1981

TRING, Ian
The estimation of subsoil hydraulic conductivity; a preliminary report on the DW7 investigation, by A. Armstrong and I. Tring. (Land Drainage Service Research and Development Report no. 4)
ADAS, 1980

TUCHFIELD, J.
Industrial electrical equipment. Memorandum. (NEDC (82) 48)
NEDO, 1982

TUCK, Anthony
Border warfare; a history of conflict on the Anglo-Scottish border
DoE, 1979

TUCK, D. H.
Manufacture of upper leathers. (G134)
Tropical Products Institute, 1981

TUCK, Mary
Alcoholism and social policy; are we on the right lines? (Research Study no. 65)
Home Office, 1980

Ethnic minorities, crime and policing: a survey of the experiences of West Indians and whites. (Research Study no. 70)
Home Office, 1981

TUCKEY, L.
Young disabled people: report of a seminar sponsored by the Centre for Extension Training in Community Medicine, London School of Hygiene and Tropical Medicine, in association with the Civil Service College. (Working Paper no. 29)
Civil Service College, 1981

TULEY, G.
Nothafagus in Britain. 2nd ed. (Forest Record 122)
Forestry Commission, 1980

TUPHOLME, S. M.
An introduction to steel selection: part 2, stainless steels, by D. Elliott and S. M. Tupholme. (Engineering Design Guides 43)
Design Council, 1981

TURNBULL, A. T.
Meat processing in Brittany and Normandy. Report of a study tour undertaken in France, September 1979
ADAS, 1979

TURNBULL, J.
Orchard systems: report of a study tour undertaken in Holland and Belgium, 16–21 August 1981, by J. Turnbull and M. J. Marks
ADAS, 1982

TURNER, H. A.
British overseas aid: agricultural research (crop and soil sciences) 1974–78, compiled by L. Kasasian and H. A. Turner. (Overseas Research Publication no. 26)
Overseas Development Administration, 1980

TURNER, Louis
Energy policy research register 1980–81: for Austria, Denmark, France, Federal Republic of Germany, Italy, Netherlands, Norway, Sweden and Switzerland, compiled by A. M. Walton and L. Turner
SSRC, 1981

TURNER, P.
People playing sport – the role of local authorities. (A Regional Strategy for Sport and Recreation, Report 4)
Eastern Council for Sport and Recreation, 1982

TURNER, T. P.
The application of operational research in government. (CSC Working Paper no. 17)
Civil Service College, 1979

TURNEY, A. H.
The administration of the broadcast receiving licence system. Working party report 1st April 1978–31st March 1979
Home Office, 1979

TWEEDSMUIR, Lord
The functions of the Council on Tribunals. Special report of the Council. January 1980
Session 1979–80 Cmnd. 7805

TWIGGER, R.
The November 1982 social security up-rating: a pre-budget view. (Research Note no. 61)
House of Commons, 1982

TYLER, F. T.
Production and processing of peas and other vegetables. Report of a visit to France, June 1979
ADAS, 1979

TYNAN, O.
Improving the quality of working life in the 1980's. (Work Research Unit Occasional Paper 16)
Employment Dept., 1980

UNWIN, R. J.
EEC concerted action on treatment and use of sewage sludge – meeting of working parties 4 and 5, Holland, 10–11 June 1980 and seminar on phosphorus in sewage sludge and animal waste slurries, Holland, 12–13 June 1980. Report by J. H. Williams and R. J. Unwin
ADAS, 1981

EEC workshop on problems encountered with copper in agriculture Irva-station d'agronomie, Bordeaux, October 1980. Report
ADAS, 1980

Exchange visit to New Zealand, 1978–79. Report
ADAS, 1979

URQUHART, D. J.
General information towards the better use of existing construction industry information resources. Final report of the General Information Group
DoE, 1979

URQUHART, Robert
History of the Scottish Milk Marketing Board
Scottish Milk Marketing Board, 1979

UZZELL, David
Tape-slide for public participation in planning, by P. Stringer and D. Uzzell
DoE, 1980

VAIDYANATHAN, L. V.
Seminar on isotope techniques in studies of the useful conservation and the pollutant potential of agricultural nitrogen residues, Vienna, Austria, 25–29 August 1980. Report on seminar
ADAS, 1981

VAN LAUN, John
The Clydach Gorge: industrial archaeology trails in a north Gwent valley
Brecon Beacons National Park, 1980

VARNHAM, K. B.
Greek potato production. (James E. Rennie Award Report no. 10)
Potato Marketing Board, 1981

VARWELL, Adrian
Way of life: in search of meaning. (North Sea Oil Panel Occasional Paper no. 5)
SSRC, 1981

VAUGHAN, J. S.
Caravan and camping sites on the farm. (Socio-economics Paper no. 6; Booklet 2006, rev. ed.)
ADAS, 1980

A guide to sources of non-agricultural income on the farm. (Socio-economics Paper no 13; Booklet 2013)
ADAS, 1980

VEAL, A. J.
New swimming pool for old; the impact of replacing an old pool on indoor swimming in Ashton-under-Lyne and surrounding areas. (Sports Council Study 18)
Sports Council, 1979

Research on the urban fringe, compiled by J. C. Phillips and A. J. Veal. (CURS Conference and Seminar Papers no. 6)
Countryside Commission, 1979

Six examples of low cost sports facilities; a study of centres at Rochford, Bolton, London, Nottingham, Steyning. (Sports Council Study no. 20)
Sports Council, 1979

Trends in leisure participation and problems of forecasting: the state of the art. (A Report to the Sports Council/SSRC Joint Panel on Leisure and Recreation Research)
Sports Council, 1980

VELJANOVSKI, Cento G.
Economic myths about common law realities – economic efficiency and the law of torts. (Centre for Socio-legal Studies: Working Paper no. 5)
SSRC, 1979

VENNING, Muriel
The manager in engineering. (Research Report 7)
Engineering Industry Training Board, 1979

VERNON, Tom
Gobbledegook; a critical review of official forms and leaflets and how to improve them
National Consumer Council, 1980

VICKERMAN, R. W.
Personal and family leisure expenditure
Sports Council, 1980

VLACHONIKOLIS, I. G.
Effect of ill-health and subsequent compensation and support on household income; a logistic regression approach, by Y. Brittan and I. G. Vlachonikolis. (Centre for Socio-legal Studies Working Paper 6)
SSRC, 1980

VOSPER, J. D.
Safe handling of dyestuffs in colour stores
Health and Safety Executive, 1980

Safeguarding of opening machinery
Health and Safety Executive, 1981

WACHER, J. S.
Circencester Roman amphitheatre
DoE, 1981

WADDILOVE, Lewis E.
Social policy and social responsibility; record of a study day, London, February 1979
Personal Social Services Council, 1979

WADDINGTON, J. C.
General assembly of the permanent international association of navigation congresses. Report of a visit to Italy, June 1980
ADAS, 1980

Water control projects. Report of a visit to West Germany, October 1979, by K. C. Nobel and J. C. Waddington
ADAS, 1979

WADE, Brian
Retail employment change in Scotland with special reference to super-stores, by R. L. Davies and B. Wade (Central Research Unit Papers)
Scottish Office, 1982

WADSWORTH, Jack
Cutlery and flatwear industry. Report of the working party
Industry Dept., 1980

WAILES, R.
Berney Arms Mill, 2nd ed.
DoE, 1982

WAIN, David B.
Inland waterways; arteries for employment and spending
Inland Waterways Amenity Advisory Council, 1980

WAINWRIGHT, G. J.
Gussage All Saints; an iron age settlement in Dorset. (Archaeological Reports no. 10)
DoE, N1979

WALKER, A. M.
People as pedestrians, by J. E. Todd and A. M. Walker. (Social Survey Div.)
OPCS, 1980

Adult dental health; England and Wales, 1968–78, by J. E. Todd and A. M. Walker. (Social Survey Div.)
OPCS, 1980

WALKER, C. D.
Orchard and plantation systems. Report on 2nd symposium on research and development, August 1980
ADAS, 1980

WALKER, Caroline R.
Lea Valley glasshouse growers' study, 1978–1979
ADAS, 1980

WALKER, E.
Enforcement of Trade Descriptions Act in Scotland, by D. Purdom and E. Walker
Scottish Consumer Council, 1980

WALKER, Graeme
Public expenditure, 1977–78: outturn compared with plan, by C. Jutsum and G. Walker. (Government Economic Service Working Paper no. 28)
Treasury, 1982

WALKER, J. O.
Spraying systems for the 1980's. Proceedings of a symposium held at Royal Holloway College, March 1980. (Monograph no. 24)
British Crop Protection Council, 1980

WALKER, Robert L.
Canvassing rent allowances in Bristol and Westminster
DoE, 1979

WALKER, S. D.
The role of planning units in departments and lessons from management reviews. (CSC Working Paper no. 22)
Civil Service College, 1980

WALKER, T.
Metal melting and heat treatment operator training guide book
Foundry Industry Training Committee, 1979

WALKLAND, Iris
Byker community development project, 1974–78. A report by W. Hampton and I. Walkland. (Newcastle upon Tyne Council for Voluntary Service)
Home Office, 1980

WALKLEY, Clive
Music materials for the primary (a bibliography) 1979 supplement. (Schools Council Project: Music Education of Young Children)
Schools Council, 1979

WALL, J. R. D.
Management plan for the Acelhuate River catchment, El Salvador: soil conservation river stabilisation and water pollution control. (Land Resource Study 30)
Land Resource Development Centre, 1981

WALLACE, C. K.
Skills in demand: a report on manpower recruitment in the mining machinery industry. (Mining Machinery SWP)
NEDO, 1980

WALLACE, J. G.
Scottish health authorities priorities for the eighties. Report by a working party of the Scottish Health Service Planning Council
SHHD, 1980

WALLER, George S., Lord Justice
The age of consent in relation to sexual offences. Working paper by the Policy Advisory Committee on Sexual Offences
Home Office, 1979

The age of consent in relation to sexual offences. Policy Advisory Committee on Sexual Offences Report, April 1981
Session 1980-81 Cmnd. 8216

WALLER, W. M.
Land restoration following mineral working with particular reference to the Polder method of restoration. Report of a study tour undertaken in West Germany, June 1979, by W. M. Waller and D. A. J. Hanbury-Tracey
ADAS, 1979

WALLIN, S. C.
Sludge incinerator emissions. Report of a sub–committee of the standing committee on disposal of sewage sludge. (Water Division 2, Technical Note no. 15)
DoE, 1980

WALMSLEY, Roy
Sexual offences, consent and sentencing, by R. Walmsley and K. White. (Research Study no. 54)
Home Office, 1979

Supplementary information on sexual offences and sentencing, by R. Walmsley and K. White. (Research Unit Paper 2)
Home Office, 1980

WALSH, K.
The methodology of labour market analysis: a handbook for labour market studies in the Health Service, by K. Walsh, D. McGill and R. Pearson. (Manpower Planning Series 6)
DHSS, 1982

The Tyne labour market: Health Service recruitment on Tyneside, by K. Walsh and D. McGill. (Manpower Planning Series 6)
DHSS, 1982

WALTERS, P. R.
Jojoba: an assessment of prospects, by P. R. Walters and others. (G128)
Tropical Products Institute, 1979

WALTON, Ann-Margaret
Energy policy research register 1980–81: for Austria, Denmark, France, Federal Republic of Germany, Italy, Netherlands, Norway, Sweden and Switzerland, compiled by A.-M. Walton and L. Turner
SSRC, 1981

WANKLYN, J.
Research in corrosion. A review of projects supported by the Engineering Board of the Science and Engineering Research Council
SERC, 1982

WARBURTON, R.
Safety in paper mills. Fourth report of the joint standing committee for paper mills
Health and Safety Executive, 1979

WARD, A. G.
Food standards committee. Second report on food labelling. (FSC/REP/69)
MAFF, 1979

WARD, A. J. R.
A developing strategy for the West Midlands. Updating and rolling forward of the regional strategy to 1991. Report of the Joint Monitoring Steering Group, July 1979. (D. T. Routh and A. J. R. Ward, ch.). 2 vols.
West Midlands Planning Authorities Conference, 1979

WARD, C.
Art and the built environment; a teacher's approach, by E. Adams and C. Ward
Longman for Schools Council, 1982

WARD, Murray
Mathematics and the 10-year-old, the report of the schools council project, primary school mathematics. (Schools Council Working Paper 61)
Schools Council, 1979

WARD, Paul
Quality of life in residential care
Personal Social Services Council, 1980

WARDAZE, Geoffrey
Chain of command review; the open structure. Report of a team
Civil Service Dept., 1981

WARDLOW, L. R.
Insect resistance. Report of a study tour undertaken in Holland and Denmark, May 1979
ADAS, 1979

WARE, R.
Poland under martial law (Background Paper no. 98)
House of Commons Library, 1982

WAREING, A. D.
Variety and growing system of crisp lettuce. Report of a study tour in Holland
ADAS, 1982

WAREING, A. P.
Visit by the West Sussex tomato working party to nurseries of prominent growers, by R. R. Charlesworth and A. P. Wareing. Report of a visit to Holland, 18–19 September, 1981
ADAS, 1982

WARNER, N. R.
Traffic in social security work between DHSS local and regional offices and headquarters. Report of a study for the principal establishments officer, by N. R. Warner, A. J. Laurence, R. C. Heron and L. T. Byars
DHSS, 1981

WARNER, S. A.
Examination and testing of lifting equipment: Health and Safety Diving Operations at Work Regulations 1981. (Diving Safety Memorandum no. 17/1982)
Energy Dept., 1982

Surface decompression techniques/decompression sickness. (Diving Safety Memorandum no. 15/1982)
Energy Dept., 1982

WARREN, J.
Assessment of mobilising times in fire brigade control rooms, by P. Stringer and J. Warren. (Technical Memorandum 4/80)
Home Office, 1980

WARREN, J. J.
Evaluation of the thermal imaging camera. (Scientific Advisory Branch Report 16/81)
Home Office, 1981

WARREN, M. E.
Britain and Schleswig-Holstein; trends in dairy farming, 1976–1980. (Report no. 23)
Milk Marketing Board, 1980

WARWICK, K. S.
The CAP and resource flows among EEC member states, by J. M. C. Rollo and K. S. Warwick. (Government Economic Service Working Paper no. 27)
Treasury, 1979

WATERFIELD, Albert
Self blanching celery (protected cropping). (Booklet 2062)
ADAS, 1979

WATERMAN, J. J.
Torry research station, 1929–1979; a brief history
MAFF, 1979

WATERS, R. L.
Work on transplanting sugar beet. Report of a study visit to Eire, April 1980
ADAS, 1980

WATSON, C. E.
Guarding of foundry machinery. Joint Standing Committee on Health, Safety and Welfare in Foundries. Seventh report of the Sub-committee on machinery safety
Health and Safety Executive, 1979

WATSON, E. D.
Oestrous behaviour, ovarium morphology and hormone profiles in dairy cattle. Report of a study tour undertaken in West Germany, 3–13 September, 1981
ADAS, 1982

WATSON, H. B.
Sheep slaughter and hygiene. Report of a study tour undertaken in France, 1979 series
ADAS, 1979

WATSON, W.
Symposium on managerial and economic aspects of large livestock holdings, and technical, economic and sanitary aspects of buildings and equipment: report of a visit to Spain, 19–23 October 1981, by W. Watson and D. Sisson
ADAS, 1982

WATT, Joyce
Primary – secondary liaison; the Blackburn project. Scottish Committee on Home – School – Community Relations.
Committee on Primary Education
Consultative Committee on the Curriculum, 1981

WAY, A. A.
Promoting sport in villages. (A Regional Strategy for Sport and Recreation, report 3)
Eastern Council for Sport and Recreation, 1982

WAY, H. C.
Credit cards and automated transfer of funds. (Guides to Computing Standards no. 21)
National Computing Centre, 1981

WEATHERITT, Mollie
The prosecution system; survey of prosecuting solicitor's departments. (Research Study no. 1)
Royal Commission on Criminal Procedure, 1980

WEATHERITT, N. T.
International Society for Horticultural Science: 4th international symposium on timing of field promotion of vegetables, Nyborg, Denmark, 27–31 July 1981. Report by J. D. Whitwell and N. T. Weatheritt
ADAS, 1982

WEBB, Kenneth
Kina Holdings Ltd. Investigation under the Companies Act, 1948. Report by W. Denny and K. Webb
Trade Dept., 1981

WEBB, Michael G.
Power sector planning manual
Overseas Development Administration, 1979

WEBB, T.
Role of foreign-owned multinational companies in the UK computer industry. Report of the Computer Sector Working Party Multinational Sub-committee
NEDO, 1979

WEBBER, Richard
Census enumeration districts: a socio-economic classification. (Occasional Paper 14)
OPCS, 1979

WEBSTER, N.
Police interrogation; tape recording, by J. A. Barnes and N. Webster. (Research study no. 8)
Royal Commission on Criminal Procedure, 1980

WEDD, G. N.
Bottle banks. Report of the joint working group of the London Borough Association
DoE, 1982

WEDDELL, Jean M.
Planning for stroke patients, a four-year descriptive study of home and hospital care, by J. M. Weddell and S. A. A. Beresford
DHSS, 1979

WEDDEN, R.
Geographic variations in the cost of health service inputs. (Government Economic Service Working Paper no. 35)
DHSS, 1980

WEDGE, P.
Continuities in childhood disadvantage, by J. Essen and P. Wedge. (Studies in Deprivation and Disadvantage 6)
Heinemann for SSRC, 1982

WEEDON, B. C. L.
An examination of asbestos in relation to food and drink. (Food Additives and Contaminants Committee) (FAC/REP/30)
MAFF, 1979

Metals in canned foods. Report of the Food Additives and Contaminants Committee. (FAC/REP/38). (Agriculture, Fisheries and Food, Min.)
HMSO, 1982

Modified starches. Food Additives and Contaminants Committee Report. (FAC/REP/31)
MAFF, 1980

Review of the colouring matter in food regulations, 1973. Interim report of the Food Additives and Contaminants Committee. (FAC/REP/29)
MAFF, 1979

Review of remaining classes of food additives used as ingredients in food. Report on the review of bulking aids. (Food Additives and Contaminants Committee). (FAC/REP/32)
MAFF, 1980

WEEKS, J. M.
Cornish beef, pt. 1, by A. C. Emery and J. M. Weeks
MAFF, 1979

WEINREICH, Peter
Manual for identity exploration using personal contacts. Research Unit on Ethnic Relations
SSRC, 1980

WELCH, J. A.
Electronic mail systems: a practical evaluation guide, by J. A. Welch and P. A. Wilson. (Office Technology in the '80s)
National Computing Centre, 1981

WELCHMAN, Rosemary
Learning at work; the Tavistock guide, by L. Hilgendorf and R. Welchman (Special Programmes Research and Development Series no. 9)
MSC, 1982

WELLINGS, Jack
Construction Equipment and Mobile Cranes Sector Working Party. Progress report.
NEDO, 1979

WELLS, A. C.
Assisting the vision of firemen in smoke: the development and trial of a thermal imaging system, by A. G. Lindfield and A. C. Wells. (Research Report no. 17; Central Fire Brigades Advisory Councils for England and Wales and for Scotland: Joint Committee on Fire Research)
Home Office, 1981

WELLS, Terry
Creating attractive grasslands using native plant species
Nature Conservancy Council, 1980

WELSH, B. J.
Consolidated Gold Fields Ltd. Report of investigation under the Companies Act, 1948, by B. J. Welsh and M. C. A. Osborne
Trade Dept., 1980

WELTMAN, A. J.
Pile load testing procedures. (DOE and CIRIA Piling Development Group Report PG7)
Property Services Agency, 1980

Piling in 'boulder clay' and other glacial tills, by A. J. Weltman and P. R. Healy. (Report PG5)
Property Services Agency, Piling Development Group, 1978

Site investigation manual, by A. J. Weltman and J. M. Head (PSA Civil Engineering Technical Guide, no. 35)
PSA, 1982

Survey of problems associated with the installation of displacement piles, by P. R. Healey and A. J. Weltman. (Report PG8; Civil Engineering Technical Guide 26)
Property Services Agency, 1980

WEMYSS, Lord
The ancient and historical monuments of Argyll, vol. 3: Mull, Tiree, Coll and northern Argyll. 21st report of the Royal Commission on the Ancient and Historical Monuments of Scotland. July 1980
Session 1979–80 Cmnd. 7678

Ancient and historical monuments of Argyll, vol. 4: Iona. 22nd report of the Royal Commission on the Ancient and Historical Monuments of Scotland
Session 1981–82 Cmnd. 8420

WENBAN-SMITH, Hugh
Magazine publishing: a case of joint products. (Government Economic Service Working Paper no. 16)
Price Commission, 1979

WERNER, J. B.
Mortality in the British rubber industries 1967–76, by P. J. Baxter and J. B. Werner
Health and Safety Executive, 1980

WEST, J. J.
Boscobel House
DoE, 1981

WEST, L. C. W.
Experimental coal-dust explosions in the Buxton full-scale surface gallery XII, by D. Rae and L. C. W. West. (Research Paper no. 16)
Health and Safety Executive, 1982

WESTLAKE, H. J.
On-farm computer terminals: report of a visit to Denmark, 7–9 October 1981. (FR6791)
ADAS, 1982

WESTLEY, C. B.
Thermal screens and programmed control. Report of a visit to Holland
ADAS, 1982

WHELAN, Christopher
The law and the use of troops in industrial disputes. (Centre for Socio-legal Studies: Working Paper no. 2)
SSRC, 1979

WHELAN, Edward
Young persons' work preparation courses – a systematic evaluation, by Barbara Speake and Edward Whelan
Employment Service Agency, 1979

WHINNEY, John
Cornhill Consolidated Group Ltd. Report of investigation under the Companies Act, 1948, by D. Calcutt and J. Whinney
Trade Dept., 1980

WHIPP, J. I.
Management of high yielding dairy herds. Report of a study tour in USA and Canada, October 1979, by M. J. Ecclestone and J. I. Whipp
ADAS, 1979

WHITE, D.
Pay negotiations in six overseas health services
DHSS, 1980

WHITE, John
About Westonbirt: a short guide
Forestry Commission, 1979

WHITE, Karen
Sexual offences, consent and sentencing, by R. Walmsley and K. White. (Research Study no. 54)
Home Office, 1979

Supplementary information on sexual offences and sentencing, by R. Walmsley and K. White. (Research Unit Paper 2)
Home Office, 1980

WHITE, M.
Shorter working time through national industry agreements. (Research Paper no. 38)
Employment Dept., 1982

WHITE, Peter
Sherborne old castle, Dorset
DoE, 1979

WHITEHEAD, W. D. J.
The construction of a transportable charcoal kiln. (Rural Technology Guide 13)
Tropical Products Institute, 1980

WHITEMAN John
Direct access to financial markets for financing nationalised industries' investment, by M. Breech and J. Whiteman (Economic Working Paper no. 6)
NEDO, 1981

North Sea oil and the U.K. economy (Economic Working Paper no. 5)
NEDO, 1981

WHITTINGHAM, E. C. J.
Developing strategy for the West Midlands. Updating and rolling forward of the regional economy; problems and proposals. Report of the Council and West Midlands Planning Authorities Conference, July 1979, by J. A. Pope and E. C. J. Whittingham
West Midlands Planning Authorities Conference, 1979

WHITWELL, J. D.
International Society for Horticultural Science: 4th international symposium on timing of field promotion of vegetables, Nyborg, Denmark, 27–31 July 1981. Report by J. D. Whitwell and N. T. Weatheritt
ADAS, 1982

WHYTE, R.
Employment growth in small manufacturing units, 1954–1974. (ESU Discussion Paper no. 14)
Scottish Economic Planning Dept., 1982

WICKENS, R.
Sugar beet transplanting in the Republic of Ireland. Report by R. Wickens and K. A. McLean
ADAS, 1982

WIDDOWSON, E. M.
Foods which simulate meat. The nutritional aspects of vegetable protein foods which are meat analogues. Report of the panel on novel foods; committee on medical aspects of food policy. (Report on Health and Social Subjects 17)
DHSS, 1980

WIGHT, G.
Report on 3rd European Veterinary Convention, Avignon, France, 9–11 October 1980, by G. Wight, L. H. Green and J. T. Blackburn
ADAS, 1981

WIGODER, Basil Thomas, Lord
Relocation of pay bed authorisations at hospitals of the Argyll and Clyde Health Board. Proposals made by the Health Services Board. October 1979
Session 1979–80 HC 215

Relocation of pay bed authorisations at hospitals of the Durham area health authority. Proposal made by the

Health Services Board under section 17 of the National Health Service Act, 1977
Session 1978–79 HC 292

Relocation of pay bed authorisations at hospitals of the Kent area health authority. Proposal made by the Health Services Board. July 1979
Session 1979–80 HC 138

Relocation of private practice facilities at national health service hospitals of the Ealing, Hammersmith and Hounslow area health authority (teaching). December 1979
Session 1979–80 HC 311

Relocation of private practice facilities at national health service hospitals of the Wolverhampton area health authority. Proposals made by the Health Services Board under section 71 of the National Health Service Act, 1977. April 1980
Session 1979–80 HC 527

Relocation of private practice facilities at national health service hospitals. Proposals made by the Health Services Board. February 1979
Session 1978–79 HC 189

Withdrawal of authorisations for the use of NHS hospital accommodation and services by private patients. Health Services Board's fourth set of proposals. February 1979
Session 1978–79 HC 188

Withdrawal of authorisations for the use of NHS hospital accommodation and services by private patients. Health Services Board's fifth set of proposals. May 1979
Session 1979–80 HC 17

Withdrawal of authorisations for the use of NHS hospital accommodation and services by private patients. Health Services Board's 7th set of proposals. October 1979
Session 1979–80 HC 212

WIJERATNE, W. V. S.
European colloquim on cytogenetics of domestic animals, Uppsala, Sweden, 10–13 June 1980. 4th report
ADAS, 1981

WILCOX, H. J.
Potato diseases, by G. H. Brenchley and H. J. Wilcox. (RPD 1)
MAFF, 1979

WILCOX, J. C.
Spring meeting of the Irish grassland and animal production association, Kilcoran, Fermoy, Eire. Report of a visit to Eire, February 1980
ADAS, 1980

WILDGOOSE, James
A framework for assessing the economic effects of a green pound devaluation, by S. Dickinson and J. Wildgoose. (Government Economic Service Working Paper no. 23)
Treasury, 1979

WILDING, P.
A guide to the assessment of trend movements in new vehicle registrations from seasonally adjusted data. (Internal Note ST(79)5)
DoE, 1979

WILDING, R. W. L.
Legal entitlements and administrative practices: a report by officials
Civil Service Department, 1979

WILDING, Richard
The professional ethic of the administrator. (CSE Working Paper no. 10)
Civil Service College, 1979

WILKES, E.
Terminal care. Report of a working group. Standing Sub-committee on Cancer
DHSS, 1980

WILKIE, Elaine
A history of the Council for the Education and Training of Health Visitors: an account of its establishment and field of activities 1962–1975
Council for the Education and Training of Health Visitors, 1979

WILKINSON, B.
World climate conference, February 1979. Report of a visit to Switzerland
ADAS, 1979

WILKINSON, Diana
Rent arrears in public authority housing in Scotland. (A Scottish Office Social Research Study)
Scottish Office, 1980

WILKINSON, Judith
The overhead projector
British Council, 1979

WILKS, S. R. M.
Register of research into relations between government and industry
SSRC, 1981

WILLEY, Richard
Multi-ethnic education: the way forward, by A. Little and R. Willey. (Schools Council Pamphlet 18)
Schools Council, 1981

WILLIAMS, Alwyn
A heritage for Scotland. Scotland's national museums and galleries: the next 25 years. Report of a committee
Scottish Office, 1981

WILLIAMS, Bernard
Committee on obscenity and film censorship report. November 1979
Session 1979–80 Cmnd. 7772

WILLIAMS, Charles C. P.
Area electricity boards. Electricity prices and certain allied charges. Price Commission report, July 1979
Session 1979–80 HC 132

BOC Ltd. Compressed permanent gases and disolved acetylene sold in cylinders, cylinder rentals and fixed charges. Price Commission report, February, 1979
Session 1978–79 HC 223

BP Oil Ltd. Oil and petroleum products. Price Commission report, May 1979
Session 1979–80 HC 87

British Gas Corporation: gas prices and allied charges. Price Commission report, July 1979
Session 1979–80 HC 165

Butlin's Ltd. Tariffs of the main holiday centres in the UK. Price Commission report, February 1979
Session 1978–79 HC 181

Daily Telegraph Ltd. Cover price of The Daily Telegraph. Price Commission report, March 1979
Session 1978–79 HC 241

Dollond and Aitchison group. Prices, charges and margins for optical products. Price Commission report, January 1979
Session 1978–79 HC 134

Esso Petroleum Co. Ltd. Oil and petroleum products. Price Commission report, May 1979
Session 1979–80 HC 88

Perkins Engines Co. Diesel, gasoline, reconditioned and 'short' engines. Price Commission report, April 1979
Session 1978–79 HC 345

Prices, costs and margins in the distribution of video tape recorders and their accessories. Price Commission report, April 1979
Session 1978–79 HC 331

Prices, costs and margins in the manufacture and distribution of portable electric tools. Price Commission report, February 1979
Session 1978–79 HC 204

Prices, costs and margins in the manufacture of floor and furniture polishes. Price Commission report, May 1979
Session 1979–80 HC 13

Prices, costs and margins of metal doors and windows for domestic properties. Price Commission report, April 1979
Session 1978–79 HC 340

Rugby Portland Cement Co. Ltd. Cements. Price Commission report, April 1979
Session 1978–79 HC 346

Shell UK Oil. Oil and petroleum products. Price Commission report, July 1979
Session 1979–80 HC 178

Thermos Ltd. Vaccuum ware. Price Commission report, January 1979
Session 1978–79 HC 135

United Biscuits (UK) Ltd. Biscuits, crisps, nuts and savoury snacks. Price Commission report, April 1979
Session 1978–79 HC 347

WILLIAMS, D. T. E.
An education and training technology service for the National Health Service
National Training Council for the NHS, 1981

WILLIAMS, Helen M.
The management of publicly-owned land in the Hertfordshire/Barnet experiment area. (Working Paper 17)
Countryside Commission, 1979

WILLIAMS, J. B.
Soil water investigation in the Gambia. (Land Resources Development Centre Technical Bulletin 3)
Ministry of Overseas Development, 1979

WILLIAMS, J. H.
EEC concerted action on treatment and use of sewage sludge – meeting of working parties 4 and 5, Holland, 10–11 June 1980 and seminar on phosphorus in sewage sludge and animal waste slurries, Holland, 12–13 June 1980. Report by J. H. Williams and R. J. Unwin
ADAS, 1981

Treatment and use of sewage sludge. Reports of visits to France, October 1978 and February 1979
ADAS, 1979

WILLIAMS, Kevin
Aftermath of tribunal reinstatement and re-engagement, by K. Williams and D. Lewis. (Research Paper 23)
Employment Dept., 1981

WILLIAMS, N. P.
Influences on the profitability of twenty-two industrial sectors. (Bank of England Discussion Paper no. 15)
Bank of England, 1981

WILLIAMS, R.
Berwick-upon-Tweed environmental and traffic problems. Working Party Report
DoE, 1979

WILLIAMS, Richard
Career management and career planning: a study of North American practice
Civil Service Dept., 1981

WILLIAMS, Sir Robert
Genetic Manipulation Advisory Group 3rd report. 1982
Session 1981–82 Cmnd. 8665

Hepatitis in dentistry. Report of the expert group.
DHSS, 1979

WILLIAMSON, Peter
Early careers of 1970 graduates. (Dept. of Employment Research Paper no. 26)
Employment Dept., 1981

WILLIS, Carole F.
Race, crime and arrests, by P. Stevens and C. F. Willis. (Research Study no. 58)
Home Office, 1979

WILLIS, G.
Modem interfaces and connectors. (Guides to Computing Standards no. 22.2)
National Computing Centre, 1981

Modems. (Guides to Computing Standards no. 22.3)
National Computing Centre, 1981

WILLIS, Margaret
The environment movement, conservation and the future. (with postscript February 1981)
DoE, 1980

WILLMOTT, Phyllis
Participation in local social services; an exploratory study, by R. Deakin and P. Willmott. (Studies in Participation 1)
Personal Social Services Council, 1979

WILMOT, Carole E.
Classification/thesaurus for sport and physical recreation (and allied topics), compiled by Carole E. Wilmot. (Development edition)
Sports Council, 1981

WILSON, Alexander
How to start exporting; a guide for small firms, by A. Wilson and G. W. Lockhart. (Small Firms Service Series)
Industry Dept., 1980

WILSON, C. I.
Potential for a large coastal quarry in Scotland. Preliminary research report, by C. I. Wilson and C. D. Gribble. (Planning Services)
Scottish Development Dept., 1980

WILSON, D. R.
North Leigh Roman villa, Oxfordshire, by D. R. Wilson and D. Sherlock
DoE, 1980

WILSON, Duncan
Modern public records: selection and access. Report of a committee appointed by the Lord Chancellor, March 1981
Session 1980–81 Cmnd. 8204

WILSON, Geoffrey
From governments to grass roots. Report of the advisory committee on relationships between the official and unofficial commonwealth
Commonwealth Secretariat, 1979

Socio-legal research in Germany. An account of work in the socio-legal field in the Federal Republic of Germany
SSRC, 1980

WILSON, Sir Harold
Committee to Review the Functioning of Financial Institutions.
Report and appendices, June 1980. 2 vols.
Session 1979–80 Cmnd. 7937

Second stage evidence. Vol. 1
Treasury, 1979

Second stage evidence. Vol. 2: insurance company associations, Lloyd's, Committee on Invisible Exports
Treasury, 1979

Interim report: financing of small firms. March 1979
Session 1978–79 Cmnd. 7503

The distribution of films for exhibition in cinemas and by other means. Fifth report of the Interim Action Committee on the Film Industry, 1982
Session 1981–82 Cmnd. 8530

Film and television co-operation. Fourth report of the Interim Action Committee on the Film Industry, April 1981
Session 1980–81 Cmnd. 8227

Financing of the British film industry. Second report of the Interim Action Committee on the Film Industry, June 1979
Session 1979–80 Cmnd. 7597

Statistics, technological developments and cable television. Third report of the Interim Action Committee on the Film Industry, March 1980
Session 1979–80 Cmnd. 7855

Studies of small firms' financing. (Committee to Review the Functioning of Financial Institutions, Research Report no. 3)
Treasury, 1979

WILSON, James
Northern Region Working Party on Aggregates second report, November 1979
DoE, 1979

WILSON, Jill
Careful storage of yams. Some basic principles to reduce losses
Commonwealth Secretariat, 1981

WILSON, K. W.
Removal of tree stumps. (Arboricultural Leaflet 7)
Forestry Commission, 1981

WILSON, M.
Tenants Associated: a survey of tenants groups in Scotland
Scottish Consumer Council, 1981

WILSON, M. F.
International meeting on the Groupe Polyphenols, J.E.P. '82, Toulouse, September/October, 1982. Report
ADAS, 1982

WILSON, M. S., Mrs.
New Zealand Veterinary Association Conference 1981, Queenstown, South Island, New Zealand, February 1981. Report
ADAS, 1981

Sheep production. Report of a visit to New Zealand and Australia, December 1978/January 1979
ADAS, 1979

WILSON, Mary D.
Education of disturbed pupils, by M. D. Wilson and M. Evans. (Working Paper 65)
Schools Council, 1980

The curriculum in special schools. (Programme 4: Individual Pupils)
Schools Council, 1981

WILSON, P. A.
Electronic mail systems: a practical evaluation guide, by J. A. Welch and P. A. Wilson. (Office Technology in the '80s)
National Computing Centre, 1981

WILSON, Paul
Drinking in England and Wales. An enquiry carried out on behalf of the DHSS. (Social Survey 1128)
OPCS, 1980

Free school meals: a survey carried out on behalf of the Dept. of Education and Science. (Social Survey Div. Occasional Paper 23)
OPCS, 1981

WILSON, Paul *(continued)*
Scottish licensing laws; a survey, by I. Knight and P. Wilson. (SS 1094)
OPCS, 1980

WILSON, R. S.
The use of chironomid pupal exuviae for biological surveillance of water quality, by R. S. Wilson and J. D. McGill. (Tech. Memo no. 18)
Water Data Unit, 1979

WILSON, Sheena
An investigation of difficult to let housing. Volume 2: case studies of post-war estates, by Sheena Wilson and Keith Kirby. (HDD Occasional Paper 4/80)
DoE, 1981

An investigation of difficult to let housing. Volume 3: case studies of pre-war estates, by Sheena Wilson and Keith Kirby. (HDD Occasional Paper 5/80)
DoE, 1981

WIMBUSH, Erica
Leisure and the over 50's, by J. A. Long and E. Wimbush. (A Review for the SC/SSRC Joint Panel on Leisure and Recreation Research)
Sports Council, 1979

WINETROBE, B.
'Alternatives to domestic rates': responses to the Green Paper. (Research Note no. 76)
House of Commons, 1982

WINFIELD, R.
Public transport planning – the end of an era?
Welsh Consumer Council, 1982

WING, J. K.
Two reports on research into services for children and adolescents (2): Helping disturbed children and adolescents. Report of the Joint Sub-group
DHSS, 1980

WIRZ, H.
Sheltered housing in Scotland: a research report, by H. Wirz, with M. McGinn and G. Wilson. (Central Research Unit Papers)
Scottish Office, 1982

WITZENFELD, S.
Review of the government statistical services. Initial study of the Office of Population Censuses and Surveys, by S. Witzenfeld and J. Craig
Central Statistical Office, 1981

WOLFERS, E. P.
Decentralisation; options and issues, a manual for policy-makers
Commonwealth Secretariat, 1982

WOLSTENHOLME, Sir Gordon
Genetic Manipulation Advisory Group. Second report. December 1979
Session 1979–80 Cmnd. 7785

WOOD, A. M. M.
Long-term research and development requirements in civil engineering
Science and Engineering Research Council, 1981

WOOD, Douglas
Men registering as unemployed in 1978; a longitudinal study. (DHSS Cohort Study of Unemployed Men, Working Paper no. 1)
DHSS, 1982

WOOD, E. G.
Marketing: a guide for small firms. (Small Firms Service)
Industry Dept., 1981 (reprinted 1982)

WOOD, Sir John
New towns staff. (Standing Commission on Pay Comparability Report no. 12)
Session 1980–81 Cmnd. 8109

WOOD, L.
A study of the departure flow regulator at the London Air Traffic Control Centre, August 1980. (CAA Paper 82004)
Civil Aviation Authority, 1982

WOOD, Malcolm
Tourism marketing for the small business
English Tourist Board, 1980

WOOD, Michael B
Introducing computer security
National Computing Centre, 1982

WOOD, P. C.
The disposal of sewage sludge to sea, 1975–78. Report of the sub-committee. (Standing Technical Committee Reports no. 18)
National Water Council, 1979

WOODING, M. G.
Agricultural applications of aerial photography and remote sensing: report of a study tour undertaken in Holland, 5–8 May 1981
ADAS, 1981

International geoscience and remote sensing symposium, Munich, June 1982
ADAS, 1982

OECD symposium on terrain evaluation and remote sensing for highway engineering in developing countries. Report of a visit to France, September, 1979
ADAS, 1979

WOODROFFE, G.
Service please: services and the law: a consumer view, by B. Lantin and G. Woodroffe
National Consumer Council, 1981

WOODROOFE, Ernest
Review body on doctors' and dentists' remuneration.
Ninth report. June 1979
Session 1979–80 Cmnd. 7574

Supplement to ninth report. October 1979
Session 1979–80 Cmnd. 7723

Second supplement to ninth report. December 1979
Session 1979–80 Cmnd. 7790

WOODROW, David
Guide for NHS administrative and clerical staff on qualifications, study facilities and courses. (National Staff Committee for Administrative and Clerical Staff; Working Party on Training of Administrators)
National Staff Committee for Administrative and Clerical Staff, 1980

WOODS, Philip
Getting primary care on the NHS, by K. Jones and P. Woods
Welsh Consumer Council, 1979

WOODWARD, Nicholas
Unemployment in West Cornwall, by R. McNabb and N. Woodward. (Research Paper no. 8)
Employment Dept., 1979

WOOLF, Myra
The reliability of fertility data obtained from pregnancy histories. (Studies on Medical and Population Subjects no. 40)
OPCS, 1979

WOOLLACOTT, P. N.
Prospects for improved fuel economy and fuel flexibility in road vehicles. Report by R. J. Francis and P. N. Woollacott. (Energy Paper no. 45)
Energy Dept., 1981

WOOLLEY, E. W.
Winter barley and other cereals, by E. W. Woolley and D. J. Yarham. Report of a study tour undertaken in West Germany and Denmark, 1979 series
ADAS, 1979

WOOTTON, H.
Patients' rights: a guide to the rights and responsibilities of patients and doctors in the NHS, by H. Wootton, P. Griffiths and H. W. Thomas, ed. by B. Guthrie
National Consumer Council, 1982

WORSWICK, G. D. N.
Factors underlying the recent recession, by G. D. N. Worswick and Dr. A. Budd. (Papers Presented to the Panel of Academic Consultants no. 15)
Bank of England, 1981

WORTHING, Charles R.
The pesticide manual. A world compendium. 6th ed.
British Crop Protection Council, 1979

WOZNIAK, E.
Origins and consequences of default; an examination of the impact of diligence, by M. Adler and E. Wozniak. (Res. Rep. for the Scottish Law Commission no. 5)
Scottish Office, 1981

WRAGG, S. R.
Making decisions with the aid of market information
Meat and Livestock Commission, 1980

WRATHALL, A. E.
31st annual meeting of European association for animal production – West Germany, 1–4 September 1980. Report
ADAS, 1981

WRAY, C.
British council cultural exchange programme between Britain and the German Democratic Republic: report of a visit to the German Democratic Republic, 7–20 September 1981
ADAS, 1982

Veterinary research institutes in Moscow. Report of a visit to USSR, September 1979
ADAS, 1979

WREN-LEWIS, S.
Role of money in determining prices; a reduced form approach. (Government Economic Service Working Paper 42)
Treasury, 1981

WRIGHT, E. D.
Non-home department police forces. Report of the Committee of Inquiry Into Pay and Conditions. July 1979 Session 1979–80 Cmnd. 7623

Rank structure of the police. Report of the joint working party. Part 1: ranks from constable to chief superintendent.
Police Advisory Boards of England and Wales and Scotland
Home Office, 1972

WRIGHT, E. N.
Bird problems in agriculture. The proceedings of a conference 'Understanding agricultural bird problems' held at Royal Holloway College, April 1979, ed. by E. N. Wright and others. (Monograph no. 23)
British Crop Protection Council, 1980

WRIGHT, Edmund Kenneth
Larkfold Holdings Ltd. Report of investigation under the Companies Act, 1948, by D. J. Nicholls and E. K. Wright
Trade Dept., 1979

WYNNE-EDWARDS, V. C.
Captive hawks. Report of the joint working group
DoE, 1979

YARHAM, D. J.
Winter barley and other cereals, by E. W. Woolley and D. J. Yarham. Report of a study tour undertaken in West Germany and Denmark, 1979 series
ADAS, 1979

YELLOWLEES, Henry
Recommended daily amounts of food energy and nutrients for groups of people in the UK. Report by the Committee on Medical Aspects of Food Policy. (Report on Health and Social Subjects 15)
DHSS, 1979

YEOMANS, J. L.
Training for skills questionnaire. Analysis of results, March 1979
Man Made Fibres Producing Industry Training Board, 1979

YOUEL, Alex J.
Parks and people. Report on the European conference at Losehill Hall, September 1978
Peak Park Joint Planning Board, 1979

YOUNG, C. E.
Small-scale enterprises – project handbook
Overseas Development Admin., 1979

YOUNG, C. J.
Guidelines for the processing and publication of Roman pottery from excavations. (Directorate of Ancient Monuments and Historic Buildings Occasional Papers no. 4)
DoE, 1980

YOUNG, Elizabeth
Starter homes; a report of a DoE survey of new small houses and flats for sale, by R. Mainwaring and E. Young. (HDD Occasional Paper 2/80)
DoE, 1980

YOUNG, Frank
Nutritional aspects of bread and flour. Report of the panel on bread, flour and other cereal products; committee on medical aspects of food policy, by Frank Young and J. H. Cummings, *ch.* (Report on Health and Social Subjects 23)
DHSS, 1981

YOUNG, Ken
Public policy research; a review of qualitative methods, by K. Young and L. Mills
SSRC, 1980

Urban governments and economic change, by K. Young and others. (The Inner City in Context 11)
SSRC, 1980

YOUNG, Kirkpatrick L.
Ferguson and General Investments Ltd.; C. S. T. Investments Ltd. Report on investigations under the Companies Act, 1948, by J. Jackson and K. L. Young
Trade Dept., 1979

YOUNG, N. A.
The European potato industry: a descriptive account of the potato sectors of the member states of the EEC-10, Spain and Portugal
Potato Marketing Board, 1981

YOUNG, Michael
Building societies and the consumer. A report, by M. Rigge and M. Young
National Consumer Council, 1981

YOUNG, Stephen
European development strategies of US-owned manufacturing companies located in Scotland, by N. Hood and S. Young
Scottish Economic Planning Dept., 1980

YUILL, D.
Regional development agencies in Europe; an overview, by D. Yuill and K. Allen. (ESU Research Paper 4)
Scottish Economic Planning Dept., 1981

ZANGWILL, O. L.
Behaviour modifications. Report of a joint working party to formulate ethical guidelines for the conduct of programmes of behaviour modification in the National Health Service. A consultative document with suggested guidelines
DHSS, 1980

ZUCKERMAN, Lord
Badgers, cattle and tuberculosis. Report
MAFF, 1980